TEACHING READING COMPREHENSION

TEACHING READING COMPREHENSION:

From Theory to Practice

■ **THOMAS G. DEVINE**
University of Lowell

Allyn and Bacon, Inc.
Boston   London   Sydney   Toronto

Library of Congress Cataloging in Publication Data

Devine, Thomas G.,
   Teaching reading comprehension.

   Bibliography: p.
   Includes index.
   1. Reading comprehension.   I. Title.
LB1050.45.D48   1986   428.4'3   85-28660
ISBN 0-205-08746-9 (pbk.)

Printed in the United States of America

10 9 8 7 6 5 4 3 2 1 91 90 89 88 87 86

to Susanne F. Canavan

About the Book

"What happens in students' minds as they read stories and textbook assignments? As they listen to me talk in class? How do they make sense of what they hear and read? How do I really know when they have comprehended?"

These and similar questions have bothered me since I first began to teach. Periodically, I checked the professional literature in reading instruction and came away with no firm answers.

Two years ago I decided that such questions were central not just to my teaching but to all education, and that I needed some reasonable answers to help me make sense of my continuing career as a teacher.

I discovered then that many others have been bothered by these same questions and that—particularly during the past decade—answers have been suggested by researchers working in such fields as cognitive psychology, psycholinguistics, information processing, artificial intelligence, and rhetorical analysis. Their findings, I discovered, contribute to what may be seen as a gigantic information explosion, one that has led to unprecedented speculation, theorizing, and research in reading comprehension.

Today much is finally known about key factors that influence the ways students comprehend both spoken and printed texts—linguistic competence, prior knowledge, knowledge of word meanings, knowledge of textual structure, and memory. Enough is now known, too, to discount some widely shared beliefs about reading comprehension—that there are discrete "reading comprehension skills," that there are "levels" of comprehension, that reasoning may be equated with comprehension, and that comprehension may be measured by available "reading comprehension" texts.

This book, in short, recounts my search through the often exciting theoretical and research literature of the past few years and my subsequent synthesis. Specifically, it:

- Examines critically the factors that clearly affect (and do not affect) reading comprehension.
- Suggests a coherent explanation, based on the recent research, of what really happens when students try to understand their reading materials.
- Describes hundreds of teaching/learning strategies that positively influence the reading comprehension of children and young adults.

It should help other teachers make more sense of the theory and research and thus better comprehend comprehension. It also offers a wide variety of effective ideas for teaching students to better understand what they read and hear in class.

Brief Contents

Part One **Theoretical Background** **1**

1 Research and Theory — Reading Comprehension
   Instruction Today   3
2 Research and Theory — Major Factors
   Affecting Reading Comprehension   23
3 Research and Theory — What Is Reading Comprehension   49

Part Two **Teaching/Learning Strategies** **73**

4 From Theory to Practice: Relating the New to the Known   75
5 From Theory to Practice: Developing Word Meaning
   Knowledge   113
6 From Theory to Practice: Improving Comprehension
   of School Reading Assignments   145
7 From Theory to Practice: Understanding the Ways
   Texts Are Organized   187
8 From Theory to Practice: Thinking about and beyond
   the Printed Text   229

Appendix **Testing Reading Comprehension** **273**

Index   **287**

Contents

Activities in Idea Boxes   *xii*

Preface   *xiii*

Part One   Theoretical Background   1

1   Research and Theory—Reading Comprehension Instruction Today   3

Introduction and Overview   3
Suggested Study Questions   4
The Importance of Reading Comprehension   5
Problems in Teaching Reading Comprehension   6
Recent Research and Theory in Reading Comprehension   8
Four Basic Assumptions about the Comprehension Process   11
Recapping Main Points   19
End-of-Chapter Activities   19
References   21

2   Research and Theory—Major Factors Affecting Reading Comprehension   23

Introduction and Overview   23
Suggested Study Questions   24
Prior Knowledge and Its Effect on Comprehension   24
Word Knowledge and Its Effect on Comprehension   29
Memory: Where Prior Knowledge Is Stored   33
Schema Theory and Reading Comprehension   39
Recapping Main Points   45
End-of-Chapter Activities   46
References   47

3   Research and Theory—What Is Reading Comprehension?   49

Introduction and Overview   49
Suggested Study Questions   50
What Other Factors Affect Comprehension?   50

What Happens As Students Try to Comprehend?   60
Recapping Main Points   68
End-of-Chapter Activities   69
References   70

Part Two   Teaching/Learning Strategies   73

4   From Theory to Practice: Relating the New to the Known   75

Introduction and Overview   75
Suggested Study Questions   76
Teaching Guidelines   77
Finding Out What Students Already Know   77
Activating Students' Prior Knowledge   83
Idea Box   88
Increasing Students' Prior Knowledge   90
Idea Box   99
Relating the New to the Known   101
Recapping Main Points   109
End-of-Chapter Activities   110
References   111

5   From Theory to Practice: Developing Word Meaning Knowledge   113

Introduction and Overview   113
Suggested Study Questions   114
Teaching Guidelines   114
The Importance of Word Meaning Knowledge   115
Identifying Potential Verbal Trouble Spots   116
Building Word Meanings Independently   121
Idea Box   131
Building Word Meaning Knowledge from the Ground Up   133
Recapping Main Points   141
End-of-Chapter Activities   141
References   143

6   From Theory to Practice: Improving Comprehension of School Reading Assignments   145

Introduction and Overview   145
Suggested Study Questions   147
Teaching Guidelines   148
Effective Prereading Comprehension Strategies   148
Idea Box   160

Effective During-reading Activities   163
Idea Box   170
Postreading Activities for Comprehension   172
Teaching Strategies versus Learning Strategies   179
Recapping Main Points   181
End-of-Chapter Activities   181
References   183

7   **From Theory to Practice: Understanding the Ways
    Texts Are Organized   187**

Introduction and Overview   187
Suggested Study Questions   188
Teaching Guidelines   189
Comprehending Sentences: Problems and Solutions   189
Idea Box   194
Comprehending Paragraphs: Problems and Solutions   200
Idea Box   211
Comprehending Extended Discourse: Problems and Solutions   213
Comprehending Textual Materials: Three Other Considerations   222
Recapping Main Points   223
End-of-Chapter Activities   224
References   225

8   **From Theory to Practice: Thinking about and beyond
    the Printed Text   229**

Introduction and Overview   229
Suggested Study Questions   230
Teaching Guidelines   230
Improving Comprehension through Better Inference-Making   231
Idea Box   241
Improving Comprehension through Better Reasoning   243
Idea Box   256
Improving Comprehension through Self-Monitoring   258
Recapping Main Points   268
End-of-Chapter Activities   268
References   269

Appendix   Testing Reading Comprehension   273

Index   287

Activities in Idea Boxes

Activating prior knowledge   167, 168, 169, 170
Advance organizers   168
Analogies   243
Critical thinking   439, 440, 441
Developing word meaning knowledge   189, 241, 242, 243, 244
Direction following   419
During-reading activities   290, 291, 305
Extending and sharpening prior knowledge   187, 188, 189, 190
Inferencing   410, 417, 439, 440
Listening   168, 439
Main ideas   306, 370
Oral language   188, 190, 289, 290, 291, 306, 350, 351, 439
Outlining   290, 305, 371, 372
Paraphrasing   351
Patterns of organization   350, 370, 372, 439
Plot   371
Predicting   291, 417, 439
Prereading activities   289, 290, 291, 292, 417
Problem solving   419
Purposeful reading   190
Semantic mapping   167, 168, 169, 170, 189
Sequencing   305, 306, 372, 419
Signal words   370
Summarizing   292
Writing   170, 189, 244, 292, 305, 306, 439, 441, 449
Visualizing   169, 305, 306, 371, 440

Preface

What does it mean to understand something? to get meaning? to comprehend? How do people understand? get meaning? comprehend? Can they learn to do these things better? How? Questions like these stimulated the writing of this book, which presents the answers its writer found.

The book is organized, as briefly and coherently as possible, around these and similar questions and the answers found in the rich and exciting research literature of the past decade or so. This remarkable period in human thought has seen the coming together (with all expected clashing and flying sparks!) of a number of areas of study—cognitive psychology, artificial intelligence, psycholinguistics, communications theory, and others. This coming together has led to an Ideas Explosion of sorts and, as might be expected, to the growth and development of new insights into the ways people understand, comprehend, get meaning, and think.

The questions that serve as an organizational framework for these chapters tend to reflect the concerns of teachers, particularly reading teachers—rather than, say, those of specialists in psycholinguistics or computer science. Thus, "How do people comprehend?" becomes "How may students better comprehend school reading assignments?" The answers, too, reflect these shared concerns. Thus, "How may students better comprehend school reading assignments?" is answered in terms most teachers will readily recognize.

There are a few points readers should note before they begin to read *Teaching Reading Comprehension:*

1. Writers of doctoral studies have long been advised to include early in their proposals and dissertations both a statement of purpose and a paragraph or two (usually labeled "Scope and Limitations") which note in advance not only those topics to be studied but also those the writer does *not* intend to study. This is considered an academic safeguard. If, the reasoning goes, the writer tells readers exactly what is and is not intended, they can hardly fault him later for not doing what he had never set out to do in the first place.

The purpose of *this* book, discussed at greater length in Chapter 1, is twofold:

- To review, as concisely as possible, recent research and theory related to reading comprehension.
- To suggest effective teaching/learning strategies, growing out of this research and theory, for the improvement of students' reading comprehension.

This book does *not* intend to examine (despite occasional references) such important areas as child growth and development, developmental psychology, the sociology of reading, literacy, classroom management, or the organization and supervision of the reading program.

These limitations may be better appreciated if prospective users know the intended readership of the book. It is planned for teachers, practitioners and practitioners-in-the-making, and designed for use both as a resource for teachers in schools and as a supplementary textbook in undergraduate and graduate courses in reading instruction. It is assumed, always, that readers either already know a good deal about the teaching of reading or have other, more comprehensive, books available.

2. The first three chapters, all labeled "Research and Theory," review recent research and speculation in the area of comprehension, focusing particularly on linguistic competence, prior knowledge, word meaning knowledge, memory, and schema theory. The remaining chapters, all labeled "From Theory to Practice," describe teaching/learning strategies suggested by recent theory. The strategies are grouped under Relating the New to the Known, Developing Word Meaning Knowledge, Improving Comprehension of School Reading Assignments, Understanding Ways Texts Are Organized, and Thinking about and beyond the Text. The measurement and evaluation of instruction are considered separately at the end of the book.

Each separate chapter includes an Introduction and Overview, Teaching Guidelines, Suggested Study Questions, a summary Recapping of Main Points, End-of-Chapter Activities, and References. The "From-Theory-to-Practice" chapters also include Idea Boxes interspersed throughout. These contain additional teaching activities and strategies.

3. The book rests on an interactive theory of the comprehension process, one that suggests three "texts" are involved in reading:

- One which the writer has "in-the-head" as the written version is developed.
- The actual printed text—which may or may not (depending upon the writer's rhetorical competence) reflect the original, writer's text-in-the-head, and which, in any case, takes on a life of its own once it has left the writer's hands.
- The text-in-the-head the reader develops using his or her linguistic competence, prior knowledge, knowledge of word meanings, cognitive skills, and knowledge of the ways texts-on-paper are organized.

Comprehension, from this view, is the process of using syntactic, semantic, and rhetorical information found in the printed text to reconstruct in the reader's mind (using his or her prior knowledge, as well as needed cognitive skills) another "text"—one that resembles the writer's text-in-the-head when the printed text was prepared. This theory, explained in Chapter 3, is not unique to this book but may be new to many readers.

4. The explanation of the comprehension process found here rests, in turn, on schema theory, a theory which seems to account best for the ways knowledge is encoded and stored in memory and later retrieved and used by writers and readers. Schema theory and its importance in reading comprehension are explained in Chapter 2.

5. This book, it should be noted here, tends to downplay some beliefs long held by many teachers and various authorities in reading:

- That there are separate, discrete, identifiable reading comprehension skills.
- That these may be sequenced hierarchically.
- That "levels" of comprehension exist.
- That comprehension must necessarily involve "thinking."

Discussions of these issues are found in Chapters 3 and 8.

6. *Teaching Reading Comprehension* focuses on *school* reading, particularly the reading of school assignments in basal readers and content area textbooks. The explanation of the comprehension process presented in Chapter 3 and the many strategies suggested throughout the "From-Theory-to-Practice" chapters relate to *all* reading. It is important, for example, to be able to activate prior knowledge or figure out the meaning of an unfamiliar word when reading the daily newspaper; to use one's knowledge of the ways texts are organized when reading a technical report; to make inferences and predictions when reading a novel for pleasure. However, given the space constraints of the book, it was decided to focus primarily here on *school* reading assignments. It is assumed that teachers of reading will help students make transfers from basals and school textbooks when they can. It is also assumed that, given the constraints of the typical school and the typical school day, most teachers have influence upon only school reading assignments anyway.

7. No attempt has been made here to program or sequence teaching/ learning strategies by age or grade levels. The suggested teaching ideas and activities found throughout the "From-Theory-to-Practice" chapters (and in the Idea Boxes) are presented in the context of the discussion, in places that seem most appropriate. Thus, while describing the importance of inference to the comprehension process, a specific suggestion is made for improving students' ability to make inferences; in a discussion of textual organization, a specific idea for teaching paragraph patterns may be introduced. These suggestions may refer in one place to fourth-graders and in another to eighth-graders. The assumption throughout these pages is that teachers use the suggested teaching ideas as "triggers" to stimulate their own creative processes. The description of an effective teaching game in a second-grade group, for example, may stimulate a seventh-

grade teacher to develop a somewhat similar game more appropriate for her age group; a suggestion for an activity that works for eighth-graders may provoke a fourth-grade teacher to create a comparable one for her children.

Listing strategies in a carefully sequenced program from kindergarten through high school is a worthwhile project but is outside the scope of this book. Here it is assumed that the creative teacher, like the cutpurse Autolycus in *The Winter's Tale*, takes what he or she finds, changes it a bit here and a bit there, polishes it up, and reshapes it to fit the needs of a particular group of students.

Finally, a word about masculine and feminine pronouns. Elementary teachers are usually (but not always) referred to by feminine pronouns. This is done because the vast majority of elementary school teachers are, indeed, women. When referring to students (who are rather evenly balanced by sex in schools), *he* and *she, him* and *her,* are interchanged regularly and, it is hoped, sensibly.

This book, as noted, is the result of a search to find answers to questions about reading comprehension, particularly about the teaching of reading comprehension in schools. The search took its writer through most of the important research and theory of the past two decades. Clearly, the end result, *Teaching Reading Comprehension,* has been shaped by the search. Even the "original" explanation of the comprehension process given in Chapter 3 owes much to the research and speculation of others. The writer has taken and reshaped the ideas of many theorists and researchers, who are all noted in the chapter references.

Special note must be made here to individuals who gave (knowingly or unknowingly) *special* help. They include Susanne F. Canavan of Allyn and Bacon, Inc., who encouraged the writer from the first three-page proposal to the final typescript; Dr. Anne M. McParland of the University of Lowell who generously shared her professional materials; and those reviewers whose comments throughout proved valuable beyond measure: Margaret Early, Syracuse University; JoBeth Allen, University of Kansas; Gary Anderson, Arizona State University; John M. Kean, University of Wisconsin at Madison; Sam Sebesta, University of Washington; Clyde G. Colwell, Kansas State University; Timothy Shanahan, University of Illinois at Chicago; Patricia L. Anders, University of Arizona; Richard L. Allington, SUNY Albany; and Roger DeSanti, University of New Orleans.

T.G.D.

PART ONE

Theoretical
Background

The development of effective teaching/learning strategies for reading comprehension needs to rest upon some kind of reasonable theoretical framework.

The three chapters of Part One look at reading comprehension in today's schools, at some of the problems that get in the way of successful instruction, at various factors that influence reading comprehension, and at one explanation of the comprehension process. The teaching/learning strategies and approaches presented in Part Two grow out of the theoretical framework outlined here.

Research and Theory—
Reading Comprehension
Instruction Today

▪ INTRODUCTION AND OVERVIEW ▪

What happens in students' minds as they try to make sense of reading assignments? Do they have to *say* print to understand it? In what ways does what they already know affect their comprehension? How important is it for them to have knowledge of word meanings? How does the author's text influence their comprehension? Is comprehension simply thinking? Are there levels of comprehension? special comprehension skills? What role does memory play in student comprehension? How do teachers know if their students understand what they have read? How do students themselves know if they have understood it?

What, in short, is reading comprehension? Can teachers teach it? Can students learn to do it better?

These are some of the questions that underlie the organization of this book. They are questions that have vexed reading teachers for years. Some of these questions have been partially answered, but not to the complete satisfaction of all teachers and reading specialists. Today they are being answered in ways that will lead to many improvements in classroom practices of reading comprehension.

Teachers today live in the midst of a gigantic information explosion, one that has led to unprecedented speculation, theorizing, and research in reading comprehension. This activity has resulted in new ways of viewing reading instruction, measurement and diagnosis, program development, and the creation of instructional materials.

The purpose of this book is twofold:

- To review much of the current theory and research related to reading comprehension

- To identify and describe effective teaching/learning strategies growing out of this theory and research

Its chapters are intended to offer teachers enough information for them to evaluate theories they encounter in courses, at conferences, and in the professional literature; and enough workable teaching ideas to help them organize comprehension instruction more effectively in their classrooms.

Chapter 1 looks at reading comprehension instruction in schools today, discussing specifically its importance as well as some of the problems that are inherent in all approaches to improved teaching. It includes a brief overview of recent research and speculation and concludes with a closer look at four assumptions that must underlie all attempts to develop a viable theory and effective teaching/learning strategies.

Chapter 1 includes Suggested Study Questions, and then discussions of

- The Importance of Reading Comprehension
- Problems in Teaching Reading Comprehension
- Recent Research and Theory in Reading Comprehension
- Four Basic Assumptions about the Comprehension Process
    Students must know the coding system
    Students must want to figure out the code
    They must have texts that they can decode
    Prior knowledge plays a role in comprehension

Chapter 1 also includes

- Recapping Main Points
- End-of-Chapter Activities
- References

▪ SUGGESTED STUDY QUESTIONS
FOR CHAPTER 1 ▪

1. In what ways is sounding out print different from comprehending it?
2. Why should comprehension be the major goal of all reading instruction?
3. Why has comprehension instruction been neglected until recently? Why has it now become a major concern of researchers and teachers?
4. What are some recent explanations of the comprehension process? How does a *top-down* model work? a *bottom-up* model? an *interactive* model? Which approach underlies this book?
5. What assumptions about comprehension must underlie any reasonable explanation of the process?

6. What is meant by *linguistic competence?* What are its three components?
7. What role do writers' texts play in readers' comprehension of them?
8. What is *prior knowledge?* In what ways does it seem to affect comprehension?

THE IMPORTANCE OF READING COMPREHENSION

Many teachers have probably encountered at least one student like Richard. As a sixth-grader Richard could easily read pages of his teacher's graduate school textbooks aloud. Highly specialized technical terms might have caused him to hesitate momentarily, but he would skillfully sound them out and move on through the text, pausing briefly at commas and stopping at periods. When questioned about ideas and information on these pages, he admitted no knowledge and seemed chagrined at adult expectations that he have it. Richard's oral reading ability was impressive, but for him words, phrases, and sentences represented only opportunities to demonstrate his superb mastery of well-taught rules and generalizations about graphemic-phonemic correspondences.

Students like Richard may be relatively rare, but all teachers have worked with students who can sound out print without always being able to understand that print. Many of their most successful readers, they recognize, are often able to *say* what is printed in their schoolbooks but remain unable either to tell in their own words what an author intends or to use a text to stimulate their own thinking.

As they react to some of the criticisms in the media of today's reading instruction, teachers must sometimes recall not only the few Richards but also the many otherwise successful readers in their classrooms who have occasionally substituted word calling for comprehension. To many of the critics of the schools, the Richards of the world can *read.* To them, relating the graphemes of the printed page to the phonemes of the spoken language is all there is to reading. Most reading teachers, however, have always been sure that reading involves more than this simple kind of decoding. Reading, for reading teachers, has always been a matter of understanding and making sense of printed texts, not just saying print aloud.

Most teachers know that too many of the nation's illiterates can effectively match sounds to letters and *say* print; and that these unfortunates are illiterate in that they are unable to comprehend what they have read *or said.* Literacy, as reading teachers know, involves more than basic decoding skills; it requires that readers comprehend printed language and use it to infer, generalize, predict, and evaluate.

Above all, teachers know that their students—despite the ubiquity and powerful influence of radio, television, and film—must become comprehending readers to survive and be successful in our society. They know that the boys and girls and young adults in our schools today must be able to make sense of

newspapers, books, and magazines, in order to supplement the ideas and information they get from non-print sources;

advertisements, insurance and tax forms, applications for loans and mortgages, menus, bus and airline schedules, instructional manuals, employment notices, union contracts, pension and health plans, plus a wide variety of printed forms encountered daily by all citizens;

political, economic, and commercial propaganda and advertising skillfully designed to persuade and promote not only products and people but ideas, trends, and ideologies;

all kinds of imaginative literature to help them extend their horizons, stimulate their minds, and broaden their sympathies and to provide them with insights into the human condition; and

materials to help them with life-coping situations, in their careers, in their homes, and in all aspects of their daily lives.

However, many teachers are now developing an awareness of the complex interrelationships that exist between print and all other forms of communication in all other social contexts. They now realize that neither sounding out print nor even making sense of commonly found printed texts is enough. Decoding and comprehension in reading are parts of a far larger package—literacy itself. Many reading teachers now see literacy not as a collection of "basic" skills to be developed, sharpened, and measured but as a means of exploring and expanding human potential. They agree with Harste and Mikulecky (1984) that literacy is a system of knowing, a way of learning, growing, and sharing, and that "to study language and literacy outside of or separate from other forms of communication and separate from social contexts is to miss the multidimensional and transactive nature of meaning and expression" (p. 71).

PROBLEMS IN TEACHING
READING COMPREHENSION

All this is not easy. Although most teachers seek out workable teaching methodologies, they find they are not always available. As Durkin (1978–79; 1981) discovered in her studies of comprehension instruction and materials, too often the basal readers teachers use in reading classes tend to encourage teachers to be "assignment-givers" and "questioners"; they do not regularly show teachers how to teach comprehension. The professional material designed to guide instruction suggested that teachers first have students read selections and then ask them questions to test whether or not they had read—and had comprehended! Rarely did teachers' manuals define or explain what was meant by comprehension or offer help in the form of descriptions of effective methods, illustrations, demonstrations, or questions that led to more than assessment. She noted, too, that when instruction for teachers did appear in manuals "the connection between what is being taught and how to read is either minimized or entirely overlooked" (1981, p. 542).

Why is help in this important job so hard to find? One explanation is simply that reading specialists and researchers, until relatively recently, focused their attention primarily on other aspects of reading. The earliest books on reading (see, for example, Huey, 1908) emphasized comprehension; and the first tests, such as the *Gray Oral Reading Test* of 1915 (Davis, 1983, p. 504), noted that many children who could pronounce words did not know their meanings. Other matters, however, either of genuine concern or of temporary interest, led reading teachers away from comprehension. Thus, much research and theorizing in past decades was directed to eye-movements, reading readiness, grapheme-phoneme (that is, letter-sound) relationships, phonics instruction, reading interests of children and young adults, study skills, experience chart approaches, content area reading, the linguistically and culturally different, classroom organization, parental involvement, and other important aspects of reading in the schools. Strategies for improving comprehension were developed by individual teachers and specialists, but—until recently (see next section)—comprehension instruction was only one of the reading profession's many concerns, not its central one.

A second explanation for the relative lack of attention to the development of teaching/learning strategies in comprehension lies surely in the difficulties of its measurement. How does one test to discover whether or not a reader has truly comprehended a text? Popular standardized tests limit reader responses by their multiple-choice formats, usually testing simple recall or specific cognitive skills, such as inference-recognition. Criterion-referenced tests assume that the comprehension process is a complex of discrete, testable skills. Neither type (norm- nor criterion-referenced) necessarily indicates whether or not comprehension has indeed occurred. Because the most effective teaching/learning methodologies *tend* to develop when testing instruments are most valid, strategies for improving comprehension have tended to lag behind those for teaching other aspects of the school curriculum. When reading teachers find it difficult to measure their success (or failure) in teaching comprehension, they (understandably) have difficulties refining, much less sharing, specific teaching techniques. (See Appendix, Testing Reading Comprehension.)

A third explanation grows out of what may be called "the definition problem." No widely accepted definition of reading comprehension has ever been shared by teachers, specialists, researchers, or test-makers. Indeed, many define reading comprehension in terms of sounding out print, assuming that once readers turn printed language into spoken language they can then understand it. Others equate comprehension directly with memory, assuming that if readers remember what they read then they understand it as well. Still others assume that comprehending is comparable to labeling; thus, to categorize and pin a label on an idea is to understand it. Too many define reading comprehension in a circular manner: comprehension is "reading for understanding"; "reading for understanding" is "reading for meaning"; and "reading for meaning" is comprehension. Some dodge the question. They define comprehension as "getting a clear grasp of what is read." One reason teachers are not always successful in their attempts to develop and refine specific strategies for teaching is that they have always been at least somewhat befuddled by what they and their colleagues mean by *comprehension.*

RECENT RESEARCH AND THEORY
IN READING COMPREHENSION

Despite the problems of defining and measuring reading comprehension, most teachers, fortunately, have always tried to help students make sense of printed texts. Realizing from their daily experience in the classroom that word calling and memorization are not enough, teachers have tried to show students how to relate the new information and ideas they have picked up from the printed page to what they already know, how to interpret and reinterpret, and how to structure meanings from texts. Most teachers have developed, through their experience and their intuitions and by trial and error, classroom methods that have helped students go beyond basic decoding.

Today such teachers find themselves to be the beneficiaries of almost two decades of unparalleled speculation and research related to the nature and process of reading comprehension. Reading specialists and researchers have joined with cognitive psychologists and psycholinguists to explore what some have called that "elusive entity" (Pearson and Johnson, 1978, p. 5). Reading comprehension now is becoming less and less elusive as new insights into its nature are uncovered. In the past decade alone fresh and potentially useful perspectives have been derived from such areas as pragmatics, schema theory, transformational grammar, artificial intelligence, discourse theory, textual analysis, rhetoric, memory, metacognition, and information processing. Although complete explanations of the comprehension process are not yet available, teachers in the classroom find that their search for better teaching strategies is now guided by some carefully thought-through theories and many actual research findings.

Several theoretical models of the comprehension process have been suggested: some are primarily text oriented (resting on the assumption that the text itself has the most influence upon readers' comprehension); some are completely reader oriented (resting on the assumption that what readers bring to a text is more important than the text itself); some are *interactive* (assuming that comprehension is both text based and knowledge based at the same time). A few models seem to owe more to one area of study than to another (that is, some are primarily psychological, some linguistic, some rhetorical), but most are interdisciplinary in that their originators use information from several fields of study. (Descriptions of recent models may be found in Massaro, 1984; Samuels and Kamil, 1984; and Flood, 1984.)

At this time three general approaches to comprehension theory and research exist. Each has its proponents and critics; each should be understood by reading teachers as they work to develop more effective strategies for their students.

One approach, once referred to as the *bottom-up* point of view, holds that reading begins with the decoding of words and goes on to meaning. It rests clearly on a text-based, or text-oriented, model of comprehension. Theorists holding this view say that reading starts with simple letter identification and goes from there to sound–letter correspondences; it proceeds when readers put sounds together to make words and then sentences that, for them, have meaning.

This approach in its simplest form was popularized two decades ago by the "Let's Read" series developed by Leonard Bloomfield and Clarence L. Barnhart (1961). In this series children are introduced systematically to the graphemes of the printed language and are then encouraged to relate them to the corresponding phonemes of the spoken language. Thus the spelling "CAT" is decoded as the spoken word /kăt/. If children have semantic meaning for the spoken word, they can—according to proponents of this approach—transfer it to the printed spelling. In essence reading from this point of view is relating "new" language in print to spoken language already possessed and understood by readers. This view of reading has always had great influence on some parents and teachers (it provides a quick-and-easy definition of reading, as well as a ready measuring instrument) and, as a model for learning sound–letter correspondences, remains viable. Clearly this view cannot serve as a model of the comprehension process unless one assumes that language-users always comprehend everything they hear.

A second approach holds that reading starts with what is already in the reader's head, not with the printed page. Resting on reader-based, or reader-oriented, models of the comprehension process, this *top-down* view assumes that meaning is in the reader's mind and is used to figure out letters, words, and sounds. Thus, to top-down theorists, it is of primary importance that a reader know that falling into a body of water may cause wet clothing in order to decide that P _ _ _ is *pond* in the sentence, "The boy's jeans got wet when he fell into the P _ _ _." Readers in this case may be helped by knowing that the grapheme (letter) "P" usually in English represents the phoneme (sound) /p/, but the knowledge of the consequences of falling into water is more important for reading *comprehension* than the information about letter–sound correspondences.

Top-down theorists assume that meanings are already in the minds of readers and that readers go to the print to gain confirmation of what they have already guessed. Frank Smith (1978), for example, suggests that comprehension takes place before individual words are identified. To explain this he uses the sentence, "We should *read* the *minute* print on the *permit*." None of the highlighted words may be said aloud until they have been understood in the context of the sentence. He says that readers tend to read several words ahead and behind the actual word their eyes focus on; and he quotes research to demonstrate that, when lights are turned out, readers generally can predict accurately the next few words of the print they actually cannot see. Smith stresses the importance of *prior knowledge* (which he calls *non-visual information*), noting that the more knowledge readers have acquired about the subject of a given text the better they understand it and the less likely they are to need specific information about letter–sound correspondences.

A third approach—and the one underlying these chapters—is often referred to as *interactive*. It accepts that both so-called bottom-up and top-down theorists are probably correct; letter–sound correspondences, letter–sequence correspondences, and the syntactic structures of sentences are used in parallel by readers to help them get meaning from a string of words; however, at the same time, readers use information held in long-term memory and certain cognitive skills (such as inferencing and predicting) to check and double-check the syntactic structures of sentences and both letter–sound and letter–sequence correspondences.

The present book rests on the belief that comprehension begins as readers use the information that writers have put into their printed texts in order to create for themselves their own personal texts, texts they construct in their minds. Underlying the explanation presented here is the related belief that to understand the comprehension process one needs to distinguish among three texts: *that in the mind of the writer before and during the process of composing and encoding the printed text; the actual printed text itself; and the text readers create for themselves as they use the printed text.* Thus a writer may have a message to share and, using all the linguistic and composing (or rhetorical) skills at her command, encode it in print. A reader, then, using all his linguistic competence, his knowledge of the ways texts generally get encoded, his thinking skills, plus his previously acquired knowledge of what the writer is discussing, tries to reconstruct the original text that was in the mind of the writer. Such an approach is *interactive* in the sense that it highlights writer, text, and reader, as well as the interaction that takes place among them. (This explanation of the reading comprehension process is discussed in Chapter 3.)

In the next chapter some results of recent speculation and research are examined in greater detail as factors affecting reading comprehension are de-scribed. Some of the research findings and theorizing support aspects of a text-based (or bottom-up) view of the comprehension process; others a reader-based (or top-down) view. Much of the information currently available suggests that the interactive approach—on which this book is based—may present more ad-vantages to teachers seeking effective teaching/learning strategies for their students.

Before examining factors that affect comprehension, it is important to look at four basic assumptions upon which any theory of comprehension must rest.

FOUR BASIC ASSUMPTIONS ABOUT THE COMPREHENSION PROCESS

Consider the following:

EXIT

Ruth fell. She hurt her knee.

To be, or not to be: that is the question.

$S = K \log W$

The first example of "reading material" is almost universally recognized in English-speaking countries as a sign over an egress. The second might have been lifted from a basal reader. The third, out of context though it is, is recognized by most adults as a line from a play by Shakespeare. The fourth, known to relatively few educated adults, is Ludwig Boltzmann's response to the second law of thermodynamics. Considered by many of those who know it as the essence of simplicity, it represents entropy mathematically and symbolizes possi-ble arrangements and measures of entropy. (S stands for entropy; K is a universal constant known as Boltzmann's constant; W has to do with the number of ways in which parts of the system can be arranged; *log* is, of course, *logarithm*.)

What may be said commonsensically (that is, without prior knowledge of the intense, unprecedented research and theorizing of the past decade on reading comprehension) about these four examples of reading material? Most would probably agree with the following observations:

- *These are all written texts.* Unlike scenic views, they were deliberately concocted by one human being for another human being to com-prehend. Some written texts seem to have been intended for the writ-er's eyes alone (lists of things-to-do, memory joggers, at-tempts—possibly for therapeutic reasons—at self-expression); they may serve a useful purpose for their author but cannot be said to be written for "another human being to comprehend."

- *They are all written in some kind of code.* Texts to be read and comprehended use a language or symbol system that allows their "concoctors" to take information or an idea from their minds and "spell it out" on paper. Sometimes this is done in a language like English; sometimes in a symbol system such as that used by a trigometrician or a symbolic logician.

- *Writers and readers must share the same code.* No reader can make sense of a writer's text unless he shares the code system. If the "code" is a language, like English, both must know the words used, the ways they may be arranged in sentences, and, sometimes, the ways letters may be sounded out to make words. They need to share the same grammar system.

- *Readers must want to "crack the code."* All comprehension rests on the desire of the reader to figure out the text. (Common sense, again.) Unless the desire is present, attention cannot be maintained long enough to "crack the code."

- *"Cracking the code" is not comprehension of the text.* "T frvbmt L mph X" might be "decoded" by most elementary school children as "S equals K log W"; "Uif dfoufs dboopu ipme" as "the center cannot hold." Few elementary school children will comprehend either text. Many adults may decode "Criterion-referenced tests are valid only if the comprehension process is composed of separate, discrete testable mental processes." Not all will comprehend it.

- *Readers do not have to say the texts aloud.* "Exit," as a matter of fact, occurs infrequently in the speaking or listening vocabularies of English speakers. (Most adults may hear the word only once or twice a decade and never say it.) "S = K log W" may be said aloud but it is probably better comprehended visually. (The sounds of it may actually interfere with comprehension.)

- *It may help if readers can say texts aloud.* A child learning to read may more easily comprehend the two sentences in the second example when she says them aloud. The words are already in her speaking-listening vocabulary, and their syntactical arrangement is one she is familiar with at her age. Translating print to sound may help beginning readers. It may also help experienced readers when they read poetry (which relies on sound for much of its impact) or prose that tries to transfer spoken language to print.

- *In every case, readers must know something already to understand the text.* Enthusiastic advocates of the bottom-up point of view tend to downplay prior knowledge, but common sense indicates that readers must know certain things before they can begin to make sense of these four texts. Readers of the first need to have some prior knowledge of the need for speedy ways out of public buildings. To truly comprehend the second, even beginning readers need at least some knowledge of the consequences of falling. Readers of the Shakespearean line need to know that the common *be* verb represents here (and elsewhere) living or existence. Readers of Boltzmann's equation must have specialized knowledge (of what *S* and *W* represent) and a more general knowledge of the mathematical "coding system" (to understand what is intended by the equal sign and *log*).

These eight commonsensical observations may be extended and explored further (in a sense, the next chapters do just that). They lead to at least four basic assumptions about reading comprehension—assumptions that, from the point of view of this book, must underlie any model, theory, or approach to the comprehension process:

1. Students must know the coding system used by the writer of the text.
2. They must want to figure out the code.
3. They must have texts that they can decode.
4. Prior knowledge does indeed play a role in comprehension.

These four assumptions need to be examined in greater detail.

Students Must Know the Coding System

To comprehend a mathematical formula, readers must know the symbol system (that is, " = " represents the concept "equal"; *log* is *logarithm*, etc.). To comprehend texts in English, students must know how its language system works. This means that they must have *linguistic competence*. Briefly, students need the following three components of linguistic competence:

- *Phonological knowledge.* The knowledge of the different *phonemes*, or individual sounds, and how they are blended together to make words, as well as the *suprasegmental phonemes* of pitch, stress, and juncture. (Pitch refers to the relative position of a tone in a scale, as in music; stress to the volume of emphasis; juncture to the pauses.) Phonological knowledge is important for the comprehension of spoken language; it is important to reading comprehension only to the extent that knowledge of sound–letter correspondences helps children (and sometimes adults) "say" print.
- *Syntactic knowledge.* The knowledge of the ways words can be arranged in sentences. Readers need to know that (in English) subjects *tend* to come before predicates, adjectives before nouns, and so on. Such knowledge is important to reading comprehension, but seems to

come easily and so is rarely taught. Children come to school knowing 80 to 90 percent of basic sentence patterns and recognize "Ruth fell" and "She hurt her knee" as grammatical arrangements of words and "Hurt fell knee her she and" as incomprehensible. More sophisticated syntactical arrangements of words in sentences, such as are frequently found in high school textbooks, demand more of readers and may need to be taught. (See Mellon, 1969, for examples of sentence-combining instructional methods.)

- *Semantic knowledge.* The knowledge of the definitions of words shared by writers and readers. It is crucial to comprehension. When Lewis Carroll writes

> 'Twas brillig and the slithy toves
> Did gyre and gimble in the wabe,

students easily answer questions such as "Who gyred and gimbled?" or "Where did they gyre and gimble?" or "When did they gyre and gimble?" However, to comprehend the lines; to be able, for example, to tell someone else what they read; students must have more than syntactic knowledge. "Brillig," "slithy," "toves," "gyre," "gimble," and "wabe" need definitions shared by students and their listeners. *Both* must share semantic knowledge.

Initial reading instruction has traditionally focused on phonological knowledge, specifically knowledge of sound–letter correspondences. Children learned to match the sounds they already knew with letters and letter combinations. Enormous expenditures of time, effort, and money have been directed toward codifying these phonemic–graphemic relations and developing more effective instructional material for children to master them. At its best "phonics" instruction has helped generations of children "say" print; at its worst it has been a regular drain on teacher and student time and energy. Long chapters in professional books on reading tell teachers how to teach such items as consonant clusters, digraphs, syllabication, and the schwa sound; unfortunately, many tend to outline countless rules, generalizations, and exceptions.

The problem with decoding approaches of this nature is, simply, that sounding out letters and words is not reading comprehension. It is not the end of reading instruction, as some popular writers on the subject allege, but only a bare beginning. Comprehension is more than "sounding letters."

This point has been stressed in recent years by the work of investigators like Smith (1978) and Goodman (1973). Both have demonstrated that readers find *cues* in the printed text from which they theorize possible meanings and then read ahead to find evidence to support their theories. Goodman sees reading as a cycle of "sampling, predicting, testing, and confirming." Smith argues that reading is not decoding to sound but rather that semantic and other non-visual processes intercede between visual processes and reading aloud.

All this is not to downplay decoding skills such as mastery of sound–letter correspondences! Phonics instruction may have been overemphasized in the past, and the ability to "sound out" may not be enough to comprehend. However, readers, especially in the early stages of learning to read, must have enough technical skill in translating print to sound to find enough useful cues in the text to allow them to theorize and predict possible meanings. A simple analogy may make this clear. Most sixth-grade children can "say aloud" passages from an Italian newspaper (because most of the graphemes may be sounded out as English phonemes). With a modicum of practice, a student might mislead fellow students so that they believed she was "reading aloud" in/from Italian. (A native Italian speaker might understand what was being read!) Clearly the student is not comprehending what she reads. However, if the news story included a few Italian words that were cognate with English words she knew (*fortuna, poeta, timido*), the student could use these as cues to guess at what the news story was about. If there were enough cognates (and if she could gain a general idea from the accompanying photographs of what the writer was writing about!), she might come remarkably close to the intentions of the reporter who prepared the passages.

Students Must Want to Figure Out the Code

Readers must pay attention to a text before they can comprehend it. Even a relatively simple text, like EXIT, requires a moment of the reader's attention. A more sophisticated text—such as a poem or lines from a textbook—may demand considerable attention because it uses common words in uncommon ways, unfamiliar words, unusual syntactical arrangements, or fresh analogies. Many school textbooks in the content areas often require sustained attention on the part of student readers.

Psychologists in recent years have explored this important topic and have developed several theories about it. One widely accepted theory suggests that attention is a "limited mental resource." An explanatory metaphor says it is "energy limited": attention is powered by a fixed electrical current, allocable to only so many tasks. According to this belief, when the current is spread too far, a fuse is blown. It is, the explanation continues, "single-minded"; that is, one cannot focus well on two matters at once, and one cannot perform two demanding tasks simultaneously (Anderson, 1980). Another metaphor has attention as a spotlight, dimmed at times by fatigue, sleep, medication, or drugs, but more or less on and moving around all the time. It focuses on one thing, then another, then another; sometimes lingering for a while, and sometimes stopping longer.

Out of the research and speculation comes a question of great concern for reading teachers: What causes the "spotlight" to linger and stay? The best answers seem to relate to purpose and interest. Students pay attention to what interests them at a given moment or when they have a definite purpose.

Students will take the trouble to decode a text when they have a purpose for doing so. In schools, their purposes frequently include those created by their teachers or by the authors of teaching materials. Basal reader teachers' manuals and the instructor's handbook accompanying textbooks frequently suggest such questions as "Why did Robert take the book?" or "When did the president decide to veto the bill?" These are assumed to provide a purpose for reading. Often, under the heading "Purpose for Reading," students are told to *read to discover the causes of an event* or *read to identify the arguments used against a proposal.* Such questions and attempts to set up a reading task do indeed provide a purpose for reading, enough to sustain usually some modicum of attention. However, purpose for reading as articulated in many instructional materials and in many teachers' lesson plans is artificial and seldom related to the purposes students *really* have for reading assignments: pleasing the teacher, getting high grades, pleasing parents, getting into college, and so on.

Purposes for reading that emanate from the students themselves are more apt to focus their attention. Such purposes grow out of students' natural desire to learn something new; to make discoveries about themselves and the world around them. They most often manifest themselves as readers look for answers to questions they want answered. Thus a fourth-grader who thinks he has found a dinosaur egg in his backyard tends to focus his attention on the encyclopedia article as he reads to find the answer to *his* question: "Did dinosaurs ever live in North America?" Any strategies, such as SQ3R, that cause students to read to find answers to their own questions (see Devine, 1981, pp. 44–46) clearly encourage readers to keep the metaphorical spotlight of attention on the printed page.

Attention is contingent, too, upon the interest students have in the content of printed texts. Sometimes content is so attractive to them that cumbersome syntax and unfamiliar words are not deterrents; at other times, simple language and appealing stylistic devices fail to make a text hold the interest of readers. Interest, as reading teachers know, is an individual matter, varying widely from one student to another. What fascinates John may bore Jack. It becomes extremely difficult to control interest in the classroom because the content of a passage may differ among individual students. (It is often difficult for adult readers to pinpoint the topic or theme of a particular passage: several readers reading the same text cannot always say what it is about; see van Dijk, 1980, pp. 131–142.) Much of the "content" of any text seems to be as much in the mind of the reader as on the printed page.

Through the years reading teachers have tried to control the interest factor in a variety of ways. Some have favored *individualized reading programs* (in which students read only what interests them). Some have used *high interest-low vocabulary* books (which are written about topics of known interest to young readers). Others have used strategies (like SQ3R) that involve the student as much as possible in the reading act. The relationship of interest to motivation has been examined in a number of professional books for teachers (see Weber, 1974; Kolesnik, 1978; Devine, 1981). Interest remains a key issue in reading comprehension: students must be interested enough to figure out the code.

Students Must Have Texts That They Can Decode

Too often the texts students are given in school are inappropriately or poorly encoded. Their authors use sentences that are syntactically too advanced for children or young adults; load them with unfamiliar terms and concepts; fail to organize them in patterns that are perceived by readers; and fail to relate their content to information in the minds of young readers.

The syntactic form in which content is encoded is sometimes beyond students' competence. As Hunt (1965) has demonstrated, a relationship exists between maturity and the ability to process certain syntactic constructions. Boys and girls entering school may know the grammatical arrangements of words in basic sentences, but they "grow into" the ability to understand sentences with many clauses. They may be able to "say aloud" the surface structures of such sentences without awareness of their deep structure clauses, which represent actual psychological meaning units. They may, in other words, be able to read aloud syntactical forms in which content is encoded beyond their competence. (See Huggins and Adams, 1980, pp. 87–112.)

The semantic complexity of the content sometimes requires words, phrases, and terms students do not yet know. Good authors provide contextual definitions and glossaries; good teachers preview and teach words they suspect their students may not know. However, many authors assume vocabulary and concept knowledge on the part of children and young adults that these readers have yet to acquire. Examinations of secondary school content area textbooks reveal regular vocabulary overload. Readability formulas, which measure semantic as well as syntactic complexity, indicate books for tenth-graders written at 12th- or 13th-grade levels, and books for ninth-graders written at 10th- and 11th-grade levels.

The organizational patterns used by authors are sometimes not the patterns with which students are most familiar. Early research in secondary reading, for example, indicated that certain patterns had become known to students (for example, cause-and-effect, comparison-and-contrast, enumeration, chronological, and generalization-plus-examples). Teachers had taught these patterns, as well as the skill of locating main-idea sentences within paragraph patterns (Niles, 1965). Content area textbooks (too frequently) include sophisticated mixtures of common patterns, paragraphs without clearly defined main ideas, and unorganized prose passages. As a result even highly motivated students with considerable ability to decode have trouble figuring out what are essentially poorly encoded texts.

Too many authors are so removed from elementary and secondary school students that they seem to be unable to estimate what students know and do not know. Successful writers assess the knowledge already possessed by their readers and try to make connections in their texts between new information and what readers already know. Their success seems related to how well they can think the way their readers think. Unfortunately many reading materials given students at all levels are unrelated to student interest, student need, or students' existing knowledge of the world or that portion of the world treated in the texts.

As they examine factors affecting student comprehension of texts, teachers should remember that text does play a role in its own comprehensibility. Many writers have not sufficiently thought through, defined, and structured their texts in their own minds prior to or during the encoding process; many lack the rhetorical skills necessary to skillfully encode. Resultant texts may be disorganized, distorted, or unfocused; many may fail to highlight key points, offer illustrations and examples, connect part to part, use appropriate patterns, or provide synonyms or contextual clues for words that may be unfamiliar to their readers. Sometimes they fail to define their own purposes or to suggest to readers a purpose for them to read.

The textbooks students are given in school too often display characteristics of ineffective writing. (See Anderson, Armbruster, and Kantor, 1980.) In a recent study of schoolbooks, Estes (1982) found that many of them lacked unity, coherence, and emphasis: two or more unrelated issues are raised in a single section of a chapter, sometimes in ways that are irrelevant and disconcerting; and often main ideas are buried in irrelevancies or left to inference. Textbooks, he concluded, might try to say what they mean: "Unfortunately, they don't always do so for the people who are assigned to read them" (p. 94).

Prior Knowledge Plays a Role in Comprehension _____

Advocates of an overly simplistic bottom-up approach to reading and reading comprehension (often disproportionately represented by articles in popular magazines) have insisted that sounding out print is enough. Readers, they say, need bring nothing to the printed page except their knowledge of letter-sound correspondences and their skill in using phonics. However, any examination of printed texts indicates that readers must have some information about the world around them to understand even the simplest printed language. A beginning reader may be able to sound out "Jane fell and hurt her knee," but to truly understand the sentence a child needs to know that (1) Jane is a person, probably a young girl, (2) *fall*, in this instance, probably means to drop without restraint, (3) falling may injure parts of the body, (4) a knee injury may be painful, etc. Adult readers need not sound out "EXIT" but they need some prior

knowledge (of fires, possible panics, the toxicity of smoke, etc.) to really comprehend the sign.

Recent examinations of the role readers' prior knowledge plays in the comprehension process have stimulated many teachers to look again at the information their students bring into the classroom. They question more: In what ways
does previously acquired information influence how students understand basal
reader selections and content area textbooks? What kinds of prior knowledge are
most important for reading? How do children encode and store new information
in their memories? How do they retrieve it? How does human memory work?
This topic is so important to the development of a teacher's understanding of
reading comprehension that an extended discussion of it is presented in the
following chapter.

▪ RECAPPING MAIN POINTS ▪

Although comprehension lies at the center of all reading instruction, it had been
somewhat neglected until recent years. Researchers and teachers were concerned
with other aspects of reading instruction, had trouble agreeing on a definition
for *comprehension,* and had few ways of measuring the impact of instruction.
Now a virtual explosion of information has stimulated enormous interest in
both research and practice. Cognitive psychologists, linguists and psycholinguists, researchers in artificial intelligence and information processing, and
others in a variety of fields have gained fresh insights into the ways the human
mind works. These have helped reading researchers and teachers begin to see
how readers comprehend written texts.

Some of the new theories stress the primacy of the written text; some, the
knowledge readers bring to these texts. Others are interactive: they see comprehension taking place as readers interact with writers' texts. Recent examinations of texts and readers suggest that any defensible theory of the comprehension process must rest on at least four assumptions: that readers share
comparable linguistic competence with writers; that they must want to figure
out texts; that they have texts that can be figured out; and that the prior
knowledge they bring to each reading experience affects their comprehension.

END-OF-CHAPTER ACTIVITIES

1.   Three reasons are given here to account for the comparative neglect
     of comprehension instruction in past decades. What other reason(s)
     might you add to the list? Why?

2. How does the chapter explain the recent "gigantic information explosion" related to reading comprehension? In what other areas of contemporary life have there been similar explosions of speculation, theory, and research? Do you see similarities between reading comprehension and these areas? What are they? Are the underlying causes the same? similar?

3. Summarize in your own words the three general approaches to reading comprehension today. Note the distinct classroom advantages and disadvantages of each. Which makes the most sense to you? Why?

4. Explain in your own words the interactive approach underlying this book. What aspects of it do you find acceptable? unacceptable? Why?

5. Eight observations are made of the four short printed texts given on page 11. What other observations can you add? Why do you think these might have been omitted?

6. What is *linguistic competence?* Summarize this information briefly, using your own language as much as possible.

7. In what ways is linguistic competence necessary to comprehending *spoken* language? In what ways is listening similar to reading?

8. Children cannot learn to read unless they know oral language. The discussion of linguistic competence in this chapter implies that phonological knowledge (along with semantic and syntactic knowledge) is necessary for comprehension. Not all linguists agree. Read, for example, "Language Development and Reading" by Paula Menyuk (1984), or any other recent article on the subject, and try to answer this provocative question.

9. Why is motivation essential to comprehension? Can learners learn if not motivated? Defend your answer with specific examples from your own life as a learner.

10. Some adults have been heard to say "Children don't pay attention the way they used to!" Why is this an unfair accusation? In what ways is attention linked to motivation? to interest? How is attention related to reading comprehension?

11. Find examples of texts that are incomprehensible to you. What makes them incomprehensible? Find examples of texts that were incomprehensible to you in the past but that you can understand now. What about you has changed to make you a better comprehender of these texts?

12. What is reading comprehension? On the basis of your reading so far in this book, prepare a short defensible definition.

13. This chapter suggests that readers create their own personal texts-in-the-head on the basis of information writers build into the printed

texts. Write a brief paper explaining how you interpret this point of view.

14. With fellow students or colleagues, conduct an informal survey to determine the causes of comprehension failure in daily life. Each member of the survey team should watch for examples of people failing to understand one another and note these instances in a log, with suggested reasons for the comprehension failures. After a period of time (perhaps one week), pool the team findings and, together, try to determine the primary causes for such failures. What roles seem to be played by linguistic *in*competence (that is, failure to recognize word meanings, to note phonological clues or sentence structure)? by inattention? by lack of motivation? by insufficient prior knowledge? by fuzzy thinking?

15. If you are presently teaching, collect examples of comprehension failures in your own class. Write a brief paper citing the kinds of problems you observed and the probable reasons that may account for them.

REFERENCES

Anderson, John R. *Cognitive Psychology: Its Implications.* San Francisco: Freeman, 1980.

Anderson, T. H., B. B. Armbruster, and R. N. Kantor. *How Clearly Written Are Children's Textbooks? Or, of Bladderworts and Alfa.* (Reading Education Report No. 15.) Champaign, Ill.: Center for the Study of Reading, 1980. (ERIC Document Reproduction Service No. ED 192 275; 63 pp.)

Bloomfield, Leonard, and Clarence L. Barnhart. *Let's Read: A Linguistic Approach.* Detroit: Wayne State University Press, 1961.

Davis, Arnold R. "A Historical Perspective." In J. Estill Alexander (Ed.), *Teaching Reading,* 2nd ed. Boston: Little, Brown, 1983.

Devine, Thomas G. *Teaching Study Skills: A Guide for Teachers.* Boston: Allyn and Bacon, 1981.

Durkin, Dolores. "What Classroom Observations Reveal about Reading Comprehension Instruction." *Reading Research Quarterly* 14 (1978–79): 481–533.

Durkin, Dolores. "Reading Comprehension Instruction in Five Basal Readers." *Reading Research Quarterly* 16 (1981): 515–544.

Estes, Thomas H. "The Nature and Structure of Text." In Allen Berger and H. Alan Robinson (Eds.), *Secondary School Reading.* Urbana, Ill.: ERIC Clearinghouse on Reading and Communications Skills, 1982.

Flood, James. "Introduction." In James Flood (Ed.), *Understanding Reading Comprehension.* Newark, Del.: International Reading Association, 1984.

Goodman, Kenneth. "Psycholinguistic Universals in the Reading Process." In Frank Smith (Ed.), *Psycholinguistics and Reading*. New York: Holt, Rinehart and Winston, 1973.

Harste, Jerome C., and Larry J. Mikulecky. "The Context of Literacy in Our Society." In Alan C. Purves and Olive Niles (Eds.), *Becoming Readers in a Complex Society. 83rd Yearbook of the National Society for the Study of Education.* Chicago: University of Chicago Press, 1984.

Huey, Edmund Burke. *The Psychology and Pedagogy of Reading.* New York: Macmillan, 1908. (Reprinted Cambridge, Mass.: The MIT Press, 1968)

Huggins, A. W. F., and Marilyn Jager Adams. "Syntactic Aspects of Reading Comprehension." In R. J. Spiro, B. C. Bruce, and W. F. Brewer (Eds.), *Theoretical Issues in Reading Comprehension*. Hillsdale, N.J.: Lawrence Erlbaum Associates, 1980.

Hunt, Kellogg W. *Grammatical Structures Written at Three Grade Levels.* Urbana, Ill.: National Council of Teachers of English, 1965.

Kolesnik, Walter B. *Motivation: Understanding and Influencing Human Behavior.* Boston: Allyn and Bacon, 1978.

Massaro, Dominic W. "Building and Testing Models of the Reading Process." In P. David Pearson (Ed.), *Handbook of Reading Research*. New York: Longman, 1984.

Mellon, John C. *Transformational Sentence-combining: A Method for Enhancing the Development of Syntactic Fluency in English Composition.* Urbana, Ill.: National Council of Teachers of English, 1969.

Menyuk, Paula. "Language Development and Reading." In James Flood (Ed.), *Understanding Reading Comprehension*. Newark, Del.: International Reading Association, 1984.

Niles, Olive S. "Organization Perceived." In Harold L. Herber (Ed.), *Developing Study Skills in Secondary Schools*. Newark, Del.: International Reading Association, 1965.

Pearson, P. David, and Dale D. Johnson. *Teaching Reading Comprehension.* New York: Holt, Rinehart and Winston, 1978.

Samuels, S. Jay, and Michael L. Kamil. "Models of the Reading Process." In P. David Pearson (Ed.), *Handbook of Reading Research*. New York: Longman, 1984.

Smith, Frank. *Understanding Reading,* 2nd ed. New York: Holt, Rinehart and Winston, 1978.

van Dijk, Teun A. *Text and Context: Explorations in the Semantics and Pragmatics of Discourse.* New York: Longman, 1980.

Weber, Kenneth J. *Yes, They Can!: A Practical Guide for Teaching the Adolescent Slower Learner.* Toronto: Methuen, 1974.

Research and Theory— Major Factors Affecting Reading Comprehension

▪ INTRODUCTION AND OVERVIEW ▪

This chapter focuses on two major factors that have an indisputable influence on the ways readers comprehend texts of all kinds.

- The *general knowledge* of the world and how it works that each individual reader brings to each reading experience
- The *more specific knowledge* of words and their meanings that each reader needs to make sense of printed pages

Human memory plays a crucial role in the encoding, storage, and retrieval of such information. For this reason, recent research and speculation in the areas of memory and schema theory are also examined.

Chapter 3 examines other major factors affecting reading comprehension. It also presents a possible explanation of what happens when readers try to comprehend.

Chapter 2 includes Suggested Study Questions, and then discussions of

- Prior Knowledge and Its Effect on Comprehension
    Background and definition
    Examples of prior knowledge at work
    Examples from the classroom
- Word Knowledge and Its Effect on Comprehension
    The importance of word knowledge
    How do words get meanings?
    How do children know word meanings?
    Words as labels for concepts
    Implications

- Memory: Where Prior Knowledge Is Stored
    Kinds of memory
    Memories are often reconstructions
    Semantic versus episodic memory
    Memory and prior knowledge
- Schema Theory and Reading Comprehension
    What is schema theory?
    Some functions of schemata
    How readers use schemata
    Where do schemata come from?

Chapter 2 also includes

- Recapping Main Points
- End-of-Chapter Activities
- References

■ SUGGESTED STUDY QUESTIONS
FOR CHAPTER 2   ■

1. In what ways does what one already knows influence reading comprehension?
2. Where is prior knowledge acquired? Why do some readers have more than others?
3. Why are physicists better comprehenders of physics textbooks than other readers?
4. What is the most important kind of prior knowledge for reading?
5. How do children get meanings for words?
6. How is prior knowledge stored? retrieved?
7. In what ways does *schema theory* account for the storage and retrieval of knowledge?
8. Why are schemata called "the building blocks of cognition"?
9. What are some functions of schemata?
10. Why is *assumptive teaching* dangerous?

PRIOR KNOWLEDGE AND ITS EFFECT
ON COMPREHENSION

Most investigators now agree that what readers bring to the printed page affects their comprehension of it. Some insist that the prior knowledge of readers is the single most important component of the reading process. A few claim that the printed page of the writer merely serves to stimulate ideas already in readers' heads and may cause, at best, only highlighting and possible restructuring of these ideas in fresh ways. Some believe that text is simply a blueprint from which readers build their own meanings.

Because almost all current theories of comprehension recognize the importance if not the primacy of prior knowledge, teachers need to be aware of research and speculation in this area.

Background and Definition

The term *prior knowledge* refers to all the knowledge of the world readers have acquired through their lives. Some theorists prefer the term *world knowledge* and use it synonymously with prior knowledge; a few use equivalent phrases such as *pre-reading knowledge* or *life memory storage,* as well as more traditional terms such as *background knowledge* or *experiential background.* Smith calls it both *non-visual information* and "the theory of the world in our heads" (1978).

Such largely synonymous terms help define what is meant by prior knowledge: It is all the information and ideas, all the perceptions and concepts, the images and ideational propositions, as well as the intellectual residues of emotional experiences, held in long-term memory by readers. It is, in short, everything held in memory. It varies from reader to reader: younger ones, by definition, will have less prior knowledge than older readers; all readers, regardless of age, will have different prior knowledge backgrounds (because everyone has a different biography). Some will have richer backgrounds (more has happened to them); some poorer (less has happened to them); some may have eccentric backgrounds (strange things have happened to them). All will vary in what they have learned, or failed to learn, in life. Each is unique.

Each reader's prior knowledge—whether of a specific item of information, a specific skill or concept, or some aspect of life in general—must have some influence on how he or she approaches the printed page. In fact, as Johnston and Pearson (1982, pp. 128–129) have noted, prior knowledge probably influences the comprehension process at all levels: at the decoding-word recognition level by delimiting the set of words that could possibly appear in a sentence slot; at the short-term memory level by determining the amount that can be stored in working memory; at the inference stage by determining which inferences, if any, should be made; and at the storage level by determining which information will be stored, in what form it will be stored, and whether or not it will be retrieved. If all this is true, then there should be a strong relationship between prior knowledge and comprehension on test scores, and, as the same researchers have discovered, there is. A brief measure of prior knowledge can indeed account for a large proportion of reading comprehension score variance, even after reading ability has been taken into account (1982, p. 129).

Once one comes to recognize the role of prior knowledge in reading comprehension, one is reminded of the importance of each individual student's (1) chronological age, (2) home and family background, (3) social and community background, (4) previous educational experiences, (5) reading, film-viewing, and televiewing habits, (6) hobbies and recreational activities, as well as all the other myriad experiences which shape individual readers and make up their prior knowledge. Reading teachers are reminded, once more, of the uniqueness of each individual student.

Examples of Prior Knowledge at Work

Examples of the influence of prior knowledge at work in daily life are not difficult to find. This first comes from Jeremy Campbell, who calls it a beautiful example of a message encoded in a way that enabled a particular reader to predict its full information content on the basis of knowledge already in his possession but not in the possession of another person who read the same message (1982, pp. 64–65). His friend Tribus received a Western Union cable from Paris from his daughter who was traveling in Europe:

> PLEASE SEND ME FIFTY DOLLARS AMERICAN EXPRESS
> NICE LETTER OF EXPLANATION FOLLOWS LOVE LOU.

This message, as Campbell tells it, presented no problem to Mrs. Tribus, although she did think the word "nice" was a trifle odd. To her, it seemed like a straightforward request for money to be sent to Paris. To Tribus himself, however, it looked wrong. He knew that there were three American Express offices in Paris and that the cable should have specified which one. The cable should have contained more information. Then he realized that "nice" was not an adjective describing the expected letter but the name of a town on the French Riviera. As Campbell noted, the code of the message was not the correct one for someone who did not know that there are three American Express offices in Paris; it did not enable such a reader to predict on the basis of probability that the word "nice" should really have been "Nice." Because of Tribus's prior information, Nice was more probable than "nice" in the context of the whole message.

A frequently quoted example of prior knowledge at work in the world comes from an early study in this area by Bransford and Johnson (1973). Readers are asked to read the following passage and tell what it is about:

> The procedure is actually quite simple. First you arrange things into different groups. Of course, one pile may be sufficient depending on how much there is to do. If you have to go somewhere else due to lack of facilities, that is the next step, otherwise you are pretty well set. It is im-

portant not to overdo things. That is, it is better to do too few things at once than too many. In the short run this may not seem important but complications can easily arise. A mistake can be expensive as well. At first the whole procedure will seem complicated. Soon, however, it will become just another facet of life. It is difficult to foresee any end to the necessity for this task in the immediate future, but then one can never tell. After the procedure is completed, one arranges the materials into different groups again. Then they can be put into their appropriate places. Eventually, they will be used once more and the whole cycle will then have to be repeated. However, this is part of life. (p. 400)

At a typical gathering of adults (a PTA meeting or faculty social), some who read the passage will recognize immediately what is being discussed; others will not. Some will find it extremely difficult to understand until told that it is about washing clothes. Clearly, the text demands certain prior knowledge on the part of readers.

Another example, this time from the research literature, comes from Hayes and Tierney (1982). They required American high school students to read and recall newspaper articles about cricket matches in Australia. Before reading the articles, some students were given information about cricket and baseball, some were given information that specifically stressed explicit comparisons between the two sports, and some were given information in related readings that was irrelevant to the articles about cricket. At the time the researchers were primarily interested in discovering the instructional effects of analogy as an interpretive bridge between unfamiliar material and knowledge students already possessed. What they found was that analogies do indeed aid students in learning and remembering (for further discussion of this point, see Chapter 4), but the greatest single influence on student comprehension was specialized information about cricket given to them before they read the articles. Students who had acquired prior knowledge of the game before reading performed better on written recall tasks as well as on prediction and discrimination tasks (p. 274). The researchers concluded that their findings supported "assertions by educators, philosophers, and psychologists that attempts to increase background knowledge facilitate learning unfamiliar material" (p. 279).

Examples from the Classroom

Durkin (1983, p. 290) cites two apparently simple sentences: *Ruth fell. She hurt her knee.* What may be overlooked with "simple" sentences such as these, she points out, is "that our knowledge of the consequences of falling (based, perhaps, on personal experience) give us the ability to link the two sentences into a cause-effect relationship." Young children may be able to "say" the sentences to the satisfaction of their teacher but be unable to comprehend them unless they have the appropriate world knowledge.

Two "simple" lines from a poem widely taught in middle schools again demonstrate the importance to comprehension of children's prior knowledge of the world:*

Whose woods these are I think I know.
His house is in the village, though;

Although Robert Frost's "Stopping by Woods on a Snowy Evening" (1967, 224–225) is often selected because of its simplicity, it should be apparent that these two lines are "easy" only if readers know that farmers, especially New England farmers, sometimes own land or work fields in outlying areas. (One may say that "complete" comprehension is possible only to readers who include a thorough knowledge of the economics of New England agriculture in their heads.) Urban children without this kind of information in their long-term memories need to have it supplied by teachers or infer it on the basis of *other* appropriate knowledge they possess.

Three—again, seemingly simple—sentences selected from a sixth-grade social studies book demand even more world knowledge for comprehension:

When a house is built the priest must find out the favorable time for laying the foundation. Without this the construction work is usually not started. There is always a fear that if any accident or other mishap took place this would be because the religious ceremony was omitted. (Davis, 1971, p. 282)

To comprehend this passage students must have at least a modicum of knowledge about construction procedures (which they may have), plus considerably more knowledge about the religious beliefs of the builders (which they may or may not have). A careful examination of preceding pages reveals some treatment of religious practices and beliefs but no references to the importance to the particular people of propitious timing of ceremonies or of ceremonies related to significant events in their lives. A child who, because of absence or lack of attention, had missed reading earlier sections of the book or class discussions of them would have insufficient prior knowledge to cope with this passage, even though it is written at sixth-grade level (according to various readability formulas).

Another three-sentence example again illustrates the importance of information students bring to the text:

A patrol plane flies 220 miles per hour in still air. It carries fuel for 4 hours of safe flying. If it takes off on patrol against a wind of 20 miles per hour, how far can it fly and return safely?

---

*From "Stopping by Woods on a Snowy Evening" from *The Poetry of Robert Frost* edited by Edward Connery Lathem. Copyright 1923, © 1969 by Holt, Rinehart and Winston. Copyright 1951 by Robert Frost. Reprinted by permission of Holt, Rinehart and Winston, Publishers.

It is apparent that before students can understand this "word" problem from a mathematics textbook, they must already have a good deal of world knowledge in their heads: about patrol planes, about still air, about fuel tank capacities, about the effect of wind currents on fuel consumption, about the writer's notions of "safe" and "unsafe" flying. Good math teachers sense gaps in their students' background and take steps to fill them, but many teachers assess student ability to read mathematical problems solely on the basis of student response to text.

The constraints of prior knowledge become more apparent as students move into secondary school and college. Content area textbooks regularly present passages that can only be comprehended if readers have specific world knowledge. Authors of textbooks in mathematics, the sciences, and humanities regularly assume that their readers already have information they do not yet possess. (Similarly, some teachers unfortunately assume students have knowledge they have yet to acquire; for discussions of "assumptive teaching," see Herber, 1978, or Devine, 1981.) Ironically, students who have picked up background knowledge on a topic (often through wide reading, televiewing, adult conversations, and other sources) sometimes impress their teachers as first-rate comprehenders, even though they may lack many "basic reading skills." As Durkin points out, "Physicists are better comprehenders than we are of physics textbooks not so much because they have superior reading skills as because they have greater knowledge about their specialization" (1983, p. 190).

WORD KNOWLEDGE AND ITS EFFECT ON COMPREHENSION

Of all aspects of prior knowledge, word knowledge seems to be the most important for reading comprehension.

Phonetic knowledge may help students sound out *feckless* in a sentence such as "Fred is feckless," but it cannot help them comprehend the sentence unless they have a meaning for the word *feckless*.

Syntactic knowledge may assist them in figuring out that it was the *slithy toves* that *gyred* and *gimbled*, but they still cannot comprehend the first lines of this famous poem unless they have some meanings for the words *slithy, toves, gyre,* and *gimble*.

General or even specific knowledge of the world allows students to make inferences about texts such as these, but the quality of their inferences is directly related to the number of words in a text to which they can attach meanings.

The Importance of Word Knowledge

Any examination of texts used in schools reveals the crucial role played by word knowledge in reading comprehension. Children, adolescents, and young adults cannot begin to comprehend unless they have meanings held in memory for such words as *fell, hurt, knee, be, question,* or *log.* Neither competence in relating letters to sounds nor syntactic sophistication—both important to decoding and eventually to comprehension—can compensate for lack of knowledge of word meanings. A look at a randomly selected page from a school textbook surely supports this observation: one paragraph from a middle school geography book contains *rainforest, sunbeams, woven, vegetation, decayed, odor, stalk,* and many more words for which students must have meanings to make comprehension possible.

Research findings from studies of reading and school success support the belief that knowledge of words and word meanings is crucial (see, for example, Deighton, 1959, or Dale and O'Rourke, 1971). Correlational studies of comprehension factors all highlight the importance of word knowledge. Davis, for example, conducted factorial studies to discover the relationships to one another of various hypothesized reading comprehension skills (1968). He carefully selected items designed to measure eight skills, developed a two-form test (with each form containing twelve items measuring each of the eight skills), and, using a technique called "uniqueness analysis," identified five unique skills. *Recalling word meanings* led the list. He later applied factor analysis to the same data and identified four key factors (1972). Again, *recalling word meanings* led the list. Davis's original data were reanalyzed by Spearritt using a "maximum likelihood" factor analysis procedure; he, too, found that word meanings was the best differentiated of all factors (1972).

How Do Words Get Meanings?

Words are seldom created with meanings attached. (*Polaroid, radar, antibiotic* and similar technical, scientific, and trademarked commercial terms are exceptions to the generalization.) People attribute meanings to existing words, or use existing words or recombinations of them to hold meanings they want held. Thus *father,* which seems to have its root in a hypothesized Indo-European language spoken by wandering Asiatic tribes in Europe in prehistoric times (and which has cognates in other languages; e.g., the German and Dutch *vater* and *fater* and the French and Sanskrit *pere* and *pitar*), is an existing word to which most English speakers attribute a rather specific meaning. Thus, too, *record,* "an account made in enduring form, especially in writing" (from the Latin word for remember), proved a useful word to have around when sounds were captured on shellac cylinders for the early phonographs, and *disk,* a "thin, flat plate" (from the Greek word for throwing), was available for the computer industry at a later time.

Meanings are in the heads of speakers, listeners, readers, and writers. Words are arbitrary symbols speakers, listeners, readers, and writers use to represent their knowledge of objects, situations, events, actions, and sequences of events and actions, to represent—as will be explained in the next section—their own personal "models" or "theories" of objects, situations, events, actions, and sequences of events and actions. When all agree upon certain meanings for certain words, comprehension is easy—or relatively easy. When language users attribute different meanings to certain words, comprehension becomes more difficult (as in "The child is father of the man" or "Floppy disks are not for throwing").

How Do Children Know Word Meanings?

The quick-and-easy answer to this question is, "They don't,"—at least, not beyond the shadow of a doubt. They may know the meaning attributed to a given word at a given point in time by a certain group of language users. They can never be completely sure, because the meaning associated with the word by speakers and writers may not be the one they hold in their memories. If all writers of English agree that *father* means a "male parent" and only a male parent, readers of English might comprehend the word; unfortunately, writers tend to use even ordinary words metaphorically, give them idiosyncratically chosen meanings, or use one word to represent two or more meanings.

Children (and adults) learn word meanings through experience. They hear and read words, test them out in a variety of contexts by speaking and writing them, and over a period of time begin to attribute certain meanings to certain words. As children have more and more experiences in the world with other language users, the more accurately *their* meanings begin to conform to the meanings given words by others.

Language is, without doubt, shaped by social, not personal, experiences. While it is theoretically possible for an individual to develop semantic knowledge that is peculiarly his or her own, the resultant language would have little use as a communication tool. For readers to make sense of writers' texts, both must share meanings (and shades of meanings). Because meanings constantly shift and are affected by such a wide variety of societal forces, it may be said that children (and adults) only *know* a word's meaning(s) within certain temporal and social contexts.

Words as Labels for Concepts

Because words serve as labels for concepts, reading teachers need to know ways in which researchers have tried to explain concepts linguistically. One way (discussed in greater detail later) is the so-called *feature-list model,* which attempts to account for the meaning of a word by demonstrating the direct and indirect connections it has with related words in a "semantic network" (Smith, Shoben, and Rips, 1974). Thus, *defining features* are listed (birds, for example, "have feathers") along with *characteristic features* (they "fly"). Such an approach to word meaning helps teachers understand how children and adults, through experience, sharpen their meanings for given concepts and the words that label them. Children learn through direct experience (observation) and/or indirect experience (reading or film-viewing) that a bat is not a *true* bird because, although it has the characteristic feature of flying, it lacks the defining feature of feathers.

Another way of describing the organization of concepts is in terms of class relations, example relations, and property relations (see Pearson and Johnson, 1978, pp. 25–26). *Class relations* refers to a group of things (objects, situations, events, actions) that have recognizable characteristics or properties; thus dogs are related to pets and animals in that they belong to a class of things called animals and are likely to belong to a class of things called pets..An *example* refers to either a particular dog (Fido) or group within the class (collies). *Property relations* are attributes or characteristics: dogs, for example, bark and have four legs, tails, hair, and cold noses. These property relations relate back to class relationships: if Spot or Fido is indeed a dog, then it probably has four legs, hair, a tail, and the ability to bark.

These relationships—among classes, examples, and properties—*are* the concepts that children and adults have about the world around them. The relationships may be sharp and accurate, reflecting those shared by other language users; they may be fuzzy, incomplete, inappropriate, or idiosyncratic and thus detrimental to an individual's thinking and communication. (Another account of how words become labels for concepts may be found in Salus and Salus, 1984, pp. 122–139.)

Implications

Several implications may be drawn from recent research and discussion of word knowledge.

Word Knowledge Cannot Be Assumed   Because students are reading at a given grade level does not mean that they all share a common vocabulary. The meanings attributed to words are highly individualized; Ellen's meaning for *father* is not necessarily the same as Robert's; Tom's *disk* is not Arnold's. "Common" words, assumed to be in the reading vocabulary of every fifth-grade child, may not be in Richard's or Jane's; and the meanings students have attributed to commonly used words may not be the meanings shared by teachers and other adults.

Assessment Is Important   Before making reading assignments, teachers need to discover the nature and extent of readers' prior knowledge of the topics treated in the selection; preassessment of vocabulary knowledge is equally important. Fortunately a variety of techniques is available: synonym tests, informal inventories, maze tests, various games (see Chapter 4).

Assessment of concept development is more difficult. Paper-and-pencil tests are of less value than are interviews, observations, and simple, informal measures. One technique is first to identify concepts in the reading assignment that seem crucial to it and then, through discussion, pinpoint those concepts individuals—or the group as a whole—seem not to understand. (The teacher may ask "What does it mean to *you* when it says *a priest must find a favorable time to lay the foundation of the building?* What do you think of when you hear the word *priest? foundation?*") Once incomplete or imprecise meanings are discovered, teachers must go back and do some concept-building, remembering as they do that knowing word labels for concepts is not the same as understanding the concepts themselves.

Direct Experiences Are Paramount Firsthand experiences (visual, auditory, tactile, and psychomotor) are essential for word and concept development. Children (and even adults) need to see, hear, and touch birds or dogs before they best apprehend those relationships (among classes, examples, and properties) noted earlier. The best way to develop a rich, accurate concept for the action *cross-country skiing* or the object *water ski* is to engage in cross-country skiing or see and touch an actual water ski.

Vicarious Experiences Must Be a Major Component of All Schooling Unfortunately the constraints of time, energy, and budget do not allow children enough firsthand experiences to develop all the words and concepts they need to comprehend the texts they encounter. Teachers need to provide as many experiences as they can through field trips, opportunities to manipulate tools, toys, and equipment, role-playing, and class demonstrations and laboratory work. These need to be supplemented, however, by vicarious experiences in the form of film-viewing, televiewing, and wide reading. Children can learn about cross-country skiing, surfing, or bird-watching "second-hand" through incidental or teacher-controlled viewing and reading. Direct methods of instruction in vocabulary can supplement such vicarious experience: explanation and discussion, lessons in classification and analogy-making, exercises in using context clues and word roots and affixes, as well as the study of the dictionary and of multiple meanings.

Word knowledge, especially knowledge of words as labels for concepts, is indispensable; it is a key factor in reading comprehension.

MEMORY: WHERE PRIOR KNOWLEDGE IS STORED

Most teachers now realize that their efforts to improve reading comprehension are influenced in various ways by the quantity and quality of knowledge their students retain from prior school learning and life experiences. Prior knowledge clearly rests on the endurance and availability of memory.

Because of its crucial importance to our efforts to better understand the comprehension process, recent theory and research about how information is encoded, stored, and retrieved is reviewed here.

Kinds of Memory

Recent research on human memory identifies several kinds:

- *Free recall.* Students tell, without prompting, what they remember from their reading.
- *Aided recall.* Students remember what they read after having been given some clues or assistance.
- *Recognition.* Students identify material from their reading when it is shown to them.
- *Reintegrative memory.* Material is remembered in total context (for example, a student recalls the entire plot, setting, and characters from a novel read several years before and after hearing her teacher mention a single incident from the book).

Psychologists recognize, in addition to these four kinds of remembering, an even more basic group of three kinds of memory. The first, *sensory storage memory*, holds information for less than a second. Divided into *iconic* memory when concerned with visual stimuli and *echoic* when auditory, the sensory storage system plays an important role in all language activities. Echoic is needed to retain individual phonemes in memory while the mind begins to make sense of speech. Iconic is needed to retain letters and graphemes as decoding begins to take place in reading. Sensory storage memory seems to operate in an automatic way, and there is little that can be done to hang onto data at this stage. It is used instantly or is gone forever.

Short-term memory, the second kind, can be controlled. Usually information is retained here for a few seconds, unless a deliberate attempt is made to hold it. Such an attempt, often called *rehearsal,* may occur when a person repeats a telephone number over and over again until it is dialed (or a page number while searching through a set of encyclopedias). Short-term memory is clearly important in all language activities. A listener, for example, must retain the subject of a long sentence in order to relate it to the predicate spoken later; a reader must remember the topic sentence of a paragraph while going through its supporting sentences or the central point of a longer passage while examining related points in subsequent paragraphs. Researchers have been especially interested in discovering why information survives in short-term memory for only a few seconds. The *trace decay hypothesis* holds that without rehearsal information simply fades out, as a light bulb fades when electricity is shut off. The *interference hypothesis* holds that other stimuli interfere and make for confusion.

(Many psychologists object to the first hypothesis on the grounds that time alone cannot account for "fading out"; a piece of information, they say, would remain indefinitely unless replaced by other information; see Baron, Byrne, and Kantowitz, 1977, pp. 156–159).

Long-term memory, the third kind, is the more or less permanent repository for all the data that have somehow moved to it from short-term memory. It is where all readers' prior, or world, knowledge resides. Unlike short-term memory, which retains only a few items for a few seconds, long-term memory holds masses of information for long periods (perhaps a lifetime!). Nothing needs to be pushed aside or discarded to make room when new data comes into it. Its capacity seems infinite.

The problem psychologists have with long-term memory is accounting for *retrieval.* All information stored there seems to be *available* (that is, it is capable of being taken out) but not *accessible* (the means of hooking onto it and pulling it to the surface of awareness are not always handy). As the psychologist Tulving says, "Accessible information is always available, but available information cannot always be accessible" (1968). One way of explaining retrieval possibilities is to think of long-term memory as *self-addressable* (Shiffrin and Atkinson, 1969); that is, the same plan that is used to encode and store information is also used at a later time to retrieve it. This method of retrieval may be illustrated by thinking of how one locates a book on, say, children's reading interests from a large university library. The teacher who wants the book goes first to that section of the library where she knows books on education are shelved. This section has been divided by the librarian into separate subsections: History of Education, Philosophy of Education, Administration and Supervision, Curriculum and Instruction. The teacher (using her past experiences in the library as a guide) goes to the Curriculum and Instruction section and finds those books on Reading Instruction. Here she finds books on Elementary School Reading, Secondary School Reading, Content Area Reading, Psychology of Reading, Reading Interests, and so forth. Eventually the teacher locates a book on children's reading interests and leaves satisfied. Without realizing it, she has just retraced the same plan used by the librarian in shelving the book. Its location depended on its contents. Many psychologists now believe long-term memory is organized in much the same way a library is organized. The teacher's knowledge of the correct subtopic got her to the shelf where she then had to search to find the exact book she needed. Similarly, the self-addressing properties of memory may take us to the area of long-term memory where certain information resides, but then we must search a bit for the exact item. Sometimes the storage location is not easy to find, and we must do a great deal of searching in the "shelves" of our long-term memory; sometimes—because the system of organization is askew or unknown—items are not retrieved, although they are "available."

Meaning clearly plays a pivotal role in encoding for storage, actual storage, and later retrieval. Just as the librarian made a decision on where to store the book on children's reading interests on the basis of its contents and subject matter (encoding) and placed it on a shelf with other books on reading interests (storage), and the teacher found the book she wanted on the basis of its contents and subject matter (retrieval), so do students file, store, and retrieve information in long-term memory on the basis of meaning. People tend to remember what makes sense to them in some way, and they recall it from memory for the same reason—because it has made sense to them in some way. Information may be stored temporarily in short-term memory by acoustic features (how the words *sound* when spoken), but it is organized in and retrieved from long-term memory primarily in terms of meaning (Baron, Byrne, and Kantowitz, 1977, p. 160).

To better understand the role meaning plays in memory, one might think of a single piece of information from a first college course in reading instruction; for example, *the vowel sounds in unstressed syllables are often, but not always, reduced to the schwa sound.* This information may have been held in short-term memory for a few seconds during a class lecture; long enough, perhaps, for the student to put it into his written notes. It went into long-term memory if (1) the student had wondered about the nature of the schwa sound and found in the lecture an immediate, satisfying answer to his personal question about it, or (2) later review of lecture notes had highlighted the information at a moment when the student thought "This helps me understand several matters about phonics instruction that puzzled me" or "The professor says it's important" or "This will help me be a better teacher" or "It will be on the final exam." This information is taken into long-term memory as part of an organized structure (related to phonics instruction, to reading instruction in general, to teaching, to one's survival as a college student) and may later be retrieved not as an isolated piece of information but as part of a meaningful larger structure. The reason for storage in long-term memory may become part of the retrieval mechanism.

Memories Are Often Reconstructions

People reconstruct their memories on the basis of whatever incomplete information is retrieved. Memory, like perception, is often a total picture built from fragments. Sometimes the fragments are more readily retrievable because of personal, dramatic, or visual impact they possess; sometimes they are reassembled to conform to current beliefs or prejudices. As Bartlett's famous experiment (1932) demonstrated, meaning is indeed crucial to long-term memory storage and retrieval, but other forces affect the final outcome. Bartlett had his subjects read a simple folk tale twice and then tested their ability to remember it after fifteen minutes, two months, and two and a half years. He found that the basic meaning of the story, its general outline (an Indian warrior believes incorrectly that he has been hit by enemy arrows and dies), remained in the memory of most of his subjects, but, as time went on, they tended to simplify or distort the story to conform to their personal prejudices. The basic *meaning* (strong belief that death was coming actually led to death) frequently remained but details were omitted or distorted as subjects rebuilt their memories.

Semantic versus Episodic Memory

Bartlett's study leads to an important distinction made in current memory study: *Semantic memory* (knowledge of conceptual relations about the world) is different from *episodic memory* (one's personal record of individual experiences). Both are aspects of long-term memory but reflect different kinds of memories. For example, Bob's knowledge that carrots grew underground is part of his semantic memory, but Sally's knowledge that she is destined to have them for dinner (and that she hates them) is part of her episodic memory. Her knowledge that clouds contain water is part of semantic memory, and his knowledge that he got caught in a rainstorm yesterday is episodic. Idiosyncratic interpretations of text are usually the result of readers' reliance on their episodic memories. Failure to comprehend the sentence "November is the penultimate month of the year" is probably due to inadequate semantic memory; the reader does not include in his or her prior knowledge a commonly accepted definition of the word *penultimate.*

Prior knowledge includes both semantic and episodic memories. Both affect comprehension. Semantic memories in prior knowledge tend to be shared with others ("George Washington was the first president"); episodic memories are personal and unlikely to be known to others ("I was elected president of my third-grade class at the George Washington Elementary School in Hightsville, Maine"). Therefore when readers use prior knowledge of the world, based on semantic memory and similar to knowledge shared by writers, they have a better chance of comprehending than when they have to rely solely on their own episodic memory. (While recognizing the important distinction between the two types of memory, some psychologists note that there is no strict line dividing them. All semantic memory, they note, begins as episodic. "George Washington was the first president" was initially episodic information the first time it was learned.)

Recent studies of semantic memory have been stimulated by efforts to program computers to understand conversation. M. R. Quillian (1969) wanted the computer to use a semantic network to represent the deep structure of memory. The "full meaning" of each word was to be the direct and indirect connections it had with all other related words in the semantic network. He developed hierarchical arrangements for given concepts: *bird,* for example, was subordinate in the network to *animal* but had subordinate to it *eagle, canary, ostrich,* etc. According to his scheme, specific properties, such as "has wings," could be stored only at appropriate levels (thus, not with *animals*).

From Quillian's initial studies a variety of other approaches has developed. One, the *feature-list model* (Smith, Shoben, and Rips, 1974) uses lists of sets of elements to describe concepts. It assumes that the meaning of a word is a list of semantic features, either *characteristic features* or *defining features*. Robins and chickens are *birds* because both have defining features of birds (beaks, wings, feathers), but a chicken does not have the characteristic features of a bird (it cannot fly). A bat, according to this system, is not a true bird because, although it has the characteristic feature of flying, it lacks the defining feature of feathers. To make the system more workable, a set of *linguistic hedges* has been added to it: one can say, for example, "loosely speaking," a bat is a bird, or "technically speaking," a chicken is a bird, or a robin is a "true" bird.

Examinations of semantic and episodic memory have proved valuable to researchers in comprehension for at least two reasons: (1) they offer a relatively firm definition of that difficult-to-define term "meaning" and (2) they help clarify prior knowledge by distinguishing between the individual, personal knowledge found in episodic memory and the more "public," commonly accepted knowledge found in semantic memory.

Memory and Prior Knowledge ───────────────────────────

The knowledge of the world that readers bring to a text affects their comprehension of it, and that knowledge is found in their memories. However, as Smith has pointed out, it would be simplistic to suggest that students carry around in their heads just "memories," implying that the brain is "an audiovisual souvenir album filled with snapshots and tape recordings of the past" (1978, p. 56).

The memories that comprise prior knowledge, as this brief review indicates, are

long-term (unlike the small amount of information held for less than a second in sensory storage memory or for only a few seconds in short-term memory, this information is held indefinitely);

available (while it is not always accessible, this information remains stored and capable of being retrieved);

stored systematically (information is not tucked away in a haphazard manner; new information is related systematically to information already present so that organized networks are established);

stored in terms of meaning (the systematic networks highlight relationships; thus a new item of information takes meaning from the ways it relates—or fails to relate—to another item);

(often) *summaries of past experiences* (students do not remember that they used the encyclopedia on Monday and again on Tuesday, that they looked something up on Wednesday and again on Thursday; they remember that encyclopedias are repositories of information, places where they can "look things up");

reconstructions (they are rebuilt from the bits and pieces that are retrieved, and the rebuildings are often colored by prejudices, desires, and present perspectives of the world); and

semantic and episodic (that is, some memories are highly personal, meaningful only to the individual, and some reflect knowledge of conceptual relations about the world shared by most other people).

SCHEMA THEORY AND READING COMPREHENSION

Of all the recent research and speculation about the comprehension process, that associated with schema theory seems to have had unique impact upon the ways reading teachers now view concepts and their development and organization, upon word knowledge and world knowledge in general, and upon memory and the way it works. Because of its influence, it is important here to review some of that research and speculation.

What Is Schema Theory?

Schema theory, as it has evolved in the past decade, is a theory about knowledge, about how knowledge is represented, and about how that representation facilitates the use of knowledge in various ways. According to schema theorists, all knowledge is packaged in units, called *schemata,* and embedded into these units of knowledge (in addition to the knowledge itself) is information on how this knowledge is to be used.

Each separate schema, then, is a device for representing knowledge of a concept, along with specifications for relating it to an appropriate network of connections that seem to hold among all constituents of that particular concept. Thus, to use the simplest example, after years of using and observing pencils students develop a kind of summary of all their experiences with pencils, a theory of what a pencil is and does, a "mental model" (or schema!) for pencil. That summary-in-the-head, or theory, or mental model, allows them to better deal with new pencils and pencil-like objects when they encounter them, to more effectively store and retrieve from memory information about pencils, and to use "pencil data" in a variety of ways. When students read the word *pencil,* they have in their heads (teachers hope) a schema for the concept of pencil, one that includes all the types of pencils they have observed, all the personal experiences they have had in their lives with pencils, and all the properties of pencils they have noted (that they are for making marks, drawing, or writing, that they may be easily held in the hand, that they are usually, though not always, of wood, etc.).

However, schemata may represent more than knowledge about concepts of objects like pencils; they may represent knowledge about all concepts, those underlying situations, events, sequences of events, actions, and sequences of actions. Rumelhart (1980, pp. 35–37) explains a schema for an action or sequence of actions. The internal structure of such a schema corresponds, he says, to the script of a play. Just as a play has characters that may be played at different times by different actors, so a schema has *variables* that may be *instantiated* (or enacted) at different times by different "actors." He uses the example of the schema for the concept *buy*. Its "script" needs a SELLER, a PURCHASER, some MERCHANDISE, and some medium of exchange, MONEY. Whatever else happens in this play, some interaction, BARGAINING, must take place between the SELLER and the PURCHASER for the MERCHANDISE. The SELLER and the PURCHASER may vary in age, occupation, nationality, weight, height, race, and so on; the MERCHANDISE may vary from an automobile to a trinket to a parcel of land. The MONEY may be actual money or some object for swapping; the BARGAINING may vary in many ways. However, no matter what the variations, as long as the fundamental "plot" remains the same, the BUY play is being performed.

Rumelhart says, "This little play is very much like the schema that I believe underlies our understanding of the concept *buy* or that for *sell*" (p. 36). When people understand a situation to be a case of BUYING, they associate persons, objects, and events with the various variables of their schema for BUYING. The *instantiation of a schema* is like the *enactment of a play*. A play is enacted when certain actors say certain lines at a particular time and place; a schema is instantiated "whenever a particular configuration of values is bound to a particular configuration of variables at a particular moment in time" (p. 36). Just as it is possible, he says, to take a movie of an enactment of a play and thereby save for posterity a trace of the enactment, so it is the traces of our instantiated schemata that are the basis of our memories.

Clearly a schema is an abstraction; it must be applicable to any case of instantiation. A play script is an abstraction in the sense that when it is enacted directors, actors, designers, and others associated with the production may present highly individualized interpretations; a schema for an action or series of actions also allows for creative interpretation or even irrelevant variations. Individuals acting out (instantiating) the *buy* schema may introduce prolonged haggling, humor, assumed reluctance, anger, or other items "not scripted."

By thinking through the schema for an action or series of actions and comparing it to the script for a play, as Rumelhart does, teachers may get a better understanding of the schema for an object like *pencil*. In such a case, the schema does not specify actions but rather spatial and functional relationships. A chair, for example, IS FOR SITTING, HAS LEGS, HAS BACK, etc. Our understanding of chairs is shaped by our knowledge of these defining features.

A schema may be said to be an individual's private, unarticulated theory of an object, event, action, or sequence of actions or events. Just as researchers test out their theories by comparing them with their observation of the world around them, so do individuals constantly test their schemata. Every time we go through a supermarket checkout counter we are testing our schema for *supermarket checkout*. When we order in a restaurant we are testing our schemata for *ordering in a restaurant*. Each encounter with a chair or pencil or pair of skis provides opportunities for testing appropriate schemata. When a hitherto acceptable schema fails for some reason to account for some aspect of a situation, we either continue to hold the schema and discount our own observations and experience, or we reject it as inadequate and look for a better one. For most people, living is a process of discarding or reshaping and altering schemata.

As theories, schemata are a source of prediction about new objects, events, actions, and sequences of actions and events. All schemata cannot be tested out by observations; so people use their theories to make predictions about unobserved or nonobservable things and events. In daily life, for example, we assume that an automobile that has driven past us on the highway has headlights and a front bumper because our schema for *automobile* includes both; we assume that our pencils contain graphite because our pencil schema has graphite built into it. In reading, people regularly test out their theories. They read to discover how well their hypotheses "fit," and when they fail to find an appropriate configuration, they say the text is incomprehensible.

Some Functions of Schemata

The schemata that each person builds through a lifetime influence the processes of perception, remembering, and understanding discourse, as well as of learning and problem solving.

Perception   Considerable evidence supports the belief that people see what they are able to see (that is, what the schemata they hold in memory allow them to see). Stimuli in the environment serve as cues to trigger perceptions, but one's schemata contribute much toward the development of accurate percepts; or, to put it in other words, information from the sense organs suggests the appropriate schemata to be used for interpretation. A piece of wood is cut in one shape; a second piece in another shape; another in a different fashion. Yet a viewer *sees* a chair. Individually, the separate pieces mean little to the viewer, but, because of the way they are arranged or because of the context of the viewer's situation, they serve as cues to suggest the chair schema. (The viewer may never notice that there are idiosyncratic features of cut, shape, color, or texture; the little seen provides enough information to mentally construct what the viewer thinks a chair "ought to be.")

Studies indicate that observers' schemata may sometimes lead them astray. Stereotypes and other preconceptions regularly encourage people to see what they think they should see (welfare chiselers, mismanagement in Washington, alcoholic Irishmen, teenage irresponsibility, etc.). Such premature commitment to inappropriate or incorrect schemata may lead to distortions and illusions (see Baron, Byrne, and Kantowitz, 1977, pp. 75–107). Thus young readers often "see" words that are not on the page, and experienced readers "read" information into stories and news articles that authors did not include in their actual texts.

Understanding Discourse   Understanding spoken or written discourse may be seen as the process of finding a pattern of schemata that provide a reasonable account of the passages comprising the discourse. The Indian folk tale used in Bartlett's 1932 experiment "makes sense" only to those readers or listeners who share certain schemata (specifically, "theories" accounting for death in general, death by arrow, "mind over matter," etc.). Cues from the story suggest possibilities which readers and listeners treat as hypotheses and test out as the story moves along. They suggest possible interpretations (or *instantiations of schemata*) that are checked out against successive sentences until eventually a consistent interpretation is discovered.

Rumelhart (1984, p. 18) suggests three reasons, implicit in schema theory, to account for a reader's failure to comprehend a passage of discourse:

1. *The reader may not have the appropriate schemata.* A very young child, for example, may have no schema for death or death by arrow wound. An unsophisticated adult may have no schema for "mind over matter" and thus no way of hypothesizing that the Indian died because he believed he should die. In such cases the reader cannot understand the story at all.

2. *The reader may have the appropriate schemata, but the author may not have provided enough clues to suggest them.* In the passage cited earlier (from Bransford and Johnson, 1973) people who have washed clothes may find enough clues in the text to support their hypothesis; many others may not find a single clue to "activate" the proper schema (although they, too, may have washed clothes many times). In such a case the reader will not comprehend the text as it stands but, with the help of additional information, might come to understand it.

3. *The reader may find a consistent interpretation of the passage of discourse but not the one intended by the author.* Rumelhart tells of a Washington bureaucrat who insisted that he did indeed comprehend the clothes-washing passage: it was, he said, about his particular

job—"pushing papers." In a case such as this the reader "understood" the text but misunderstood the author.

Memory Clearly schemata play major roles in both perception and understanding discourse; they may also be the guiding forces behind remembering as well. Schemata affect perceptions; people do not, for example, see individual chairs or teenagers; they see the chairs and teenagers their schemata allow them to see. What goes into memory is not the vision of the "real" chair or young person but the viewer's interpretations of the perceptions as shaped by the schemata. In other words, people hold in memory not the actual perceptions but summaries or interpretations (based on their schemata) of the perceptions. As Smith (1978, p. 56) puts it, a person does not remember that he sat on a chair on July 16th and again sat on a chair on July 17th and again sat on a chair on July 18th. He remembers that chairs are for sitting on, a summary of the experience.

Schemata also affect the way material is recalled from memory. People do not always remember actual chairs or real teenagers; they recall their generalized versions. The forms of the *memorial fragments* have been shaped by the very schemata that shaped original perceptions. A child will not remember her fifth or eighth birthday party but her birthday-parties-in-general (perhaps all the birthday parties she has attended). An adult will not remember each specific time she drove to work but a summary of all the times she drove to work. Research suggests that the more time elapsed between the event and recall, the fewer memorial fragments are available, so people tend to rely on generic knowledge of similar situations; that is, on their schemata (Rumelhart, 1980, p. 50). In other words, just as comprehension involves selecting and verifying conceptual schemata to account for the situation to be understood, so remembering involves the process of selecting and verifying an appropriate configuration of schemata to account for the memorial fragments located in memory.

How Readers Use Schemata

Consider the following passage:

Today was decidedly not a good day for her to come. His "stars"—David and Martin—were not here. Already the coming holidays were affecting behaviors. Last night had been a long one. When he'd finally arrived back from Jean's, he'd had to read three sets of papers. He hadn't planned a thing, hoping to "wing it" through the hour. And maybe, if inspiration failed, having them do an in-class theme. But with old "Hawk-eye" Doyle sitting back there, he'd never get away with it.

This is clearly a fragment (from a novel, a short story, or possibly a journal). Many ordinary adult readers will make little sense of it. Most teachers, however, will agree on an interpretation: the narrator is expecting a visit from his supervisor, possibly his department head, principal, or coordinator; he is, unfortunately, unprepared for the visit (no lesson plan, vague ideas of extemporizing or assigning a composition), and, to make matters worse, he is still tired from a long evening, the coming holidays have infected the students with skittishness, and his two best students, who might carry some of the burden for him, are absent.

Why might teachers agree, more or less, with this interpretation? Why might non-teachers be perplexed (unless they included in *their* world knowledge considerable information about teachers and teaching)? What seems to happen here—and elsewhere in reading—is that certain items in the passage (words and phrases) activate schemata already in the minds of readers. As they continue to read on through the sentences, they test out the different activated schemata to see if they fit, discarding inappropriate ones and eventually adopting ones that pass the tests. The first sentence *might* suggest a newly married woman dreading the arrival of her mother-in-law! The reader may have a schema for a newly married woman's dreading the arrival of mothers-in-law but quickly discards it on encountering the "His" beginning the next sentence. "Stars" may suggest a sporting event, a team, and the arrival of a major league scout. The reader may have a schema for visits-from-major-league-scouts but discards this because scouts are unlikely to be women. "Behavior" may suggest a prison, hospital, or other institutional setting, but with the reference to "three sets of papers," a familiar pattern begins to emerge—for teachers and readers who know something of their working conditions. This pattern becomes another hypothesis to be tested and possibly confirmed by the reference to an "in-class theme."

Sometimes readers seem to use a *bottom-up* approach to their theory-testing. They note details (such as the three sets of papers and the in-class theme) and guess at a theory that could account for them. (This is called *data-driven processing*.) Sometimes they make a good initial guess at what seems to be happening (because, for example, they know beforehand that the writer is a teacher or an illustration shows a schoolroom) and verify their guess as they read; thus using a *top-down* approach (also called *conceptually driven*). Probably most readers use both approaches simultaneously.

The process of comprehension, as seen by schema theorists, seems much like the process of developing a theory with all its attendant hypotheses-making and hypotheses-testing. In reading, however, the hypotheses are schemata already in the memories of readers and include all the prior knowledge they bring to texts.

Where Do Schemata Come From?

People acquire their schemata through their experiences—both real and vicarious. They seem to abstract common elements from experiences, encode them in memory, and use them later as predictors when they encounter similar-appearing experiences. These schemata thus become theories or "mental models" (or "scripts") explaining how the world works. People have schemata then for pencils, chairs, teachers, and automobile salesmen, as well as for writing, sitting, teaching, and selling cars. They even have schemata for motives for writing, sitting, teaching, and selling, as well as schemata for the kinds of responses they may make to these motives.

Schemata change. As people have more and more experiences, they refine, reshape, correct, and restructure their schemata. An adult's schema for *teacher* is seldom the same as a first-grader's; a newspaper reporter's schema for *writing* is rarely comparable to that held by a college freshman. One of the major problems involved in comprehension is that all people hardly ever share the same schemata; one of the problems in reading comprehension is that readers do not always hold the same schemata as do writers.

Rumelhart calls schemata "the building blocks of cognition," noting that they are the fundamental elements on which all information processing depends. They are used, as he points out, in interpreting sensory data, in retrieving information from memory, in organizing actions, in determining goals, in allocating resources, and in guiding the flow of processing in the system. He further notes that "any device capable of all these wondrous things must be very powerful indeed" (Rumelhart, 1980, p. 34).

As teachers work out their own theories of the comprehension process, they will find it difficult to avoid schema theory and its implications for reading. (Further discussions of the ways schemata are enriched, refined, and restructured may be found in Chapter 4.)

Teachers seeking more information on schema theory will find an excellent brief description in Rumelhart (1984); a fine discussion of its relationship to the reading process may be found in Anderson and Pearson (1984).

▪ RECAPPING MAIN POINTS ▪

Comprehension of print is markedly influenced by the previously acquired knowledge readers bring to texts. Because readers make sense of new information by relating it to what they already know, the quantity and quality of their prior knowledge shapes their interpretations of texts. Of all prior knowledge, knowledge of word meanings is most important; without it, comprehension is impossible.

All this knowledge, both general "world" knowledge and word meaning knowledge, is held in long-term memory. It is stored systematically, in terms of meaning, and usually as summaries of past experiences.

One recent theory that accounts for the ways learners encode, store, and retrieve knowledge is *schema theory*. It suggests that learners abstract and generalize from their experiences *schemata*, which may also influence how they interpret sensory data, organize actions, determine goals, and guide the flow of processing through the system. Because of its power to account for so many important mental activities, schema theory has had a profound effect on recent research and theory in reading comprehension.

END-OF-CHAPTER ACTIVITIES

1. Several terms are offered here as synonyms for *prior knowledge.* What others occur to you? What differences do you perceive in the meanings for these terms? Which do you prefer? Why?

2. With another student, list five common words and then, separately, write your own personal meanings for these words. Compare the personal meanings. How do you account for any differences expressed? What specific differences may be explained by your different biographies? Explain how your answers relate to the chapter's discussion of prior knowledge.

3. Find examples from newspapers or advertisements that assume readers share certain common experiential backgrounds. Find examples that assume readers have information they may not have. Explain how your examples support—or fail to support—the view of prior knowledge presented here.

4. What is your own favorite example of "Prior Knowledge at Work"?

5. Explain in your own words the term *assumptive teaching.* In what ways is assumptive teaching related to the discussion of prior knowledge?

6. List reasons for supporting the belief that word knowledge is the most important kind of prior knowledge.

7. What is the essential difference between short- and long-term memory? Can one be said to be more important than the other? Tell in your own words how information gets from short- to long-term memory.

8. It is said that memories are often reconstructions. Give an example from your own life of a present-day memory that is clearly a reconstruction. From your example, what may be inferred about the ways human memory tends to work?

9. Explain the difference between semantic and episodic memory. Give an example of each from your own life. Why do some psychologists believe no strict line divides them? Use your personal example to explain.

10. Why is knowledge about human memory important to understanding how prior knowledge affects comprehension?

11. Give a definition in your own words of *schema*. In what ways is a schema like a concept? unlike a concept?
12. The chapter gives a schema for the concept *buy*. Develop briefly a schema for *teach*. What are its *variables?* How may it be *instantiated*, or enacted? In what ways is this like a "script"? a "plot"? a "performance"?
13. Show how your schema for *teach* may express some of the functions of all schemata. In what ways may it affect *perception? understanding discourse? memory?* How might it affect *your* behavior in a classroom?
14. The chapter suggests that schema theory provides special insights into our understanding of memory and how prior knowledge affects comprehension. What are some of these insights? What specific insights did you personally derive from this discussion?
15. In what ways did your prior knowledge affect your reading of Chapter 2? Be specific.
16. Write a brief paper on "The Influence of Prior Knowledge" using your experiences with the chapter as data.

REFERENCES

Anderson, Richard C., and P. David Pearson. "A Schema-Theoretic View of Basic Processes in Reading." In P. David Pearson (Ed.), *Handbook of Reading Research.* New York: Longman, 1984.

Baron, Robert A., Donn Byrne, and Barry H. Kantowitz. *Psychology: Understanding Behavior.* Philadelphia: W. B. Saunders, 1977.

Bartlett, F. C. *Remembering: A Study in Experimental and Social Psychology.* Cambridge: Cambridge University Press, 1932.

Bransford, J. D., and M. K. Johnson. "Consideration of Some Problems of Comprehension." In W. Chase (Ed.), *Visual Information Processing.* New York: Academic Press, 1973.

Campbell, Jeremy. *Grammatical Man: Information, Entropy, Language, and Life.* New York: Simon & Schuster, 1982.

Dale, Edgar, and Joseph O'Rourke. *Techniques for Teaching Vocabulary.* Palo Alto, Calif.: Field Educational Publications, 1971.

Davis, Bertha. *The Ways of Man: An Introduction to Many Cultures.* New York: Macmillan, 1971.

Davis, Frederick B. "Research in Comprehension in Reading." *Reading Research Quarterly* 4 (1968): 499–545.

Davis, Frederick B. "Psychometric Research on Comprehension in Reading." *Reading Research Quarterly* 7 (1972): 628–678.

Deighton, Lee C. *Vocabulary Development in the Classroom.* New York: Teachers College Press, 1959.

Devine, Thomas G. *Teaching Study Skills: A Guide for Teachers*. Boston: Allyn and Bacon, 1981.

Durkin, Dolores. *Teaching Them to Read*, 4th ed. Boston: Allyn and Bacon, 1983.

Frost, Robert. Edward Connery Latham (Ed.), *The Poetry of Robert Frost*. New York: Holt, Rinehart and Winston, 1967.

Hayes, David A., and Robert J. Tierney. "Developing Readers' Knowledge through Analogy." *Reading Research Quarterly* 17 (1982): 256–280.

Herber, Harold L. *Teaching Reading in the Content Areas*. Englewood Cliffs, N. J.: Prentice-Hall, 1978.

Johnston, Peter, and P. David Pearson. *Prior Knowledge, Connectivity, and the Assessment of Reading Comprehension*. (Technical Report No. 245.) Champaign, Ill.: Center for the Study of Reading, 1982.

Pearson, P. David, and Dale D. Johnson. *Teaching Reading Comprehension*. New York: Holt, Rinehart and Winston, 1978.

Quillian, M. R. "The Teachable Language Comprehender: A Simulation Program and a Theory of Language." *Communications of the Association for Computing Machinery* 12 (1969): 459–476.

Rumelhart, David E. "Schemata: The Building Blocks of Cognition." In R. J. Spiro, B. C. Bruce, and W. F. Brewer (Eds.), *Theoretical Issues in Reading Comprehension*. Hillsdale, N. J.: Lawrence Erlbaum Associates, 1980.

Rumelhart, David E. "Understanding Understanding." In James Flood (Ed.), *Understanding Reading Comprehension*. Newark, Del.: International Reading Association, 1984.

Salus, Peter H., and Mary W. Salus. "Word Finding, Word Organizing, and Reading." In James Flood (Ed.), *Understanding Reading Comprehension*. Newark, Del.: International Reading Association, 1984.

Shiffrin, R. M., and R. C. Atkinson. "Storage and Retrieval Processes in Long-term Memory." *Psychological Review* 76 (1969): 179–193.

Smith, E. E., E. J. Shoben, and L. J. Rips. "Structure and Process in Semantic Memory: A Feature Model for Semantic Decisions." *Psychological Review* 81 (1974): 214–224.

Smith, Frank. *Understanding Reading*, 2nd ed. New York: Holt, Rinehart and Winston, 1978.

Spearritt, D. "Identification of Subskills of Reading Comprehension by Maximum Likelihood Factor Analysis." *Reading Research Quarterly* 8 (1972): 92–111.

Tulving, E. "Theoretical Issues in Free Recall." In T. R. Dixon and D. L. Horton (Eds.), *Verbal Behavior and General Behavior*. Englewood Cliffs, N. J.: Prentice-Hall, 1968.

Research and Theory— What Is Reading Comprehension?

▪ INTRODUCTION AND OVERVIEW ▪

Any explanation of the reading comprehension process must rest to some extent on the four assumptions discussed in Chapter 1:

- Readers must know the coding system used by the writer (that is, they must possess linguistic competence).
- They must be motivated to figure out the code.
- They must have texts that can be decoded by readers like themselves.
- They need at least a modicum of prior knowledge about the information in the text to be read (especially knowledge of the meanings of words used).

An explanation must also consider five other possible factors that seem to affect comprehension:

- Readers' ability to use certain cognitive skills
- Their ability to use related reading skills
- Their ability to reason
- Their knowledge of the ways writers structure texts
- Their social and cultural backgrounds

This chapter examines these factors and then explains what probably happens as readers try to comprehend.

Chapter 3 includes Suggested Study Questions, and then discussions of

- What Other Factors Affect Comprehension?
  Cognitive skills and comprehension

Related reading comprehension skills
Reasoning and comprehension
Text structure and comprehension
Readers' social-cultural backgrounds
Some parameters in theory development
- What Happens As Students Try to Comprehend?

Chapter 3 also includes

- Recapping Main Points
- End-of-Chapter Activities
- References

▪ SUGGESTED STUDY QUESTIONS FOR CHAPTER 3 ▪

1. What cognitive skills are frequently involved in comprehension?
2. In what ways are so-called *reading comprehension skills* similar to cognitive skills? dissimilar to them?
3. What is the rationale for arranging comprehension skills in hierarchies or levels? What are the arguments against hierarchies and levels?
4. What role does reasoning play in the comprehension process? Is comprehension simply ''thinking''? ''problem solving''?
5. What role does text structure play in the comprehension process?
6. Which patterns of text organization need to be taught to students? Why?
7. What kinds of patterns are found in narratives? What is *story grammar*?
8. What explanation of the comprehension process is offered here? What are its strengths? weaknesses?

WHAT OTHER FACTORS AFFECT COMPREHENSION?

The consensus today is that before readers can begin to comprehend printed texts they must have some degree of linguistic competence, be motivated, possess reasonably readable texts, and have at least a modicum of prior knowledge. Some suggest they also need ability to use certain key cognitive and related reading skills, some reasoning power, knowledge of text structures, and social-cultural backgrounds appropriate to the reading materials. We examine these five factors before suggesting an answer to the question, What is reading comprehension?

Cognitive Skills and Comprehension

Unless readers immediately and effortlessly understand texts (for example, signs such as "EXIT" and simple sentences like "Jane fell"), they evidently need to use certain higher mental processes; that is, they need to infer, predict, draw conclusions, hypothesize, and so on. Many cognitive psychologists today refer to these postulated mental processes as *cognitive skills* and suggest that they are teachable (see, for example, Anderson, 1980). Some students are relatively successful in using these skills (through life experiences, previous teaching, or learning by trial and error); others are less sophisticated. Readers' ability to use cognitive skills, however, seems to influence their success or failure in comprehending.

What are the most important cognitive skills for comprehending? Several correlational studies attempt to identify the key processes in reading comprehension (Davis, 1968; Davis, 1972; Spearritt, 1972). One cognitive skill was identified in all three analyses: *drawing inferences*. (As previously noted, *recalling word meanings* proved to be the most powerful single factor in these analyses; see Chapter 2.) Several investigations of the professional literature pinpoint those skills that authorities agree are of major importance (see Rosenshine, 1980): recognizing sequence, recognizing cause and effect, identifying main ideas, drawing inferences, comparing and contrasting, and noting significant details.

Research findings in the area of cognitive skills and processes are as yet inconclusive (again, see Anderson, 1980), but it seems fairly reasonable to say that, when readers try to comprehend texts above the simplest levels ("EXIT," "REST ROOMS," "TELEPHONE," etc.), they do use certain cognitive skills. A basic list of such skills would probably include the following:

Drawing inferences

Predicting

Hypothesizing

Drawing conclusions

Recognizing sequence

Recognizing cause and effect

Identifying main ideas or key points

Comparing and contrasting

Noting significant details

Relating Reading Comprehension Skills _____

There is at present little evidence to support a belief in specific reading comprehension skills (Rosenshine, 1980). However, most reading teachers and specialists believe that at least some hypothesized reading skills do relate strongly to certain cognitive skills. "Predicting story outcomes," for example, seems to rest on the cognitive skill of predicting; "recognizing an author's inferences" seems to be related to the higher mental process of inferring. Although research findings do not yet support one-to-one relationships between postulated cognitive skills and corresponding hypothesized reading comprehension skills, there is some consensus among reading teachers that students' ability to use these reading skills does influence comprehension.

Unfortunately, some specialists sometimes substitute for comprehension instruction the teaching of discrete, specific—but still highly hypothetical—reading comprehension skills. Thus many professional books, curriculum guides, and instructional materials present *lists* of such skills rather than suggestions for teaching. The "skills approach" clearly offers advantages (especially for less experienced teachers): it appears to make the complex simple by ordering it and spelling out its parts; it provides teachers with specific objectives for individual lessons; it allows a framework for long-range curriculum planning; and so on. These advantages tend to lose their attractiveness when teachers realize that (1) authorities are unable to agree on their lists (see Rosenshine, 1980); (2) various statistical studies can identify only a single "skill" (*recalling word meanings*) consistently; and (3) readers may not use individual skills as they try to comprehend (see the following section, "What Happens As Students Try to Comprehend").

The term *skill* generally refers to the proficiency a learner achieves on a specific task or limited group of related tasks. Thus there are distinct skills involved in bicycle riding or clarinet playing. These are possibly best mastered in some orderly sequence (although few teachers of either will agree on the precise sequence). There may be distinct, discrete skills involved in decoding a text (such as moving the eyes from left to right across the page or matching letters with appropriate sounds). These too may possibly be best mastered in some orderly sequence.

That comparable "skills" are involved in comprehension is doubtful. Typical lists of skills reveal such items as *Finding main ideas, Following sequence,* or *Drawing conclusions.* Reading teachers need to be reminded that these "skills" are actually *mental constructs* postulated by theorists and hardly comparable to skills involved in swimming, typewriting, or even beginning reading. Evidence that they have been achieved by learners may be obtained but generally only in task situations unrelated to the comprehension of a given text. Thus a teacher may provide instruction in *Finding main ideas* and test to discover if children can indeed identify the *main idea* previously selected by the teacher; but the student's success in finding the *right* main idea is not necessarily the same as comprehending the text containing the main idea. The comprehension skills so often listed in the professional literature seem to be *higher mental processes* (sometimes called *cognitive skills*), which may—or may not—be involved in the comprehension process but are certainly not synonymous with comprehension.

Unfortunately, too, the belief in specific comprehension skills has led to the structuring of comprehension skills in various hierarchical arrangements according to *levels* of comprehension. Thus some are grouped (at the bottom!) under *literal*, or "on the line," comprehension skills; some as *inferential*, or "between the lines," and some as *critical*, or "beyond the lines." Such ordering (probably based on an analogy to the taxonomy of educational objectives developed by Bloom, 1956) may help reading teachers divide the sources of comprehension into three important components: they can think of literal comprehension as that which is extracted from information explicit in the text, of inferential comprehension as that extracted from information implicit in the text, and of critical comprehension as that extracted from the reader's prior knowledge.

However, several objections are increasingly being made to the ranking of reading comprehension skills in hierarchies according to levels:

1. No firm research evidence supports the belief in well-defined, separate, discrete reading comprehension skills, much less hierarchies of such skills.
2. If there were well-defined comprehension skills, there is no reason to believe that one skill or set of skills must be learned before another. (Readers do not have to learn to find main ideas before they can distinguish facts from opinions. They do not have to go through an inferential level before they can reach the critical comprehension level.)
3. Those cognitive skills that do seem to play a part in the comprehension process (for example, inferring, predicting, hypothesizing, drawing conclusions, etc.) are not learned separately, one at a time, one before the other; nor are they used separately very often. Even young readers make inferences, follow sequence, evaluate, and note main ideas simultaneously. Reading, like thinking, is a unitary or holistic activity in which all processes operate together and constantly intermesh.
4. This approach takes only the source of comprehension into account: it fails to consider the dynamic, active interaction of writer, text, and reader. (See next section, "What Happens As Students Try to Comprehend.")
5. The hierarchical, *levels* approach tends to confuse reasoning with comprehension, and these may be relatable but not equatable activities. Readers may easily comprehend a text such as "EXIT" without actively reasoning; on the other hand, they may operate exclu-

sively on the inferential and critical levels without comprehending. (A particular text may stimulate high-level intellectual activity—syllogistic reasoning, critical thinking, problem solving, etc.—but remain incomprehensible; note, for example, a technical paper out of one's field of knowledge or a literary work such as James Joyce's *Finnegans Wake*.)

Reasoning and Comprehension

As noted in the previous section, little reasoning ability is needed to comprehend texts such as "TELEPHONE" or "Jane fell." Considerable reasoning ability is needed to construct meanings for other texts. Readers often must not only use basic cognitive skills but use them in highly sophisticated ways. Certain texts demand that readers use problem-solving techniques, high-level analysis, critical thinking, and even syllogistic reasoning. The line separating advanced reasoning from comprehension is not firm, but some research findings indicate that it does exist. Some teachers are actually teaching advanced skills in logic or propaganda analysis when they think they are simply helping students to comprehend; some materials in comprehension instruction are actually designed to teach cause-and-effect relationships, statistical fallacies, synthesizing, stereotyping, and logic. Clearly readers' ability to do advanced reasoning, although it is not quite the same as comprehension, influences readers' ability to comprehend.

Two decades ago (see Carver, 1973) reading comprehension was divided by Spache into four "levels," or stages:

1. Decoding of words and determination of their meaning in a particular sentence
2. Combining meanings of individual words into complete understanding of the sentence
3. Understanding of the paragraph and its implied main idea, as well as cause and effect, hypothesis-proof, implications, unstated conclusions, and ideas associated with but tangential to the main idea of a paragraph
4. Evaluation of ideas, including questions of logic, proof, authenticity, and value judgments

The mental activity involved in the first two seems minimal. Efficient readers presumably have achieved a high degree of automaticity in decoding, and they share enough comparable word meanings with the writers they read to allow them to attain "complete understanding" of the sentences. Thus *The cat ate the goldfish* presents few (if any) "intellectual" problems to readers with linguistic competence in English. *The goldfish ate the cat,* on the other hand, presents *thinking* problems to both children and sophisticated adult readers.

Their prior knowledge (of the world) tells them that goldfish are small and cats considerably larger, thus posing major ingesting problems. Readers of this second sentence have need to cogitate: "Why," they may ask, "does the writer say *that?* Is she implying something I can't understand? Does she assume I know something I don't know? Has she some idiosyncratic definition for *cat?* for *goldfish?* Is she mad? Is she unacquainted with the normal syntax of English?" Readers may conclude that the writer is learning English, is playing tricks, is using some poetic device unknown to them, or indeed is mad.

Readers of the second sentence—children or adults—are operating on the third and fourth "levels" or stages Spache has described. They are involved with considerable mental activity: hypothesizing, inferring, guessing at implications, looking at logic, drawing conclusions, making judgments.

Some theorists say that a line may be drawn to separate the first half of Spache's description of reading comprehension from the second half. Everything above the line represents *reading;* everything below, *reasoning.* They note that sentences such as *The cat ate the goldfish* may be comprehended immediately if readers have sufficient linguistic competence and know the words, but that sentences such as *The golfish ate the cat* demand reasoning competence (which may be related to linguistic competence but not necessarily synonymous with it). Such theorists are especially concerned with reading tests that fail to distinguish between reading and reasoning. Carver (1973), for example, notes that most reading tests used in schools are heavily weighted with items measuring reasoning competence and are therefore not testing reading but rather students' powers to use cognitive skills.

This distinction is important to reading teachers. The widely accepted three-levels approach (discussed in the preceding section) *implies* a distinction: at the *literal* level readers evidently extract information explicit in the text, while at the other two levels they infer information implied in the text and evaluate it according to other information they already possess. However, most advocates of the three-level point of view seem to suggest that levels 2 and 3 are somehow more "advanced" than the first level and that readers move from 1 to 2 to 3. Reading teachers need to think about the distinction, because it does influence what happens in classrooms. Teachers need to answer such questions as: Does this particular strategy improve comprehension or thinking? When should I focus on specific thinking skills? Which ones are most valuable for my students? Do students need to master syllogistic reasoning to comprehend texts? When have I stopped teaching comprehension and started teaching critical thinking? Am I using texts as springboards into logic lessons? What am I testing, comprehension or reasoning?

Text Structure and Comprehension

Writers put their texts together in systematic, organized ways if they expect to be understood. Readers who know the plans of organization used by writers have an advantage over those who do not. When students can see that a passage is following a simple chronological sequence or is arranged in the form of a generalization with supporting evidence, they are in a better position to comprehend the text. Students who include in their prior knowledge information about standard rhetorical organizational patterns tend to more easily reconstruct in their minds what a writer may be trying to say.

In some theories of the comprehension process, text is primary; it is where comprehension begins and ends, and it shapes the process. In others, as has been noted, text serves as the blueprint from which readers build their own personal "texts-in-the-heads." All theories, however, must recognize that text plays a role in the comprehension process. Because texts play a prominent role in the explanation of the comprehension process described in the next section ("What Happens As Students Try to Comprehend"), it is important to discuss three observations about their nature and structure.

Texts Are Structured   As writers write they impose some kind of order on the ideas and information put to paper. They know (intuitively, perhaps) that unrelated sentences and lists of words and phrases tend to be meaningless to readers, that unorganized material tends to be misperceived or unperceived, misremembered or forgotten immediately. "Ordered discourse" seems mandatory if comprehension is expected.

A child relating his recollections of a birthday party usually arranges individual items into chronological sequence; a television comedian telling a joke uses a similar sequence but arranges his items skillfully to lead to a climax. The author of a short story may follow a chronological sequence but vary it with flashbacks; biographers tend to follow their subjects' lives in orderly sequence.

Many theorists today believe that there is not only a "grammar" of narration but also established patterns of organization for all expository prose. A high school senior presenting her position on a controversial issue before the student council tends to make a general statement ("Our seniors may be trusted to police their own prom") and justify it with carefully selected examples of student behavior at its best; the author of a biology textbook explains the possible causes of a given effect in a systematic manner; the writer of a letter to the college newspaper presents her position by comparing and contrasting it with other points of view. Most extended discourse evidently is developed according to some plan of organization.

"Grammars" for narratives have been studied extensively in recent years. Researchers like Stein and Glenn (1979) have noted that (1) stories have internal structures; (2) these structures may be depicted as hierarchical networks of units of information serving different functions in stories; (3) logical relations exist among these units; (4) hierarchical structures correspond to some extent to the ways readers comprehend and store information in stories; and (5) readers more easily remember items higher up in the hierarchical networks.

Much of this *story grammar* research grew out of the work of the Russian scholar Vladimir Propp, who tried to classify Russian folktales. He found that it was possible to list the functions within a tale. (A "function" would be an act of dramatis personae defined from the point of view of its significance for the course of action of the story.) One tale led to thirty-one separate functions: from "One of the family members leaves home" to "The hero marries and ascends the throne." From the thirty-one functions, Propp isolated seven *spheres of action*, each of which concerns the actions of one character. After applying this technique to many stories, he suggested that (1) functions of characters serve as stable, constant elements in a story, as its fundamental components; (2) the number of functions is limited; (3) the sequence of functions is always identical; and (4) all tales are of one type in regard to their structure (see Morgan and Sellner, 1980, pp. 181–184).

Research in story grammar makes it clear that stories have a structure. Some see parallels between such story structures and linguistic structures, suggesting that story grammar may be much like the tacit knowledge of syntax associated with the Chomskyan view of language. They postulate "rules," something that looks like a context-sensitive phrase grammar, and terminology appropriate to such a grammar (terms, for example, such as *simple story, kernel story,* and *complex story*). They imply that the structure of narratives is, like the grammar of the language, "built into" all people. (See Prince, 1973, or Rumelhart, 1975.)

Structures of other kinds of expository writing have been discussed in the professional literature for many years. Authors of high school and college composition textbooks, for example, have kept alive the traditions of medieval and eighteenth-century rhetoric, teaching that writers develop paragraphs and longer passages of discourse by exemplification, process analysis, causal analysis, comparison and contrast, and chronological order. Such rhetoric books show students how to structure their compositions according to well-established (truly time-tested) plans of organizations. (See Devine, 1981, pp. 227–237.)

Reading teachers have noted—and taught—such basic organizational patterns for many years. Niles (1965, p. 60) found four used regularly in school textbooks (enumeration, time order, cause-effect, and comparison-contrast); she recommended that reading teachers teach them to help students comprehend the books. Herber (1978) in a study of content area textbooks found the same patterns predominating and suggested that they be taught to readers. Robinson (1978) found certain organizational patterns common to certain school subjects: in science, for example, enumeration, classification, generalization, problem solution, comparison and contrast, and sequence; in mathematics, concept development, principle development, and problem solution; in social studies, topic development, enumeration, generalization, sequence, comparison and contrast, effect-cause, and question-answer. The patterns of organization noted by reading specialists and teachers tend to be the same patterns recommended by authors of composition books: process analysis becomes the reading teacher's time pattern, causal analysis becomes cause-effect, exemplification becomes generalization-supported-by-examples, and so on.

Some researchers believe that these patterns have become oversimplified, and note that no agreed-upon taxonomy of prose structures exists. Estes, for example, thinks it naive to talk about comparison-contrast, cause-effect, and enumeration as if they were unifying patterns which differentiate texts and may be taught to readers (1982, pp. 86–87). Others continue to study them and have developed useful classification schemes. Brewer, for example, sees four basic "forces" which lead to four kinds of discourse (informative, persuasive, entertaining, and literary-aesthetic) and three "structures" (descriptive, narrative, and expository). From these he has constructed a classification scheme with twelve categories, one which may be of value to teachers examining organizational patterns (Brewer, 1980, pp. 221–239). Meyer has proposed another description based on a set of hierarchically nested segments: (1) antecedent/consequent, (2) comparison or contrast, (3) collection or list, (4) description, and (5) response (Meyer, 1984). (More information about organizational patterns may be found in Chapter 7.)

Structures May Correspond to "Rules" of Thought   It may be that people tend to think in patterns. The rhetorical patterns found in composition textbooks go back 2,500 years to ancient Greek rhetoricians. Perhaps they were originated by the early philosophers and have been kept alive as part of a rhetorical tradition. However, they may be "built into" the human mind. It may be that people "naturally" put ideas and information into time sequence, comparison and contrast arrangements, cause-effect relationships, and so on. No one knows at this time if there are any "rules" of thought or mind that govern discourse, although some researchers believe this is "one of the most promising areas of psychological inquiry and one which may someday have most important educational implications" (Goetz and Armbruster, 1980, p. 217).

Text Organization Is in the Mind of the Reader As Much As on the Printed Page   Writers try to organize what they write as an aid for themselves in writing and as an aid for their readers in comprehending. Readers, however, tend to organize what they read *as they read.* The structure of a text, no matter how well established in the writer's mind, is ultimately *realized* by readers. This realization is made easier when readers' perceptions are guided by well-organized texts; thus when readers may expect a comparison and contrast plan of organization good writers guide them to see it (by using well-known transitional devices, or signal words, such as "on the one hand" and "on the other hand"). Texts, therefore, do play a part in their own comprehensibility (Estes, 1982, p. 94).

The belief that text structures are inherent, immutable attributes of texts, interpreted in the same way by all readers, is accepted by fewer researchers today. Evidence demonstrating the influence of readers' perspectives indicates that most readers organize their own texts as they read (see Pichert and Anderson, 1977; Anderson and Pichert, 1978). Theories such as Rosenblatt's (1978) have emphasized the difference between the printed text and the text-in-the-head of readers.

Some teaching implications may be drawn from these three observations:

- Although ways of organizing a text may be more complex than most reading and composition teachers have assumed, and although general agreement about the nature of these organizational plans does not yet exist, most texts do have structures.
- Readers will probably be better comprehenders if they are aware of the organizational plans used by writers when they wrote.
- Students may have an intuitive knowledge of ways discourse is organized, but nevertheless teachers should probably continue to teach basic plans of organization.
- It may be more effective to teach these plans simultaneously in both reading and writing lessons.
- Teachers need to check textbooks regularly to make sure students are given well-organized textbooks and reading materials.
- They need too to assess—through informal writing tasks or through conversation—the ways students perceive the organization of their textbooks and reading materials.

Readers' Social-Cultural Backgrounds

One other set of factors affecting comprehension involves readers' social, economic, and cultural backgrounds. Each reader brings to each reading experience information, ideas, attitudes, and perspectives derived from his family, neighborhood, community, and social group. Each student brings to each reading task word meanings, concepts, and schemata rooted in present and earlier experiences in her home and school.

Teachers sometimes ask: Don't our students from different cultures and subcultures have rather different—sometimes radically different—knowledge backgrounds? word meaning knowledge? Don't they hold different information in their long-term memories? Won't boys and girls from urban neighborhoods have different schemata from those of rural or suburban communities? Won't students from affluent homes tend to have different, possibly richer, experiential backgrounds? Won't children from educated families tend to have larger vocabularies than those from uneducated families?

The answer to these questions is—simply—yes. Social, cultural, and economic factors do affect the ways students comprehend texts. Such factors influence reading interests, attitudes toward reading, and learning achievement; but, more important, they shape the information stored schematically in memory and thus determine the prior knowledge readers carry with them to each individual reading experience. Even when students can decode all the words of a text and understand its organizational and language structures, they cannot comprehend unless they share with the text's author considerable world knowledge.

Some Parameters in Theory Development

Many theories and specific models of the comprehension process are now available to teachers. Some, as noted, are primarily text-based, some reader-based, others interactive. As individual teachers shape for themselves explanations of what happens when readers try to comprehend, they need to be guided by certain observations derived from recent research and theory:

- Readers must be fairly competent in the code used by the writer in preparing the text. Reading teachers are concerned with comprehension of texts in written language (usually—but not always—a reflection of spoken language). This means for them that readers must have linguistic competence.
- Readers must too be motivated to comprehend.
- Readers must have some prior knowledge of the subjects discussed in the texts they read. Specifically, they must have knowledge of the meanings of words used in the text and, more generally, some background information about what the writer is discussing. (The more prior knowledge they have, evidently, the greater their degree of comprehension.)
- Readers must also have knowledge of the ways writers may organize texts. Because rhetorical traditions are relatively firm and well-known, writers tend to structure discourse in certain ways. Readers therefore have an advantage when they are familiar with accepted patterns of organization.
- Readers must frequently—although not always—use appropriate cognitive skills (such as inferring and predicting) and often higher-level reasoning processes (such as logic and problem solving). Because many of these skills and processes may be "translated" into related reading skills, readers sometimes profit from knowing how to use them. (It may be that the less prior knowledge readers have about the subject of a text the more use they must make of their reasoning and cognitive skills.)

WHAT HAPPENS AS STUDENTS TRY TO COMPREHEND?

The following is less a formal model than an informal explanation of what probably happens as readers try to comprehend texts. It rests on the belief that reading is only one half of a communications act and that, to better understand reading comprehension, teachers need to know two things: what happens as writers develop texts and what happens when readers try to make sense of texts.

It suggests that readers try to reconstruct in their minds the arrangements of ideas that existed in writers' minds as they shaped their texts. It also suggests that complete comprehension occurs only when exact reconstruction is achieved. It assumes, further, that comprehension is rarely completely successful, because (1) writers do not always have the skills to say what they want to say; (2) writers' printed texts, once achieved, develop an independence of their own, affected in a variety of ways by time, place, culture, and other factors; and (3) readers do not always have sufficient linguistic competence, shared knowledge of rhetorical traditions, and the same background experience (world knowledge) as writers.

The comprehension process may be better understood when viewed as a twelve-"step" sequence, beginning with an "arrangement of ideas" in the writer's mind (the writer's text-in-the-head), going to a printed text, and ending with a reader's reconstruction of that "arrangement of ideas" (the reader's text-in-the-head).

1. Presumably, writers have something they want to say. They want to inform, persuade, or entertain; sometimes they may want to deliberately concoct a literary-aesthetic text. In any case, writers initiate (and, in various degrees, control) the comprehension process.

2. Working with data from their long-term memories, they develop and arrange a preliminary text-in-the-head according to their primary intentions (to share a specific piece of information, to present a point of view, to create a chuckle). Sometimes they may use reference books or other sources for additional material not held in their long-term memories; but this new material tends to support or reinforce basic views already part of their individual cognitive structures.

3. They—consciously or unconsciously—select key ideas, appropriate plans of organization, sequences, and so on, which they believe—consciously or unconsciously—will have the most impact on their readers.

4. They begin to encode according to their own linguistic competence. They choose syntactic structures they believe are most appropriate for their intentions; they select words and phrases they believe best verbalize their material.

5. They also begin to encode according to their rhetorical competence. They deliberately highlight key ideas, organize supporting data, arrange appropriate sequences, choose transitional elements, select standard patterns of organization, and so on. (Some writers are skilled in the logic and rhetoric of exposition; others are not.)

6. They often use inner speech, talking to themselves as they select what they believe are the best words and most effective rhetorical

and organizational structures. (Steps 2 to 5 probably occur simultaneously as writers "inner speech" their texts-in-the-head.)

7. Eventually writers may put all this on paper as printed texts. (Most people—and many writers—go through steps 1 to 6 all the time but for one reason or another never actually bother with the production of text.)

    If the writers' original intentions were relatively modest (to inform readers of the location of a fire exit or that Ruth fell), intentions may become printed texts rapidly, with little time spent internally organizing material, selecting words or syntactical arrangements, or highlighting key points. Little inner speech is necessary on such occasions: writers know what they want to say and how to say it and therefore write it down at once, effortlessly. If writers' intentions are more ambitious (to persuade readers to accept a controversial viewpoint or to explain the second law of thermodynamics), inner speech may not be enough; writers may then have to write out one, two, or more drafts on paper before they are satisfied with their texts.

    The final, printed texts are now quite independent of their writers. They are relatively timeless and "on their own." If their writers were linguistically competent, they may be well enough encoded for readers to decode them; if their writers were rhetorically competent, they may be used by readers to discover what writers' original intentions might have been.

8. The process now begins to work in reverse. Just as writers began with something they *wanted* to say, so readers approach texts because they, in turn, *want* to discover what the writers set out to say. They may want to be informed, persuaded, or entertained or to receive some literary-aesthetic gratification. In any case, they must *want* to initiate the comprehension process at their end.

9. Readers—if they indeed want to figure out what writers are trying to say—must decode at least portions of texts. Although psycholinguistic theorists are correct in asserting that readers need not know every word in texts, readers do need to know enough letters and words to allow them to predict what they think writers are trying to say and then later to confirm or discard these predictions. (American sixth-graders may "read" an Italian newspaper because they can find enough Italian words cognate with English words to provide cues for them to guess at news stories; few, if any, American children could make any sense at all of a Chinese newspaper, which gives no letters or words as cues.) Readers, in short, must share the same language system as writers and be able to decode as much of the language of texts as possible; the more, in this case, the better.

10. Readers must share much of writers' vocabularies. When writers use a word such as *record* to mean "preserving in permanent form,"

readers must know this particular meaning of the word; when writers use the same word to mean "the best performance known, as in a sport," readers must know this meaning. When writers use words as labels for concepts, readers must have developed those concepts. One of the few findings to emerge consistently from comprehension research is that readers must share knowledge of word meanings with writers.

11. Readers must share too writers' rhetorical schemata. In any given culture certain ways of organizing material have become common. In America, for many years, most writers have tended to organize paragraphs in terms of so-called topic (or main idea) sentences with supporting details and examples; in most societies writers have tended to relate stories in terms of chronological sequences. Clearly it behooves readers (who want to make sense of texts) to be sensitive to the organizational plans writers use in preparing texts.

12. Readers reconstruct in their minds a theory of what they think writers were trying to say when they prepared texts. To do this, they need linguistic competence (especially syntactic and semantic knowledge), rhetorical competence (especially knowledge of the ways writers may organize and structure texts), and much of the same world knowledge of those who put texts together.

The reconstructions readers make (their theories or hypotheses of what they think writers were trying to say) are powerfully influenced by all the prior knowledge of the world (gained through experience) that readers already possess.

The process (arbitrarily sequenced above into "steps") may be better understood by examining one writer, one text, and one reader, as follows.

Initially, a writer wanted to "say something." She had the beginnings of a text-in-the-head, which became increasingly viable as she thought about it, talked about it to herself or with others, and perhaps shaped and reshaped it in preliminary drafts. She used the language available to her (with its phonological, graphemic, syntactic, and semantic systems) to encode her now better-shaped text-in-the-head.

While she was doing this, she also used all her knowledge of rhetorical schemata to give her developing text a framework; she tried out (in her head or on paper) various organizational plans, rhetorical structures, and logical arrangements.

The reader comes to her printed text with a desire to figure it out. He must also have similar linguistic competence (especially syntactic and semantic knowledge) and comparable rhetorical schemata (that is, knowledge of the ways paragraphs and longer discourse structures may be organized).

If both writer and reader share similar world knowledge (if, that is, both retain comparable information and schemata in long-term memory), the reader may be able to reconstruct in his mind something close to the writer's original text-in-the-head. The wider the gap between their experiential backgrounds, their language competence, and/or their awareness and use of ways of structuring texts, the less chance the reader can reconstruct in his mind what he thinks the writer was trying to say. In any case, the reader's reconstruction will have been heavily affected by all the knowledge he has retained from experience and by his own view of the world and the way it works.

Specifically,

Susan wanted to tell Tom that their romance was over, that she did not want to see him anymore, that her feelings had changed. This is the kernel of her text-in-the-head. Although she did not talk this out with friends, she did talk it over with herself at length. She decided at last to write a letter.

The letter—her text-on-paper—is reasonably well done (because she has considerable linguistic competence and adequate knowledge of the ways such texts are organized). She wrote,

Dear Tom,

I can't see you Saturday night as we planned. I'll give you a call as soon as I can—maybe in a couple of weeks. You probably can re-sell those tickets. I know they were hard to get. I'm very sorry.

Sincerely,

Susan

Tom approaches this text with a strong desire to understand it. He too has considerable linguistic and rhetorical competence. He also shares similar knowledge of the world. He is immediately able to comprehend the text: his text-in-the-head says, "The Saturday night date is off; she doesn't want to see me." However, because of his prior knowledge of the world (specifically, of romance, courting, dating, love affairs, relationships between young men and women, etc.), he begins to make inferences on the basis of the information provided in the written text. He may infer (1) that Susan has another boyfriend, (2) that important family business has come up (her parents are coming to visit? she is quarreling with her parents?), (3) that she is playing hard to get, etc. The more he thinks about the printed text, the more he infers, hypothesizes, draws conclusions. He may use his deductive reasoning skills and draw a conclusion based on generalizations he has already in memory about male–female relationships; he may use his critical reading skills and think about the connotations of *sincerely* (rather than *love*). In a short time, Tom may construct a text-in-his-head quite different from the original text-in-Susan's-head.

Does Tom comprehend the printed text? Clearly, it is impossible to ascertain. He knows that the date is canceled and that "something is wrong," but the text he develops in his head is affected by his knowledge of the world and his emotions. Whether or not the printed text "worked" is another question: it may have done exactly what Susan wanted, but it may have backfired.

This example may appear simplistic and far removed from the concerns of most teachers. It does, however, highlight key aspects of reading comprehension. For *Susan,* substitute the name of a distinguished philosopher or eminent economist or any writer of school textbooks; for *Tom,* the name of any third-grader or graduate student.

This explanation of the comprehension process implies the following:

- *Readers can rarely be sure they have comprehended what a writer intended them to comprehend.* To "completely" comprehend a given text, the reader must share with the writer exactly the same long-term memory! Because each individual's long-term memory is unique, complete one-to-one correspondences are impossible between reader's and writer's world knowledge sources. Fortunately enough overlap exists among people's memories to allow for some (often, considerable) comprehension to take place, and of course most people in a society must share the same language system and often the same ways of organizing discourse.

- *Texts take on a life of their own and frequently "say" what their writers did not intend them to say.* Different readers, although they may share the same general experiential background and language, interpret texts in different ways. Each individual reader brings to a text not only a shared denotational meaning for a word in it but special connotational meanings as well. (See the earlier discussion of semantic and episodic meanings for words.) Each reader has had idiosyncratic experiences that encourage her to "read into" a text special meanings and consequently allow highly individualized reconstructions. The printed text of a well-known poem, for example, may lead to ten different texts-in-the-heads of ten different readers.

- *Writers have some control over their texts.* Although completed texts seem to have a life of their own, they can be organized by their writers to have a certain kind of impact on special groups of readers. It may be that different readers interpret texts in different ways because of their experiential backgrounds; nevertheless, while the text is being prepared, the writer may exert some control over possible interpretations. A writer who knows her readers may arrange material, choose certain organizational plans, select various transitional devices, or highlight key ideas in such a way that readers will not stray—too far—from *her* original intention. (This point is important for teachers to note, because too frequently in school situations students are blamed for comprehension breakdowns when writers are at fault.)

This explanation of the comprehension process also highlights certain important aspects of reading comprehension *instruction.*

Linguistic Competence   Sometimes students fail to comprehend school texts (basal readers and content area books) because they lack basic language ability. Their comprehension problems are not actually comprehension problems at all but language problems: they have yet to learn sound–letter correspondences, they have yet to develop appropriate syntactic knowledge, or they operate with minimal semantic knowledge of commonly used words. Such students need more language experiences before they need more reading (much less, comprehension) instruction.

Word Knowledge   If knowledge of word meanings is crucial to comprehension, meaningful vocabulary instruction is a paramount concern in all comprehension programs. Students must develop extensive vocabulary backgrounds in order to deal with reading materials. Vocabulary instruction must be an intrinsic part of every school lesson whether in reading or in the content fields. Vocabulary previews, semantic mapping, and direct teaching of roots and affixes all play major roles in comprehension instruction.

Prior Knowledge   The prior knowledge of the world readers bring to each reading assignment has a profound effect on their reconstructions of the intended messages of authors. Clearly all teachers must help students (1) develop rich and wide "personal information banks," and (2) make connections between the new material of texts and what they already do know. In the first place, this suggests that every teacher must utilize field trips, film-viewing, realia, models, demonstrations, wide recreational reading, and firsthand experiences to broaden and enrich "information banks." In the second place, it suggests that each teacher must show students ways to relate the new information they meet in texts to information they already possess, to build bridges between the unknown and the known, the new and the old.

Knowledge of Text Structure   Writers tend to organize their texts according to some plan or structure. Through the years composition teachers have taught students to use these plans (rhetorical schemata) to prepare better themes. Reading teachers need to teach the same structures so their students may more easily get at what writers are trying to say. If a writer uses a comparison and contrast plan to explain the second law of thermodynamics, readers may more readily understand the explanation if they are aware of the underlying structure.

Making Relationships   Much of comprehension depends on how well readers relate new material in a text to what they already know. Writers' and readers' long-term memories can never be the same, but they may have many common elements. Good writers know this and regularly compare and contrast new items with items they are rather sure their readers already know. The writer of a science textbook often—if she is a good textbook writer—compares a new concept in science with a concept most students have developed, stressing similarities and pointing out differences. The ability to see relationships between the new and the old may be taught in both reading and content area classes. Because it is so important in bridging the gap between writer's background (or world knowledge) and reader's background (or world knowledge), such instruction may play the major role in all comprehension improvement programs.

Summarizing If the end of the comprehension process is the reconstruction in the reader's mind of the text-in-the-head of the writer, summarizing takes on great importance in instructional programs. It is the only way teachers have of knowing what their students' reconstructions may be. The most skillfully designed questions may, at best, touch only the periphery of the students' reconstructions. Some questions may indicate if students are "way off" or "almost there," but questions alone can never reveal the text-in-the-head of the individual student. Teachers, however, can ask boys and girls to tell (in their own words) what they think the writer seems to be saying. A brief spoken or written paraphrase can indicate if students are able to build in their minds a "text" that resembles what teachers themselves reconstruct. (When, of course, ten students in a class all demonstrate different reconstructions, then either the writer is incompetent or his material demands more prior knowledge than students possess.)

Thinking When writers want only to indicate a fire egress or to note that Jane fell their texts are rarely challenging to readers' intellectual resources. In such cases not much thinking is involved in comprehension. When, as often happens, writers set out to marshal evidence in support of a controversial position or to explain a phenomenon far removed from the experiences of readers, their readers frequently need to use cognitive skills. To reconstruct the writer's text in his own head, the reader may have to make inferences, note implications, test out hypotheses, and seek evidence for writer's inferences and generalizations. Thinking, in such cases, is involved in comprehension. To the extent that the reader's reconstruction is itself a hypothesis or theory, then clearly thinking is involved with all comprehension.

This explanation also has the advantage of suggesting a definition for the term *reading comprehension* that is not circumlocutory. If the twelve "steps" cited above do indeed describe (even in general terms) what happens as writers prepare texts and as readers try to comprehend them, then it may be said that

Reading comprehension is the process of using syntactic, semantic, and rhetorical information found in printed texts to reconstruct in the reader's mind, using the knowledge of the world he or she possesses, plus appropriate cognitive skills and reasoning ability, a hypothesis or personal explanation which may account for the intended message that existed in the writer's mind as the printed text was prepared.

This definition implies *three* texts: (1) the internalized one in the writer's mind prior to and during writing; (2) the external, physical printed text with its syntactic, semantic, and rhetorical information; and (3) the internalized explanation in the reader's mind of what he or she hypothesizes is the writer's text-in-the-head.

It also implies, as noted, that success in comprehension is contingent upon (1) the writer's ability to encode his text-in-the-head; (2) the quantity and quality of syntactic, semantic, and rhetorical information the writer has encoded; (3) the desire of the reader to decode and try to comprehend the text; (4) linguistic competence on the part of the reader; (5) knowledge of common rhetorical structures on the part of both reader and writer; (6) a shared vocabulary; and (7) experiential backgrounds of both reader and writer, which overlap at least to some extent. (Explanations of the comprehension process, which also consider the writer and the writer's preparation of text, are to be found in Pearson and Tierney, 1984; Tierney and Pearson, 1984; and Devine, 1984. Interesting discussions of the differences between interactional and transactional theories of comprehension may be found in Rosenblatt, 1978 and 1985.)

■ RECAPPING MAIN POINTS ■

Other factors, in addition to prior knowledge (especially of word meanings), need to be considered as a theory of the comprehension process is developed. Readers' use of cognitive skills (such as inferencing and predicting) affects their comprehension, as does their ability to reason logically and solve problems. Readers' knowledge of the ways writers structure texts also affects their comprehension, as do more general factors such as their social and cultural backgrounds. Recent research, while supporting the belief that thinking is involved with comprehension, does raise questions about specific reading comprehension skills and particularly about the opinion that skills may be arranged in hierarchies or by levels. When readers have sufficient prior knowledge, they may need to do little or no thinking.

The explanation of comprehension developed here suggests that three texts exist: one in the writer's mind before and during writing; a second physical text printed on paper; and a third which readers construct in their minds using their linguistic competence, their knowledge of how writers prepare texts, any appropriate cognitive skills they may need, plus their prior knowledge. The suggested model is based on recent research and speculation in schema theory and related areas.

END-OF-CHAPTER ACTIVITIES

1. Give examples of instances when readers, to comprehend a text, have to *think* (that is, use certain cognitive processes). Give examples of reading that requires little or no thinking on the part of the reader. How do you explain the differences between these two kinds of examples? Is it reasonable to say, as some teachers do, that "Reading is thinking"? Explain your response.

2. What are some key cognitive (or thinking) skills? Which, in your opinion, are most important for comprehension? Why?

3. In what ways do so-called *reading comprehension skills* relate to cognitive skills? How are they similar? different?

4. What are some arguments both for and against the *skills approach* to reading comprehension instruction?

5. When does a reader need to do high-level thinking or reasoning? Is the reader at these times *reading* or *thinking?* Is there a difference? What is it? (Use the description on page 54 to help answer these questions.)

6. In what ways does the structure of a printed text influence the way readers comprehend it?

7. What is *story grammar?* Select a story from a basal reader and try to see its underlying structure. Does it have a "grammar"? Does its grammar resemble that of another story? In what ways is this kind of information important to teachers?

8. Name some of the organizational patterns underlying content area textbook prose. Who devised these patterns? How can readers use these patterns to become better comprehenders?

9. Recently researchers have approached these patterns in several different ways, suggesting a number of fresh points of view. Read a recent review, such as that by Calfee and Curley (1984), and prepare a brief research "update."

10. Explain the following two statements from the chapter: "Structures," or patterns of organization, "may correspond to *rules* of thought" and "Text organization is in the mind of the reader as much as on the printed page." Why might these assertions bother some teachers? What evidence is offered in their support? What are your responses to them?

11. *Readers' social-cultural background* is listed in the chapter as a factor affecting comprehension. In what ways may this factor be considered simply as part of readers' prior knowledge?

12. Would students from one social-cultural group tend to have different schemata in their prior knowledge background? Could reading comprehension problems be attributed to mismatches between

students from a subculture and the white middle-class people who generally write textbooks? For answers from a study conducted in Tennessee and Illinois, read Reynolds *et al.* (1982) and share your responses to the report in a brief paper.

13. Summarize in your own words the explanation of reading comprehension presented in this chapter.

14. In what ways is this explanation acceptable to you? unacceptable? Could you rework it to make what for you is a more reasonable explanation? What changes would you make? Why?

15. Several theorists in recent years have spotlighted the role of the writer in reading comprehension. Read the "composing model of reading" developed by Tierney and Pearson (1984) and compare it with the explanation given here.

16. The explanation of comprehension given in this chapter implies that reading and writing are not separate activities. Squire (1984) calls them "two sides of the same basic process." Read his article and summarize his position in a short paper.

17. Much recent theorizing about reading composition comes from the field of *artificial intelligence*. In developing computer programs that can read, paraphrase, and answer questions about texts, researchers have learned more about the comprehension process. Read more on the "AI perspective" in articles (for example, Dehn, 1984) or books (for example, Schank, 1982) and write a report on What Reading Teachers Can Learn from AI Research.

18. After reading Chapter 3 and thinking about reading comprehension, write a one-paragraph answer to the question: What is reading comprehension?

REFERENCES

Anderson, John R. *Cognitive Psychology: Its Implications*. San Francisco: Freeman, 1980.

Anderson, R. C., and J. W. Pichert. "Recall of Previously Unrecallable Information Following a Shift in Perspective." *Journal of Verbal Learning and Verbal Behavior* 17 (1978): 1–12.

Bloom, Benjamin S. (Ed.). *Taxonomy of Educational Objectives, Handbook I: Cognitive Domain*. New York: David McKay, 1956.

Brewer, William F. "Literary Theory, Rhetoric, and Stylistics: Implications for Psychology." In R. J. Spiro, B. C. Bruce, and W. F. Brewer (Eds.), *Theoretical Issues in Reading Comprehension*. Hillsdale, N. J.: Lawrence Erlbaum Associates, 1980.

Calfee, Robert C., and Robert Curley. "Structures of Prose in the Content Areas." In James Flood (Ed.), *Understanding Reading Comprehension*. Newark, Del.: International Reading Association, 1984.

Carver, R. P. "Reading as Reasoning: Implications for Measurement." In Walter H. MacGinitie (Ed.), *Assessment Problems in Reading.* Newark, Del.: International Reading Association, 1973.

Davis, Frederick B. "Research in Comprehension in Reading." *Reading Research Quarterly* 4 (1968): 499–545.

Davis, Frederick B. "Psychometric Research on Comprehension in Reading." *Reading Research Quarterly* 7 (1972): 628–678.

Dehn, Natalie. "An AI Perspective on Reading Comprehension." In James Flood (Ed.), *Understanding Reading Comprehension.* Newark, Del.: International Reading Association, 1984.

Devine, Thomas G. *Teaching Study Skills: A Guide for Teachers.* Boston: Allyn and Bacon, 1981.

Devine, Thomas G. "What Happens as Students Try to Comprehend." *New England Reading Association Journal* 19 (Autumn 1984): 15–20.

Estes, Thomas H. "The Nature and Structure of Texts." In Allen Berger and H. Alan Robinson (Eds.), *Secondary School Reading.* Urbana, Ill.: ERIC Clearinghouse on Reading and Communications Skills, 1982.

Goetz, Ernest T., and Bonnie B. Armbruster. "Psychological Correlates of Text Structure." In R. J. Spiro, B. C. Bruce, and W. F. Brewer (Eds.), *Theoretical Issues in Reading Comprehension.* Hillsdale, N. J.: Lawrence Erlbaum Associates, 1980.

Herber, Harold L. *Teaching Reading in the Content Areas.* Englewood Cliffs, N. J.: Prentice-Hall, 1978.

Meyer, Bonnie J. F. "Organizational Aspects of Text: Effects on Reading Comprehension." In James Flood (Ed.), *Promoting Reading Comprehension.* Newark, Del.: International Reading Association, 1984.

Morgan, Jerry L., and Manfred B. Sellner. "Discourse and Linguistic Theory." In R. J. Spiro, B. C. Bruce, and W. F. Brewer (Eds.), *Theoretical Issues in Reading Comprehension.* Hillsdale, N. J.: Lawrence Erlbaum Associates, 1980.

Niles, Olive S. "Organization Perceived." In Harold L. Herber (Ed.), *Developing Study Skills in Secondary Schools.* Newark, Del.: International Reading Association, 1965.

Pearson, P. David, and Robert J. Tierney. "On Becoming a Thoughtful Reader: Learning to Read Like a Writer." In Alan C. Purves and Olive Niles (Eds.), *Becoming Readers in a Complex Society: 83rd Yearbook of the National Society for the Study of Education.* Chicago: University of Chicago Press, 1984.

Pichert, J., and R. C. Anderson. "Taking Different Perspectives on a Story." *Journal of Educational Psychology* 69 (1977): 309–315.

Prince, G. *A Grammar of Stories.* The Hague: Mouton, 1973.

Reynolds, Ralph E., Marshá A. Taylor, Margaret S. Steffensen, Larry L. Shirey, and Richard C. Anderson. "Cultural Schemata and Reading Comprehension." *Reading Research Quarterly* 17 (1982): 353–366.

Robinson, H. Alan. *Teaching Reading and Study Strategies: The Content Areas.* Boston: Allyn and Bacon, 1978.

Rosenblatt, Louise M. *The Reader the Text the Poem: The Transactional Theory of the Literary Work.* Carbondale, Ill.: Southern Illinois University Press, 1978.

Rosenblatt, Louise M. "Viewpoint: Transaction vs. Interaction—A Terminological Rescue Operation." *Research in the Teaching of English* 19 (February 1985): 96–107.

Rosenshine, Barak V. "Skill Hierarchies in Reading Comprehension." In R. J. Spiro,

B. C. Bruce, and W. F. Brewer (Eds.), *Theoretical Issues in Reading Comprehension*. Hillsdale, N. J.: Lawrence Erlbaum Associates, 1980.

Rumelhart, David E. "Notes on a Schema for Stories." In D. G. Brown and A. Collins (Eds.), *Representation and Understanding: Studies in Cognitive Science*. New York: Academic Press, 1975.

Schank, Roger C. *Reading and Understanding: Teaching from the Perspective of Artificial Intelligence*. Hillsdale, N. J.: Lawrence Erlbaum Associates, 1982.

Spearritt, D. "Identification of Subskills in Reading Comprehension by Maximum Likelihood Factor Analysis." *Reading Research Quarterly* 8 (1972): 92–111.

Squire, James R. "Composing and Comprehensing: Two Sides of the Same Basic Process." In Julie M. Jensen (Ed.), *Composing and Comprehending*. Urbana, Ill.: ERIC Clearinghouse on Reading and Communications Skills, 1984.

Stein, N. L. and L. G. Glenn. "An Analysis of Story Comprehension in Elementary School Children." In R. O. Freeble (Ed.), *New Directions in Discourse Processing*. Norwood, N. J.: Ablex, 1979.

Tierney, Robert J. and F. David Pearson. "Toward a Composing Model of Reading." In Julie M. Jensen (Ed.), *Composing and Comprehending*. Urbana, Ill.: ERIC Clearinghouse on Reading and Communications Skills, 1984.

PART TWO

Teaching/Learning Strategies

Recent research and theory about the comprehension process lead to six generalizations, meant to guide reading teachers as they develop strategies and approaches for their classrooms:

1. Students need some prior knowledge of the material treated in their texts. (The more they have the more apt they are to comprehend.)
2. They need to make connections between what they already know and the new material they encounter. (The new may be understood in terms of the known.)
3. They need to be able to deal with unfamiliar words they meet in their reading assignments. (Comprehension rests to a large degree upon knowledge of word meanings shared by writers and readers.)
4. They need to develop the concepts for which these words are often labels. (Words in texts stand for schemata, which need to be in readers' memories.)
5. They need to know how writers structure texts, so that they may more easily identify writers' purposes and plans of organization. (Comprehension is facilitated when readers see the structure underlying a text.)

6. They need to be able to use key cognitive skills and reasoning processes frequently required to comprehend many kinds of texts. (When not enough prior knowledge is available, readers have to think through a text and explain to themselves what they think an author is trying to say.)

From Theory to Practice: Relating the New to the Known

■ INTRODUCTION AND OVERVIEW ■

Readers use writers' texts as catalysts to stimulate and guide them in the creation of *their own texts* (that is, *their* interpretations of what they think writers are trying to say, *their* personal versions of writers' texts, *their* texts-in-the-head). From the writers' printed texts readers find only suggestions—or at best guidelines—for creating their own. The information and ideas they use to make up their own texts-in-the-head are most often already present in their memories, part of the prior knowledge background they bring to each reading experience.

This chapter focuses on that prior knowledge, organized in schemata in readers' memories and so crucial to their interpretations and restructurings. It assumes that the prior knowledge students bring to their reading tasks is a primary influence on their comprehension, and that therefore teachers need to

discover what students already know before they begin to read;

activate that prior knowledge background;

build *more* background knowledge by refining and extending the schemata comprising the prior knowledge background; and, above all,

help students make connections between what they already know and the new ideas and information they encounter in their reading assignments.

Chapter 4 includes Suggested Study Questions, Teaching Guidelines (axioms, or instructional principles, around which discussion in the remaining chapters is organized), and then discussions on

- Finding Out What Students Already Know
  The direct approach: ask 'em

        Some less direct approaches
        Prior knowledge: general or specific?
- Activating Students' Prior Knowledge
        Class discussions and informal talk
        What-do-I-already-know sessions
        Semantic mapping
        Advance organizers
        Prequestions
        Pictorial activators
- Increasing Students' Prior Knowledge
        Build on what students already know
        Provide (orally) background information
        Show students some of what they are about to read
        Provide real-life experiences
        Encourage vicarious experiences through wide reading
        Restructure and build "new" schemata
- Relating the New to the Known
        Identify probable problem points in advance
        Try to identify comparable concepts students already know
        Show how connections may be made between the new and the known
        Help students make analogies

Chapter 4 also includes

- Recapping Main Points
- End-of-Chapter Activities
- References

▪ SUGGESTED STUDY QUESTIONS FOR CHAPTER 4 ▪

1. How can teachers discover what students know—and do not know—about the topic of an assignment *before* the students read it?
2. What is the difference between "general" and "specific" prior knowledge? Why is the distinction important?
3. How can teachers activate the knowledge students may already possess?
4. How can teachers add to and refine the knowledge students possess? How can they develop completely "new" knowledge? Why is it more difficult to develop new knowledge?

5. What does it mean to "build bridges between the new and the known"?
6. Why is analogy-making so important in the classroom?

• TEACHING GUIDELINES FOR CHAPTER 4 •

Recent research and theory in reading comprehension suggest approaches to the problems associated with reader prior knowledge: ways to add to it, refine it, and activate it and ways to help readers make relationships between what they know and what is new to them. These approaches in turn suggest four principles meant to guide teachers as they work to improve reading comprehension in their classrooms.

Chapter 4 is organized around the following four teaching guidelines derived from recent studies:

Teaching Guideline #1
    Find out as much as possible about what students already know.

Teaching Guideline #2
    Activate the knowledge they already have.

Teaching Guideline #3
    Add to and refine the knowledge they already have.

Teaching Guideline #4
    Help them relate new material to what they already know.

FINDING OUT WHAT STUDENTS ALREADY KNOW

Almost all teachers who have thought about the comprehension process in light of recent research and theory tend to agree that what readers bring to the printed page affects their understanding of it. Many think that what readers bring to the printed page is as important to their comprehension (if not more important) than the printed page itself.

If this prior knowledge is so important—from the point of view of this book, it is—then clearly teachers must be sensitive to the quantity and quality of the knowledge their students possess. However, it is not always easy to find out what people know. Paper-and-pencil tests tell something, but less than some believe. Observations may be revealing, but dangerously untrustworthy. One experienced teacher notes: "I can only get from a test what the test permits me to get, and, even after many years, I'm still not sure that I can tell from facial expressions what the boys and girls are thinking or what they bring into my class in their heads."

Yet teachers do need to find out what students bring into class in their heads. They need workable devices for assessing the quantity and quality of knowledge students have in order to effectively handle their reading materials. They must identify both those who bring to reading selections and assignments an adequate background and those who seem significantly lacking in appropriate information. Teachers who work intimately with small groups and individuals come to know the strengths and deficiencies in their knowledge of the world; those who meet regularly with large groups, or with groups for only a short time each week, need techniques for evaluating prior knowledge quickly. Several approaches to the problem are suggested here: the first seems simple, direct, and to the point; the others, more circumlocutory and sometimes cumbersome. All work to some extent, though none is completely satisfactory.

The Direct Approach: Ask 'Em

How can a first-grade teacher know what the children know about, say, jet planes? or frogs? How can a fourth-grade teacher discover what boys and girls know about Aztec burial customs? How can a high school teacher ascertain the information students possess about crustaceans? (All are topics discussed in various basal readers or content textbooks for these grade levels!) The simple answer is, "Ask 'em."

This suggestion, although simplistic, has validity. Teachers often discover much about the contents of students' long-term memories simply by talking to them and asking "What do you know about jet planes? frogs? Aztecs? burial customs? crustaceans?" Brief informal conversations with individual students can reveal considerable information about the concepts they currently have, the gaps in their knowledge, even their misinformation. By chatting with her children a teacher may discover that many do indeed know who the Aztecs were and know much about contemporary burial customs; she may also learn that certain children have gaps in their schematic networks about South and Central America, about death and burial, about Indians, about any number of related matters.

Unfortunately many teachers (especially in secondary schools and colleges) have large classes and busy schedules of five and six classes each day. Consequently they cannot spend as much time as they should in direct, personal discussions with their students. Two related procedures are recommended for such teachers: planned interviews and informal class discussions.

Planned Interviews   Although time constraints often disallow personal talks with *all* students, teachers may schedule regular interviews with individuals on a systematic basis. One middle school teacher notes that, when he observes (through facial expression, body language, oral response, inattention, or social behavior) that an individual seems to be having trouble with a reading assignment, he calls that person aside—during a silent reading or work period—to chat. During these moments he can get some insight into the student's background knowledge in the area of the reading assignment. Once he has such information he can (1) change reading assignments for some people; (2) provide necessary information orally; (3) suggest other supplementary readings if available in the classroom; or (4) help some refine and better define troublesome concepts. Other teachers, particularly in the secondary school, deliberately schedule brief interviews with individuals. One teacher systematically plans to talk to *every* one of her students in a tenth-grade science class by scheduling one a day (during a work session or lab). She can spend only a few minutes with each but finds that these moments provide her with information about student prior knowledge backgrounds that she could never obtain from pen-and-paper tests.

Informal Class Discussions   One of the simplest and most effective ways to find out what background students bring to their reading materials is informal class discussion. It combines many of the values of other assessment techniques, while often serving as a prereading motivational activity. Before reading *The Witch of Blackbird Pond,* one teacher plans a twenty-minute period to talk to her seventh-graders about the setting and period of Elizabeth Speare's novel. Before beginning his social studies unit on Mexico, one fifth-grade teacher tells briefly of his trip to Mexico—to stimulate boys and girls to tell what they know of this Latin American neighbor. He finds that many children know a great deal (from their own visits, recreational reading, previous school lessons, films, and televiewing) and others very little. One high school teacher slots twenty or thirty minutes into his schedule to allow students time to discuss each new chapter in the biology textbook. He notes that such informal classroom talk serves as a motivational device, while providing him with insights into the prior knowledge backgrounds of students.

Some Less Direct Approaches

Through the years teachers have developed a number of more formal and necessarily less direct approaches to the assessment of background knowledge. Some of these are described here.

Simple Questionnaires and Inventories   Before beginning a middle school unit on Colonial America, a teacher may have students complete a short

(20- to 30-item) duplicated sheet of questions, such as: How did people travel long distances in those days? From what European nation did most of these people come? Who governed the colonies? What did most people do for a living? How long ago was this?

Similar inventories may be prepared easily for chapters in content area textbooks and for individual basal reader selections, using

True-false items (Statements from the book are rewritten; students respond to their accuracy by labeling them "True" or "False.")

Fill-in-the-blanks items (Statements are presented with certain words omitted; students write in their choices.)

Incomplete-sentence items (Only the first part of a statement is given; students must complete it.)

Teachers using such quick-and-easy techniques can identify those students whose backgrounds are inadequate for them to comprehend a reading assignment, as well as entire classes for which specific assignments are inappropriate.

Open-Ended Inventories   Many middle school and secondary school students are competent enough to write out responses to such questions as "In what ways were people in Colonial America like us today? unlike us today?" or "What do you already know about life in Colonial America?" Many teachers use open-ended techniques such as incomplete sentences: "People in those days _____" or "One problem they had was _____." For students who do not possess ready competence in writing, many of these techniques may be used in oral language situations: teachers ask individuals to complete sentences or to answer questions for the group. Whether oral or in writing, such activities take up classroom time, and so many teachers use them only when they have serious doubts about the appropriateness of a specific text.

Informal Content Checks   Many content area teachers use pre-tests to discover how much their students knew about an area before they studied it. Such tests identify students who may require additional assistance, as well as provide a baseline for later evaluation of their own instruction. Such informal content checks also provide information about the quantity and quality of student prior knowledge. Short multiple-choice or fill-in-the-blanks tests, based on specific knowledge in the reading selection or textbook chapter, give teachers information about who knows what and how well they know it. Such tests, although they tend to give less personal information of students' sometimes idiosyncratic preconceptions, reveal much about the comprehensiveness and accuracy of the knowledge they do possess.

Informal Concept Tests   In prereading an assignment, teachers may discover several concepts that could be difficult for students. Prior to making the assignment, they can list on the chalkboard the words that label the concepts or the sentences that contain the concepts, asking "What does this mean to you?" Frequently teachers can spot students who have poorly formed or idiosyncratic schemata. A child who says *swapping* is "handing something to someone" and a high school student who says *capitalism* is the "personal freedom we have in America" either have yet to develop accepted, widely shared meanings for these words or are unable to articulate what they do know. In either case teachers are warned and so can stop to do some concept building before students read. Informal concept tests are valuable as preliminary assessing techniques and as activities for building and refining the schemata of prior knowledge.

Synonym and Definition Tests   After identifying words and concepts needed to understand a particular passage or selection, teachers can list these on the board or on duplicated sheets with a separate list of synonyms out of order. Students quickly draw lines from the words of the text to the teacher's synonyms, thus providing an approximation of their knowledge of important words. Before assigning the mathematics problem cited in Chapter 2 (page 28), for example, one teacher placed the following words and their synonyms in lists: *wind, patrol, still, fuel,* and *miles per hour.* Almost instantly she was able to pick out those children who did not know the words (and the concepts for which they stood). She was then able to take them aside and explain the words to them before the class worked on the problem. Other teachers, especially in secondary school, ask students to write brief definitions of potentially troublesome words (What do you mean by *patrol?* What does *still* mean as it is used here?).

The Cloze Procedure   Cloze is a technique that asks readers to anticipate meaning from context and to supply previously deleted words from a printed passage. Usually every "nth" word is cut out, and the student fills them in (orally or in writing). This gives the teacher a rough idea of how well the text is understood. The student's performance provides a measure of his or her comprehension.

In addition to its use as a test of reading comprehension, cloze is widely used to discover the appropriateness of reading materials. Thus a percentage of correct answers of 40 or below may be equated with the frustration level; a percentage between 40 and 50 with instructional level; and a percentage above 50 with independent level. (These levels are described on p. 102.) Cloze may also be used to assess student prior knowledge. Teachers can prepare duplicated sheets of summary passages from a content area textbook and quickly discover the extent of students' general or specific knowledge in the topic to be studied.

Potter (1968) suggests six criteria for developing cloze exercises:

1. Every "nth" word is deleted. (*n* may equal any number between 5 and 12.)
2. The minimum passage length must be 250 words.

3. At least fifty deletions are used to insure adequate sampling of content.

4. For determining instructional level, the exact word deleted must be used by the reader in order for the scoring criteria to be valid.

5. Other scoring systems (synonyms, form classes such as nouns or verbs) provide less reliability and require substantially more time.

6. The separate scoring of form classes or content and function words may provide specific information for specialized purposes.

How does cloze procedure work in a check of student prior knowledge? One middle school social studies teacher takes the summary statements that conclude each chapter of the textbook and duplicates them, omitting every fifth word. A day or two before students begin the chapter, she asks them to fill in the blank spaces as closely as they can. Because she is not trying to establish instructional levels, she accepts synonyms. By checking individual responses, she can identify students who seem to have a modicum of information about the topic and, more important, those who clearly know nothing about it. Other teachers use variations of the approach: chapter overviews, key passages from assignments, introductory paragraphs from narratives.

Prior Knowledge: General or Specific?

When readers know almost exactly what an author writes about (when, in other words, they share the same prior knowledge), the text serves merely as a *reminder,* a signal to help them pull from long-term memory specific knowledge they already possess. Many passages in this book serve as reminders in this sense. For example, the previous passages about the cloze procedure "signal" those teachers who already know about cloze procedure to retrieve appropriate knowledge from their long-term memories and look at it from a different point of view (in this case, that of prior knowledge assessment). When, on the other hand, readers have only a general knowledge of the topic of the text, the text plays a different role: it may remind them of *related* knowledge they have, which they can use to make sense of the print. Teachers unfamiliar with the cloze procedure may be reminded—as they read these passages—of prior knowledge of assessment and evaluation, of reading levels, of courses they have had in modern poetry, even of past experiences trying to read damaged or mutilated student homework papers. They can use all this other knowledge, which may be called their *general* knowledge of reading, to help them figure out exactly what the cloze procedure is.

When teachers attempt to assess student prior knowledge, are they focusing on primarily specific or general prior knowledge? The answer must be, "Both." If teachers discover that students already possess exactly the same prior knowledge as that represented by the assigned text, they may decide not to bother assigning it. If they discover that students have some general knowledge in the area, they can then utilize this knowledge to help students make connections between the new and the known. (See page 101.) If they discover that students have absolutely *no* knowledge, specific or related, they may decide that the assignment is inappropriate. A simple assessment, based on a variation of the cloze procedure, illustrates the distinction.

Fifth-grade children are asked to fill in the blanks with words they believe make sense:

> If you were living in London two ___(1)___ years ago, the only book you would have would be a hornbook. A hornbook was not really a ___(2)___. It was a single sheet of ___(3)___ nailed to a thin ___(4)___ with a handle. The alphabet and all the vowels were ___(5)___ on the paper. A clear piece of ___(6)___ covered the paper to protect it from rain or dirt. Except for the hornbook, which was really a ___(7)___ book, there were almost no books written just for ___(8)___.

Any child who could write in *hundred, book, paper, board, printed, horn, school,* and *children* probably does not have to read—as a school assignment—this basal reader selection by Mary Emerson (1982). That child has somehow picked up specific prior knowledge for this text (even though the child may have substituted *cardboard* or *vellum* for *paper, wood* for *board, written* for *printed, text* for *school,* and *kids* or *students* for *children*). Number 6 may be most significant: any child who gets *horn* evidently has the appropriate specific knowledge. Children who can fill in exact words or synonyms for several of the missing words probably have enough knowledge of associated areas (books, schooling, "olden times") to profit from reading this text with instruction. Clearly any child who cannot offer a single item is not ready for *this* text.

ACTIVATING STUDENTS' PRIOR KNOWLEDGE

When students have appropriate general prior knowledge background to make sense of a reading assignment, how can teachers help them activate that knowledge? Often a word, a phrase, an image, or an anecdote is enough. For some, expressions such as "a piece of horn covering the paper" or "thin board with handle" are enough to assist them retrieve from their long-term memories a schema for *hornbook*. For many, a picture of a hornbook, or the word itself, is adequate. Several more elaborate techniques are described here for helping students activate the knowledge—specific and general—they possess. They all serve an important purpose: they encourage students to retrieve appropriate knowledge from memory, so that they may relate it to the new ideas and information of reading assignments.

Class Discussions and Informal Talk

As noted in the previous section, class discussions, conversations, interviews, and informal talks in and out of class all serve as techniques for teachers to discover more about what students bring to their reading. Over a period of time, teachers can begin to get some notion of what their students know. Experienced teachers frequently are able to assess the prior knowledge of their students with remarkable accuracy. However, those same techniques serve another purpose: they give students opportunities to discover what they know about topics; in other words, they assist them in activating appropriate schematas. To use the hornbook example once more, one group of boys and girls did not seem to know the term; yet, after a few minutes of class discussion, many revealed to the teacher—and to themselves—that they did know a great deal about schooling in general, about ways children learn to read, and about the need for books of some kind in instruction. When they read the basal reader selection, they were able to develop a schema for hornbook and extend and refine related schemata—helped to a large extent by the prereading discussion.

What-Do-I-Already-Know Sessions

Related to general class discussions and informal talk are more structured "what-do-I-know-already" sessions. In these, teachers ask students to examine together the selection title and headnote (if available). Then, playing secretary, the teacher lists on the chalkboard all the information students say they are reminded of by the title and headnote. Individual students may be reminded of areas unrelated to the contents of the selection, but most will probably recall information the teacher knows is appropriate to the reading. In such brainstorming sessions, most classes will provide enough information for their teacher-secretary to fill a large chalkboard. These bits and pieces of data are then used to stimulate further recall, and in the process considerable knowledge will be activated. Some teachers then actually call for summary statements: "Well, we seem to have a lot of information already, and we haven't yet read the assignment! Let's try to pull it all together. Can we come up with a few sentences that summarize what we know?"

An example of such a session grows out of one teacher's prereading discussion of Isaac Asimov's story, "The Key Word." Using the headnote for the basal reader selection: "Codes might be the key to the detective case. But how does a newspaper fit in?" (Clymer, Venezky, and Indrisano, 1982, pp. 424–429), the teacher asked what ideas and words these lines triggered in people's heads. She received such items as *spies, CIA, microfilm, cyphers, FBI,* plus a plethora of data culled from student recreational reading, televiewing, or movie watching. Ten minutes of discussion filled the front board in the classroom and satisfied the teacher that most children had had opportunities to have any existing prior knowledge about codes and detectives activated.

Semantic Mapping

A more systematic way of eliciting from students their prior knowledge about a topic is *semantic mapping*. The free association of brainstorming is still done by students but is controlled and organized by the teacher (who still plays secretary). The teacher might write *hornbook* or *codes* on the top of the chalkboard and ask, "What pops into your head when you see this?". As the students offer their associations, the teacher tries to write these on the board in categories. Thus *codes* may elicit ideas such as "detectives use them," "spies send messages with them," "they keep secrets," "kids use 'em," "they're hard to crack," "they use numbers," "they're put on microfilm," and so forth. Rather than simply write these randomly on the board as in a "What-do-I-already-know" session, the teacher strives to organize them under headings as she goes along. For this topic she may have headings such as "Uses," "Kinds," "What They're Like," and so forth. The result is a semantic map; a diagram that presents visually the information elicited from students, but in such a way that qualities and relationships are evident.

Semantic maps clearly are valuable tools for activating information, but they also serve as assessment devices (teachers can learn much about what students already know about a topic) and motivational approaches (they tend to create a mood of anticipation). Semantic maps may also be used as guides *during* reading (students can add to their own personal maps in their notebooks as they read the selection) and as *post*-reading tools (students use them for review and as the basis of post-reading discussions). Many teachers find too that such maps may be used to connect students' schema (by its nature, abstract) to specific, concrete examples. Thus students may have a schema for *code;* they have knowledge that it is some kind of system for using letters, numbers, or symbols to communicate messages secretly or in brief form. As a teacher develops a map for *code,* she may list definite instances of codes which individuals give (such as the code used in one of their clubs, a code they read about in another story, a personal code they once devised, etc.). As she does this she is, of course, helping students see the difference between the abstract schema and some of the examples included in the abstraction. In content area subjects where the topic might be *gas* or *birds,* the exercise in semantic mapping becomes a sophisticated lesson in both the content area and the ways people think about content. (Because semantic mapping serves as a valuable device for further developing knowledge, it is discussed again later in this chapter and in the chapter on word meanings.)

Advance Organizers

Advance organizers were first proposed as devices "to bridge the gap between what the reader already knows and what the reader needs to know before he/she can meaningfully learn the task at hand" (Ausubel, 1968, p. 148). Their function is to provide some ideational scaffolding for the incorporation of the new material the text contains. As Bransford notes, their purpose is "to prepare readers to gain information from reading they could not have otherwise gained" (1979).

In a sense, the preparation in class of a semantic map or even a good oral discussion prior to reading are advance organizers. Each helps readers to see what is coming and to fit it into some ideational structure. Ideally an advance organizer must be written at a higher level of generality than the material to be read. One on codes, for example, would start from the abstraction, noting that codes in general were systems using letters, numbers, or symbols to transmit messages either briefly or secretly or both. It would then point ahead to the material in the text, noting how the concept is used *in the text,* and trying to account for ways this use differs from the generality or abstraction. Although some confusion exists in the research literature about their effectiveness (Tierney and Cunningham, 1984), many teachers use advance organizers or some personal variation of them. Many teachers say that it is valuable to provide students with a brief overview (orally or in print) of material to be read. Skillfully prepared, such organizers can activate knowledge students possess, while at the same time helping them to see it in relation to the material they are about to read. Many textbook authors now provide well-written advance organizers within their books to guide students. Teachers who have such textbooks should use their built-in organizers; teachers who lack them might try to write their own. An example of an advance organizer may be found in the first paragraphs of this chapter, where a generalization developed in the first half of the book is restated in such a way that readers may see how Chapter 4 applies it.

Prequestions

Whenever teachers—or the students themselves—spell out questions to be answered by the reading, they are activating prior knowledge. Such questions serve other purposes: they tend to focus attention and provide for purposeful reading. The process of examining a teacher's questions in advance of reading, or—even better—the development by students of their own questions, allows readers opportunities for activating knowledge they possess as well as for establishing purpose and focusing attention.

Here is an example of how prequestions help young readers recall what they already know: Prior to assigning a fourth-grade class a basal reader selection on *rocks and stones,* the teacher set up a class discussion of the What-do-I-already-know type. She easily filled the chalkboard with items of information, comments and observations, and autobiographical stories. Rather than systematize this material into categories as she might do in semantic mapping, she asked rather that boys and girls create questions they wanted answered by the selection. The children suggested such questions as: What is the difference between a rock and a stone? Where do they come from? Are they found everywhere in the world? Did any come from outer space? Can people make rocks? What are they good for? Will they last forever?

In this case the teacher used the children's questions to set up a purpose (*many* purposes) for reading, while providing a way of focusing their attention as they read. In addition, she found that the process of phrasing the questions from the information on the chalkboard helped boys and girls better remember all they did know about rocks and stones (from physics, chemistry, astronomy, geology, and a number of other areas). She had—through the questions—activated considerable prior knowledge.

More sophisticated versions of this prequestion technique exist. Stauffer's DR-TA or Directed Reading-Thinking Activity (1969) has students spell out their purposes for reading and frame questions they want answered. Manzo's ReQuest Procedure (1969) also uses a questioning format in which students, usually in pairs, generate their own questions. Both these approaches provide teachers and students with powerful techniques for prereading and reading. They both also tend to activate prior knowledge, as does SQ3R (all to be examined in Chapter 6).

Pictorial Activators

Whether or not pictures in basal readers and school textbooks actually facilitate comprehension is not entirely clear. Some research (Samuels, 1970; Thomas, 1978; Marr, 1979) seems to deny the positive value of including photographs, drawings, and other illustrative materials. Other research (see Tierney and Cunningham, 1984, pp. 620–621) supports the belief that *some* pictures in *some* situations help *some* learners. As Tierney and Cunningham point out, research on the topic is difficult to interpret. Too often pictures interact with other variables in experiments, and researchers can never be sure whether it is the picture or some other factor that seems to be facilitating comprehension.

However, pictures and other visual material can *activate* a student's prior knowledge. If indeed a child has some schema for hornbook or jet plane, a simple picture of a hornbook or a jet plane may serve to help retrieve appropriate knowledge from long-term memory. Pictures added gratuitously to a text to delight or add to the attractiveness of the book may not, as some researchers have found, increase comprehension, but pictures chosen carefully to trigger reader memories can have a positive effect on the reader's ability to make use of knowledge already possessed. Many teachers collect pictures. Knowing they will teach certain units in certain areas, they seek out pictures of topics to be studied. These pictures are then posted or circulated for class inspection. Thus a teacher may share a photograph of a volcano erupting before students read a science textbook chapter on volcanos, because her discussions with students indicate that they do have some informational background on volcanos. The picture serves to activate, she hopes, their volcano schemata.

Idea Box

Before reading a basal story set in a school, one second-grade teacher helps her group develop a semantic map of "Our School." She first places the phrase in the center of the chalkboard and then asks the children to think of as many words as they can that relate to it. As they suggest words, she writes them on the chalkboard *in categories.* Thus, *paper, pencils,* and *rulers* are placed in one area, *teachers, pupils,* and *principal* in another, with words like *fun, exciting, boring,* and *nice* in another. When she finishes, she has several categories, all filled with words given by students. She next asks them to suggest names for the categories: *paper* and *pencils* are listed under the heading "Tools to Learn"; *teachers* and *pupils* under "People in School"; and so on. Throughout the process the teacher encourages children to talk about the words, calls attention to the ways the words can be used in different sentences, and asks volunteers to try using each in original sentences. When the map is completed she tells the group to check it as they read the new story to see if the school in the story is like theirs or different in some way.

Before reading a story in a third-grade book—about a girl lost in a large airport—one teacher uses a version of a semantic map (1) to discover how much her students actually know about airports; and (2) to activate whatever knowledge they had prior to reading. She places "AIRPORTS" in the center of the board and asks children in the group to quickly tell of their experiences with airports. As she goes around the group, she discovers that some children know a little from televiewing, but that many had real experiences flying or visiting airports. She writes a one-sentence summary statement of each child's response, using the child's name: "Teresa flew to Los Angeles on a 747"; "Mike and his mother picked up grandmother at the airport last month"; "Jessica's uncle flew to Mexico"; and so on. The teacher then asks what problems children associate with airports and writes these down next to "their" sentences. Thus, next to Teresa's, she writes "crashes"; next to Mike's, "getting lost"; next to Jessica's, "missing planes"; and so on. The brief prereading activity also gives the children a purpose for reading, because the teacher next notes that the new story is about a problem one girl had in an airport: "As you read, be watching to find out what *her* problem is."

One third-grade teacher uses *sounds* to provide a framework for her group's prereading. She asks what sounds each child associates with airports. After writing down on the board obvious answers (such as jet roar), she presses the group to think of other sounds and obtains a variety of answers (such as voices on the intercom system, *different* voices, babies crying, baggage scraping on floors, etc.). Her board list serves to activate knowledge children already have about airports and also leads to a purpose-for-reading question: "As you read this story, be listening in your mind for all these sounds and others. Do you hear sounds we didn't mention? What are they?"

One fourth-grade teacher uses the advance organizer in a science book to provide for assessment of prior knowledge and its activation. She reads the one-paragraph "summary" of the chapter aloud as children follow. Then she notes that it sums up what they are about to read, asking: "What else do you know that's not mentioned here about the topic?" For a chapter on weather, children offer a dozen pieces of relevant information not noted in the book's headnote. She jots these on the board, allows time for discussion, and then suggests that each child read to see if the author does mention these points.

Many teachers at all grade levels assess and activate students' knowledge with *pictures.* One second-grade teacher uses the illustrations provided in the book. She asks children to examine each carefully and tell what ideas they trigger. She then lists all the ideas on the board for group discussion. A middle school teacher tells students in advance to locate appropriate pictures at home: "On Monday we begin our unit on Mexico; over the weekend, search old magazines and newspapers to find all the photographs or pictures you can find related to Mexico." On the first day of the unit he gives students a chance to show and tell about their findings and then posts these on the bulletin board. For the remainder of the period he has students write in their notebooks all the information they already have about Mexico: information that is triggered by the pictures or that "pops into their heads." Before the hour is over he goes around the group and writes this material on a master list to be duplicated and shared the next day. The list serves then as a yardstick to assess new information obtained in reading: as students read in their social studies textbook during the week they check items that they already know and add items new to them. Pictures in this case provide for assessment, activation, and purposeful reading.

Writing may be used to activate prior knowledge. One middle school teacher regularly has students write down everything that comes into their minds about the topic in a reading assignment. "Just list," he says, "every word or phrase that pops into your head." Thus, prior to reading about Westward Expansion in their social studies books, boys and girls jot down every possible bit of information they can think of pertaining to the topic. The teacher then goes around the class asking students to read their lists. Sometimes he talks about various items; sometimes he writes them on the chalkboard. He says the time spent with this activity is worthwhile, because it helps students realize how much they already know about the topic of the assignment.

Another writing activity designed to make students conscious of their own prior knowledge is *ad writing*. One junior high school teacher tells students that they constitute an advertising agency handling a new product, which—because the agency is so successful and busy—they have not yet studied in depth. "But don't let that simple fact deter you," she says, "Write the ad anyway!" She gives them time before reading to write out an advertisement for the topic of the lesson (for example, The First Transcontinental Railroad or Marconi's Magnificent Breakthrough). The "ads" are fun to read together and, when shared, help the students realize how much they already know about the material in the assignment.

INCREASING STUDENTS' PRIOR KNOWLEDGE

If the quantity and quality of readers' prior knowledge is a primary influence on comprehension, then clearly teachers' efforts to increase prior knowledge is of major importance: the more students know about the subject discussed in the text, the more apt they are to understand it; the more prior knowledge they have, the greater the speed and efficiency of their reading; the greater amount of information they bring to a text, the better able they are to evaluate it and use it to stimulate their own thinking. Expanding students' knowledge is, therefore, the primary concern of reading teachers as well as content area teachers.

However, it is easier to grant the validity of such assertions than to set up specific classroom activities designed to further develop and increase the prior knowledge students need to comprehend specific texts, basal reader selections, or content area reading assignments. When a class is scheduled to read Esther Forbes's *Johnny Tremain* and several children know little or nothing about Colonial America, a teacher must expect from them less comprehension of the novel. When a high school student has no background knowledge of the geography and history of the Midwestern states, his teachers can predict that he will have difficulties understanding a social studies unit on "America's Bread Basket" or Willa Cather's *My Antonia.* When a fourth-grade child has a poorly formed or inaccurate schema for *swapping,* her teacher cannot expect her to comprehend a story in which swapping is central to the plot. How can one teacher step in—just before students begin a reading lesson—and remedy deficiencies in real-life or vicarious experiences and provide the variety of prior knowledge needed to better comprehend a text?

Individual teachers clearly cannot, in one or several classes, develop and refine the infinite number of schemata that contribute to students' prior knowledge. Some students, because of the richness of their personal experiences or the depth and breadth of their recreational reading, approach each reading assignment with a wealth of world knowledge. Others, without vicarious or real-life experiences, are handicapped comprehenders from the start. One or two (or fifty-two) class lessons can have only a modicum of effect on building students' knowledge background.

Fortunately, that modicum counts. The prior knowledge held schematically in long-term memory may be refined, enriched, extended, and enlarged by individual teachers in individual lessons. Three processes are involved: accretion, tuning, and reconstruction.

Accretion Each time a teacher teaches something, talks about it, or even refers to it in class, traces of the "something" are left in students' memory. These traces seem to be fragments of a schema that may be stored in memory and later serve to help recall the "something." Over time enough classroom discussion and experience, combined with later recollections (however fragmentary), may lead to the development of a fully formed schema that will help students better understand a newly encountered text. For example, at various times in his course, a high school teacher discusses *laissez-faire* and the "New Deal." A student will retain portions of data each time the teacher reintroduces the terms: Laissez-faire, the student begins to realize, has something to do with freedom; the New Deal is connected with the Great Depression; Laissez-faire is related in some way to capitalism; the New Deal is somehow related to economic controls, and so on. Certain fragments will stay in the student's memory and add, piece by piece, to the slow development of the appropriate schemata that these terms label. Eventually enough classroom encounters, however casual, will lead to more-or-less fully formed schemata for *laissez-faire* and *New Deal.*

Tuning As a student encounters a term in many classroom contexts, she reshapes and modifies it, gradually refining it until it works for her in a variety of situations. Sometimes one portion of a schema is replaced (because it fails to account for a fresh situation) and generalizations are made. Thus a child's initial encounters with, say, *bank* lead to fragments of a schema (building or place; money or checks). Over time (and many experiences) she forms a primitive schema, "Place where money is kept." More encounters in various contexts help her *tune* her original schema so that it includes lending and borrowing. A fifth-grade child's schema for *division* is tuned over a period of months or years in arithmetic classes and out-of-school experiences. What may start out as a simple set of memorized procedures becomes, with a variety of new experiences, a more fully formed schema for an arithmetical process. (One fifth-grade girl announced to her class: "I've got it; it's just muliplication backwards!") Most adults tune their schemata as they too have more experiences in the world; thus few teachers today have the same schemata for *marriage, technology,* or even *teaching* that they had in college.

Reconstruction   If accretion and tuning were the only ways schemata change, no new ones could form. Actually students (and adults) create new schemata by making analogies, by learning that a newly encountered object, action, or event is like one they already know except for a few differences. Thus a student forms a fresh schema—for her—of, say, a *college freshman dormitory* by realizing that it is like a hotel or a summer camp dormitory (both of which she already understands) but with certain distinct differences. Her younger sister forms a new schema for *computer terminal* by analogy with *typewriter,* by noting ways in which the terminal is like and unlike the machine familiar to her. A high school student in English class creates for himself a theory or explanation of *noun clause* by comparing and contrasting it to a noun: How, he asks himself, is it like a noun? different? What can it do in a sentence that a noun does? What can it do that a noun can't? etc. A child *restructures* when his schema for *animal* is changed to include ants: he had thought that animals had four legs and fur, but when told that an ant is an animal he is forced to make analogies and fresh generalizations (But how is it different from a dog? a cow? How is it like them? etc.). (Further explanation of accretion, tuning, and restructuring may be found in Rumelhart and Norman, 1978.)

Of the three processes, restructuring is the most difficult for teachers to manage in their classrooms. Accretion involves putting new information into schemata students already possess; tuning involves minor changes in those schemata. Teachers have usually attended to these two assimilation processes. A teacher, for example, may have told children that the thinner a piece of horn was sliced the more transparent it became, thus adding to their hornbook schema. She may also have told them that hornbooks were generally only slightly larger than a regular-size schoolbook today and could include only so many lines of print, thus helping them refine and tune their schema. By informing students that hornbooks were replaced in time by cheaper book printing and that their use was geographically restricted to areas that maintained cows and similar animals, she helps them further build on and refine what they know. Restructuring is not so simple.

Restructuring involves *major* changes in student schemata. Students must build—"from the ground up"—a new schema; one that is necessarily analogous to other schemata they possess but still new to them. Restructuring means analogy-making (a hornbook is *like* a book but it is *not* a book, a teaching device *like* a computer but *not* a computer, etc.); but analogy-making done in such a way that a fresh structure develops. One reason why restructuring is so difficult is that *existing schemata may get in the way*. If—to use the same example—a teacher says a hornbook is a teaching device and a student has a schema for "teaching device" (one that revolves around her home computer!), it may be difficult for that student to develop the one the teacher wants to develop. As McNeil (1984) points out, people resist developing new schemata when new schemata conflict with existing ones: "We resist new information when it requires that we change a large number of other logically related beliefs in order to maintain consistency among them. Resistance to a new schema takes the form of counterarguing with the learner's current framework, treating anomalies as exceptions that prove the rule, and keeping incompatible schemata separate" (p. 65).

What can teachers do—immediately—to help students develop enough prior knowledge background to better comprehend the reading materials they are given? Six suggestions are made here.

1. *Build upon what students already know.* This involves accretion and tuning—as well as activating.
2. *Provide much background information orally.* This again represents the first two processes; teachers are adding to and refining prior knowledge.
3. *Show students some of what they are to read.* Teachers here are not only activating prior knowledge but also refining it.
4. *Provide real-life experiences.* This is of course the ultimate way to build background: teachers—if they can control the operation!—stimulate accretion, tuning, *and* restructuring.
5. *Encourage wide reading for vicarious experiences.* This again helps (and is more manageable by teachers) the processes of accretion, tuning, and restructuring.
6. *Restructure—and build—"new" schemata.*

Discussions of these suggestions follow.

Build Upon What Students Already Know

Students usually have more related (and potentially useful) information than they or their teachers realize. To comprehend selections in one basal reader, fifth-grade children need to understand, among many other terms, *crystal ball* and *potter's wheel*. Many boys and girls, without specific instruction, know both; their prior knowledge permits them to handle these concepts without a teacher's assistance. Many other children are unable to tell what either term refers to. However, in a brief prereading discussion, a teacher can elicit from students a large number of associations (for *crystal*, for *ball*, for *potter*, for *wheel*). Generally the kind of associative responses contributed by children implies some existing knowledge of the schemata that the words label. Teachers can often use the information students already have to help them develop the schemata they will need to comprehend the selections. (See the section "Relating the New to the Known" later in this chapter.)

Provide (Orally) Background Information

Traditionally most teachers' manuals accompanying basal readers include in their guided reading lessons a section called "Building Reading Background" or "Background for Reading." In these sections teachers are advised to give children information they will need to understand the selection. (This advice was found in basal manuals from the 1920s and 1930s, predating all psycholinguistic discussions of prior knowledge and world knowledge. It suggests what many reading specialists realized—without knowledge of recent research findings—the importance of readers' background knowledge.) Before children read a selection about Eskimos or sailing "round the Horn," teachers were counseled to explain about life in the frigid northwestern parts of the continent and the difficulties of maneuvering a sailing ship in treacherous seas; teachers were told to show maps and pictures, tell about the time and place, the habits, histories, and customs of the people, and so on. Such information, it was believed by manual authors, helped young readers better understand the selections. Most elementary school teachers continue to provide this valuable prereading service to children.

Unfortunately some teachers in upper grades and secondary school (and college!) neglect this vital component of every reading lesson. The vogue of individualized instruction in the middle schools, and the disparagement of too much lecturing and "teacher talk" in secondary schools, may have discouraged many teachers from providing extensive background presentations orally. Older students are too frequently told to "Read pages 90 to 120" or "Read Chapter 9 for tonight." Some of these students may have acquired (through life experiences or recreational reading) the schemata necessary to allow for some comprehension of the material; many may not. A brief verbal explanation by teachers before students begin to read can help them refine and sharpen the schemata that make up their background knowledge.

Show Students Some of What They Are About to Read

In addition to acquiring important background information through listening, students learn visually. Teachers need to show photographs, drawings, reproductions of paintings, maps, charts, graphs, and other visual representations of material to be found in reading assignments. Many teachers collect large files of *visuals:* before their students read a selection, they show pictures of Eskimos, of sailing ships, of storms at sea, of ice landscapes, and so forth. They have board maps indicating the Pacific Northwest or the Straits of Magellan. Some have attractively prepared slides or wall posters.

In an effort to help students *see* as much of the material as possible that they are assigned to read, many teachers go out of their way to locate appropriate films and videotapes. One middle school teacher regularly schedules a film about the American Revolution before children read *Johnny Tremaine;* a high school teacher always shows a videotape of a popular film about the 1920s prior to the class reading of *The Great Gatsby.* Content area teachers sensitive to the value of visualization regularly bring to class actual models (of a water wheel, an Elizabethan theatre, an internal combustion engine, an abacus). Their students not only see but touch aspects of the world they will read about in their textbooks.

Provide Real-Life Experiences

Hearing about and seeing are invaluable avenues to background building. Actual experience is better. Unfortunately actual experience of most aspects of the world are hard to come by in the classroom. Some teachers rely on field trips (to museums, hospitals, factories, restaurants, fire stations); others on simulated experiences (classroom versions of town meetings, senate hearings, jury trials, elections). Many teachers emulate their colleagues in the sciences by doing actual experiments in class if possible. One teacher has students "act out" literature (see Devine, 1981, pp. 262–263). They decide which traits differentiate various characters, what the setting seems to be, which events are central to the story, in what sequence these events occur, and so forth. They then present, in small groups, their dramatic recreations of the work. Such an approach suggests a variety of strategies in other content areas, especially history and other social studies.

Actual experience is the best way to develop and refine the schemata that make up readers' prior knowledge. If teachers want students to know about crystal balls or potters' wheels, they must let them see, touch, and use these objects; if they want students to know about swapping or banking, they must set up classroom situations where children can swap or actually bank their money. If teachers want their students to know about an action or an event, whether ordering food in a restaurant or manipulating the stock market, they need to let students order food in a restaurant or manipulate the stock market. The constraints of the school and classroom limit most teachers to field trips, simple hands-on experiments, acting out, and simulation games. Skillful building on what students already know can help them make analogies between what they already know and what is new and as yet unexperienced (thus helping them develop new schemata by restructuring); but at least one other approach remains.

Encourage Vicarious Experiences Through Wide Reading ⎯⎯⎯⎯

It may be axiomatic that, in the development of background knowledge, there is no substitute for direct experience; but no one can possibly directly experience all facets of life. Many readers acquire rich knowledge backgrounds through reading itself. They understand what it's like to use a potter's wheel or to manipulate the stock market, not because they have personally done these things but because they have read about them.

Teachers at all levels need to be sensitive to how important wide reading is in providing students with information about people, places, events, situations, points of view, and so on. Those who advocate programs in recreational (that is, non-curriculum) reading note that it is through their reading that students gain insights into the ways people think, feel, and behave. (Film- and televiewing, they note, allow viewers to observe as outsiders, not to identify with characters and engage themselves as readers can.) Programs such as *Uninterrupted Sustained Silent Reading* (*USSR*) encourage students to read what they want to read, quietly, during the school day; thus, according to advocates of such programs, fostering in students the development of lifetime reading habits as well as providing them with new ideas and information.

These five suggestions allow for the accretion and further tuning of schemata that students possess; the last two also allow for restructuring and developing new schemata. The next suggestion is, as previously noted, the most difficult to implement in the classroom.

Restructure and Build "New" Schemata ⎯⎯⎯⎯⎯⎯⎯⎯⎯⎯

A fifth-grade basal reader selection concerns a boy who is constantly swapping—a yo-yo for baseball cards, a boomerang for a bouncing ball, a skateboard for a unicycle, and finally that for a puppy (Clymer, Venezky, and Indrisano, 1982, pp. 11–19). To comprehend the story readers must have meanings for words such as *yo-yo* and *unicycle;* they must have, that is, fairly well-developed schemata for which these words serve as labels. And clearly they must know about *swapping*. In her quick assessment of what children seemed to know and not know before beginning the story, the teacher discovered that everyone knew *yo-yo,* a few apparently did not know *unicycle,* and—to her surprise—one or two seemed not to know *swapping*. She decided to take a few minutes prior to reading to discuss the setting for the story. Using the pictures in the book, she activated existing schemata: What is the boy holding in his hand? Where is he? What is that in the background? and so forth. As the children discussed the illustrations, the teacher added information about boomerangs and baseball cards and stimulated boys and girls to share information they already had about these and similar items that appeared in the pictures. During this time the teacher was helping students add to and refine certain schemata important to understanding the story, as well as activating these and related schemata.

What to do, however, about the children who seemed not to understand *swapping?* The teacher approached the concept through a semantic map. She quickly listed phrases from the class: "It's exchanging," "like buying," "no money," "not in store," and so forth. She was able to visually demonstrate that swapping was like buying in some respects but different in others. She had children make analogies between schemata they had (shopping, buying, exchanging) in such a way that—she hoped—the few children who seemed not to have a schema for *swapping* built one for themselves by analogies to similar schemata they did have. These children were developing a schema through the process of restructuring. As they meet *swapping* in new contexts they will add to it, reshape it, refine it, and as time passes construct for themselves a meaning they can use through life.

Swapping is easy. What can teachers do about schemata that appear important to the understanding of assignments in content area textbooks? The teaching approach is basically the same: the teacher needs to identify knowledge that learners already have and use it systematically to help them make analogies between the "old" and the "new" that is coming into being. The following terms (each of which labels a schema) were selected from an intermediate-grade social studies textbook: *kinship systems, castes, pastoral, civilization,* and *industrial revolution*. Most teachers can teach these terms. Many may not realize that when they are "teaching" the terms they are helping boys and girls to build schemata.

What happens when existing schemata get in the way of restructuring? This *can* happen when dealing with relatively simple items such as *hornbook* or *swapping*. A child, for example, may have a "firm" belief that a book must have pages, all the same size and numbered sequentially. Another may believe that to get something new one *must* pay money as in a store. Both of these beliefs constitute disruptive or intruding schemata. If a child is so committed to the preexisting (and interfering) schemata that the teacher cannot budge it, it is doubtful if the new schemata will get developed. Sometimes a child's *emotional* commitment is so great that he cannot see the analogies presented to him. Some older children and young adults have lived so long with certain sets of schemata that teachers find restructuring especially difficult.

McNeil (1984) recommends several approaches to restructuring problems of this nature. One, *a dialectical model,* forces students to deal with contradictions and opposing examples (Collins, 1977). It seems especially appropriate in various content area situations where students resist building or restructuring a particular schema. Using it, the teacher

brings out any facts the student knows about the issue;

determines what causal factors the student knows;

determines if the student knows how causal factors are related;

helps the student determine which factors are insufficient;

gives the student a counter-example for an insufficient one;

asks, if the student overlooks a fact, why the factor does not apply;

poses a misleading question in order to free the student to learn about exceptions to the general rule;

asks for a prediction about an unknown case; and

asks for consideration of other factors.

How does this work in practice? One teacher needed to make sure students understood the *caste system* (referred to several times in various reading assignments). Several children did understand the idea of *social class*. Indeed, their schema for social class was so well structured that it stood between them and the new schema. Following the strategy outlined by Collins, the teacher asked such questions as: What do you already know about caste? class? What causes social classes in a country? How are these causes related? Which apply in the case of social class? If Mr. X changed his caste, doesn't that mean caste is really like class? If what we have said about caste is true, what can you predict about a country with a rigid caste system?

Another approach for restructuring schemata is based on the *inquiry method* (McNeil, 1984, pp. 69–70). After focusing on the particular schema or schemata, the teacher makes certain requests of students.

1. List everything you observe or note about the topic.
2. What facts or events go together?
3. What is the common thread among these items?
4. What do you call each of the groups?
5. Do the items belong to one group only?
6. Let's try to find another way to group the items.
7. What is the common thread among the items in the new grouping?
8. In the light of these groupings, what concepts (labels, schemata) do we have now?

As students respond to these requests and questions, they

list their observations;

group the items;

give common factors for grouping;

label the groups;

examine the grouping;

consider alternative ways to group;

identify a common factor for the new grouping; and

summarize by giving final grouping.

How might a teacher use this approach for *industrial revolution?* After asking students (individually or in small groups) to list everything they can about revolutions, she asks them to group related items. Next she asks them to look for the common thread among all these groups of items. (From French Revolution, American Revolution, and Scientific Revolution the students may say the thread is *Change* or *Upset*.) Step 4 above asks for names for the groups: "political," "scientific," etc. When asked to note if some items are classifiable under two headings, students in this case must say that "scientific" and "industrial" may be classed together. As they continue through the suggested outline, students are in a sense going through the process of schema development.

Because restructuring is essentially analogy-making, it is discussed further in the next section on "Relating the New to the Old" and again in the section on developing word meanings in the following chapter.

Idea Box

To help children sharpen and extend specific schemata related to their reading, many teachers use *semantic associations.* Before reading a selection in a third-grade reader about sailing, for example, a teacher writes the words *boat* and *sail* on the chalkboard and asks children to tell as many things as they can about each. The teacher then writes down all this information. Under *boat,* she may get "crosses ocean," "Columbus's ship," "Love Boat," "races at Newport," "aircraft carrier," and so forth; under *sail,* "canvas," "catches wind," "clipper ship," "no smoke," "needed before engines invented," and so forth.

Teachers using semantic relationships can help children perceive new meanings and new relationships. Some children, for example, may never have realized that sail-power and man-power were the only means of moving a craft before the invention of the steam engine, or that modern sail boats may have gasoline engines as well as sails. Others may never have appreciated the differences in size between the Santa Maria and "Love Boat," or between an aircraft carrier and a clipper ship. Others may never have heard of the Santa Maria or clipper ships. Such simple prereading activities in semantic associations help children of all ages gain new knowledge, while at the same time sharpen and extend the knowledge they already have.

One third-grade social studies selection notes that seashells are found on mountaintops. When the teacher realizes that children are unable to understand this observation, she decides that she needs to restructure rather than refine and extend their schemata. She first tries to identify the concepts they already have, which allow them to understand "seashells on mountaintops." She selects *changes in the earth* as her discussion focus: "What forces can change the face of the earth?" Children suggest erosion, earthquakes, and volcanos. She lists these on the board and asks for examples of each. She then sets up a problem-solving situation: "How can seashells get to the tops of mountains?" She writes down all suggested hypotheses: "People carry them there in their pockets"; "Seas once covered the mountains"; "Volcanos push up mountains from under the sea"; and so forth. The group evaluates each and decides that perhaps the best explanation came from their third hypothesis. Thus for these children a new concept develops as their teacher helps them recombine knowledge they already have in fresh ways. Most never realized that volcanos grew upward by throwing melted rock from below the earth's crust, nor that volcanos could arise from under the sea. A brief exercise in schema-building leads to the development of several related schemata and consequently better comprehension of the reading assignment.

Many teachers use *semantic feature analysis* as a way of helping students relate the new to the known. One teacher needs to make sure children have a meaning for the word *oboe* as they read a selection. She could show them a picture of the instrument and play a recording of one being sounded; or, even better, she could show them a real oboe and have someone play it for them in class. Instead she makes a simple *features chart.* She lists on one side of the board several musical instruments suggested by the children (piano, drum, clarinet, trumpet, etc.). Then across the top of the board she lists "features" of musical instruments (size, color, use, source of sound, etc.). Then, working as a group, the children check in the various features of the instruments: pianos are large, heavy, used in orchestras and in solos, and their sound is derived from the vibrations of metal strings hit by small hammers; oboes are small, light to carry, used in orchestras and bands, and their sound is derived from the vibrations of two wooden reeds blown upon by the player. As they develop a *grid* for their analysis chart, children begin to see the ways one musical instrument differs from another and the ways in which they are alike.

Another way to help children develop a concept is through a "Snowball Paper." The teacher gives a starter sentence: "Volcanos change the earth's surface" or "Sails propel ships." The paper is then passed around the group for each student to add a sentence: "Volcanos throw up hot lava"; "Sailing ships need winds." As the paper goes through the group, a text grows, showing what students already know but also adding, for many, new information. Completed Snowball Papers may be duplicated to serve as the basis for prereading discussions, with the teacher adding more information and clarifying certain points.

One activity, both for activating students' prior knowledge and for encouraging them to read an assignment actively, is suggested by Jo Beth Allen of the University of Kansas. After the central topic of the assignment is identified, she has her students brainstorm together everything they "know" about the topic. She then writes on the chalkboard or on a continuous overhead the information they give, pinpointing areas where concepts conflict, helping students formulate questions from these conflicting areas, and throughout encouraging them to develop related questions, other areas of concern, and personal inquiries growing out of the discussion. Then she has students, as individuals or in groups, organize the information collected and the questions into a study guide for the assignment. The guide may be at a simple level ("Answer these questions as you read") or quite sophisticated ("After you read, note: Things We Know for Sure, Things We Are Sure We Don't Yet Know, and Questions We Still Want Answered"). Such an activity shows students that they already have considerable knowledge about topics to be studied and at the same time stimulates them to read their text thoughtfully.

RELATING THE NEW TO THE KNOWN

Most recent research and theory on the comprehension process stress the value for readers of relating the new ideas and information encountered in texts to what they already know. Pearson and Johnson, for example, define comprehension as ''building bridges between the new and the known'' (1978, p. 24); Frank Smith defines it as ''relating new information to what is already known'' (1978, p. 240).

New ideas and information are understood by readers in the light of the existing framework of schemata that constitute their individual prior knowledge backgrounds. A reader begins to understand "A" because, in certain respects, it is like "B" and unlike "C"—both of which he already knows or thinks he knows (actually, the reader's "B" and "C" may undergo reshaping and fine tuning as they are compared and contrasted with the "new" "A"). A fifth-grader comprehends *unicycle* in the ways it is like and unlike *bicycle* and *tricycle* (which he already knows); a high school student begins to figure out *laissez-faire* by comparing and contrasting it with *free enterprise* and *capitalism* (which she already understands). Readers constantly make inferences ("educated guesses") about new schemata, which they test out as they read. Their continued reading of a text allows them to develop, refine, and restructure new schemata as they pit these against ones they do know.

This ongoing mental activity takes place always, everywhere, without the help of teachers. It is the way human beings (and animals) learn. However, in their classrooms teachers frequently need to exploit the information available from recent research and theory to improve students' comprehension of specific texts. What can teachers do then to "build bridges"? Four suggestions are made here.

Identify Probable Problem Points in Advance _____

Many years ago reading teachers began to distinguish between the *independent* reading level (at which students could read easily without teacher guidance), the *instructional* level (where teachers had to provide some assistance), and the *frustrational* level (where the content and structure of the text became such a burden on the reader that ordinary instruction was not enough). These levels were characterized generally in terms of vocabulary and syntax; that is, the words and sentence structures found in materials read at the independent level were already familiar to readers; the words and syntax of texts read at the frustrational level were still mostly unknown to readers; material at the instructional level tended to include relatively few words still unfamiliar to readers and a manageable number of sophisticated sentences, all of which could be conveniently taught in regular lessons. It is suggested here that the basic difference among independent, instructional, and frustrational levels is actually the extent and quality of prior knowledge possessed by students (prior knowledge not only of words and syntactical arrangements but of the world and the way it works). Materials that are easy for students to read tell them what they already know; materials that are difficult contain ideas and information they have yet to learn. On a continuum from "easy" to "difficult," instructional reading materials cluster in the middle. They contain enough information already in memory so that students can move steadily through it, yet enough new ideas and information to demand some teacher intervention. Throughout the following discussion the focus is on material at the instructional level.

To help students build bridges between the new and the known in instructional level material, teachers need first to identify what is probably new to student readers. They need to carefully review each assignment or basal selection and list those concepts (and the words that label them) that, in their professional judgment, will probably not be known to students. Thus a high school science teacher will find, in the following passage in her science textbook, several "probable problem points":

> The most visible objects on the disc of the sun are clusters of spots, known as sun spots or simply spots. These range in size from tiny flecks visible only through a telescope to large areas which may be seen by the unaided eye. One sun spot group has been estimated to be as large as the circumference of the earth multiplied by 140 times. All have two portions, a darker one near the center called the umbra and a lighter one called the penumbra. The umbra appears darker than it really is because of the relative brightness of the surrounding area. Some penumbra have several umbra within them. Observers have traced the positions of sun spots throughout the year and have noticed two kinds of movement. Sometimes they move in straight lines and sometimes in slight curves. This is due to the inclination of the sun's equator to the plane of the earth's orbit.

Before assigning the passage, the teacher must decide if students know the meanings of the writer's words. *Umbra* and *penumbra* are explained in context; *circumference, inclination,* and *orbit* may be used and defined by the teacher on the chalkboard. However, the real problem points are not necessarily the obviously more difficult words; they are the schemata these and other words label. More than board definitions are required if students are to understand "most visible objects," "disc of the sun," "clusters of spots," "tiny flecks," "unaided eye," "estimated," "circumference of the earth," "multiplied 140 times," "two portions," "relative brightness," "inclination of the sun's equator," and "plane of the earth's orbit." If the textbook has been chosen because it is at the instructional level for the class, most students will have approximate meanings for most of these terms. But at least some will have poorly formed schemata for *disc, circumference,* or even *clusters.* Most students will have trouble understanding "inclination of the sun's equator" and "plane of the earth's orbit."

Try to Identify Comparable Concepts Students Already Know

Authors of textbooks try to be sensitive to their readers' prior knowledge but, because they write for a wide readership, often are unable to accurately predict what individual readers may or may not know. On the other hand, teachers who assign specific selections in those textbooks are not only sensitive to their own students' prior knowledge but know, within certain limits, what students will probably understand or not understand. A high school science teacher who has taught her class for a period of time will be able to predict whether students will understand *orbit, circumference, disc,* or *estimated.* She will also be able to pinpoint information students do possess that might help them understand unfamiliar concepts and words. For example, she may decide that most students will have a poorly formed schema for *orbit* but that all have played with a yo-yo. She may, therefore, explain that an orbit is the path of one body about another, and spin a yo-yo around her body on its string, noting that she represents the sun, the yo-yo the earth, and the "path" the orbit. A social studies teacher may decide that his students will not understand *supply and demand* but that they are familiar with the sale of rock concert tickets, and explain the new concept in terms of the one they do understand.

Implicit here is the belief that teachers play a key role in the reading comprehension process: they can show students how to be better comprehenders by relating the new to the old. Teachers can identify those parts of a text students probably will not readily understand, recognize information students already possess that will help them understand those parts, and then show them how to make fruitful connections.

Show How Connections May Be Made Between the New and the Known

What are the best ways of making connections? Many suggestions come from recent studies of human memory (see Chapter 2). For example, the word that represents a concept may be defined (and understood) in terms of the direct and indirect connections it has with other related words in the same semantic network or hierarchical order. Just as *bird* is subordinate in its network to *animal* and has subordinate to it *eagle* and *robin,* so *orbit, disc,* and *penumbra* may be placed in similar semantic networks with certain terms above and below them. *Disc,* or *disk,* for example, may be subordinate to "objects" and "round, flat objects" and have subordinate to it various kinds of discs, such as phonograph records, invertebral disks (as in "slipped disks"), and the central part of flower heads.

Each word and the concept it represents may be further described (and understood) in terms of specific semantic features. Robins and chickens, for example, are birds because they have the *defining features* of all birds (such as feathers, beaks, and wings), but chickens do not have all the *characteristic features* of birds (for example, they cannot fly). Thus bats are not "true" birds because, although they have the characteristic feature of flying, they lack the defining feature of feathers. A *computer disk* has the defining features of all disks (it is round and flat) and also special characteristic features (it is coated with a magnetic substance for storing data). As noted in Chapter 2, *linguistic hedges* are added to this system to make it more workable. Thus a bat is a bird "loosely speaking"; "technically speaking" a chicken is a bird; or a robin is a "true" bird.

This information is valuable for teaching. When a teacher has identified a potentially difficult concept in an assignment and, on the basis of her experience with a particular group of students, has noted which related concepts they already have as part of their general prior knowledge, she can begin to make systematic connections for learners by asking such questions as

Where have you heard the word *disk* before? (My uncle had a slipped disk. Phonograph records. They use them in computers.)

What do all these have in common? (They are usually round. They are all flat.) (*characteristic features*)

In what ways are phonograph records different from that flat, round bone in the human skeleton? (They have grooves. They record music.) (*defining features*)

Another useful approach to connection-making is to ask students to look at *class relations, example relations,* and *property relations* (Pearson and Johnson, 1978, pp. 25–26). Students are shown that a phonograph record is related to uncle's slipped disk in that both belong to a class of things called *disks.* Such relations are called class relations. John's particular recording of his favorite rock group and the particular invertebral disk "slipped" by Arthur's uncle are examples from the larger class of disks and are *example relations. Property relations* are specific properties or attributes: John's disk has grooves; Arthur's uncle's disk is made of bone.

Using this information teachers can show students how to make *specific* semantic maps. These are visual representations of the possible connections between things they already know and what may be new to them. The diagram on page 106 is meant to represent the concept to younger children. It is an incomplete semantic map for *cat.* Using such a map (or even better *making* one in class) helps children refine and extend their schema for *cat.* However, as noted in Chapter 2, schemata may represent more than knowledge about things or objects; they may also represent knowledge of situations, actions, sequences of actions, events, or sequences of events. Thus *orbiting* or *swapping* may be diagramed as a semantic map in the same way as *cat* or *disk.* To help children with *swap,* a teacher might build on their existing knowledge of *buy.* Their schema for *buy* is comparable to a "script"—with a SELLER, a PURCHASER, some MERCHANDISE, and a medium of exchange, MONEY, as well as interaction between seller and purchaser, BARGAINING. (See Chapter 2; also Rumelhart, 1980; Schank, 1982.) Working with students, a teacher may develop a semantic map showing *swap* as an example of *buy* (belonging to the

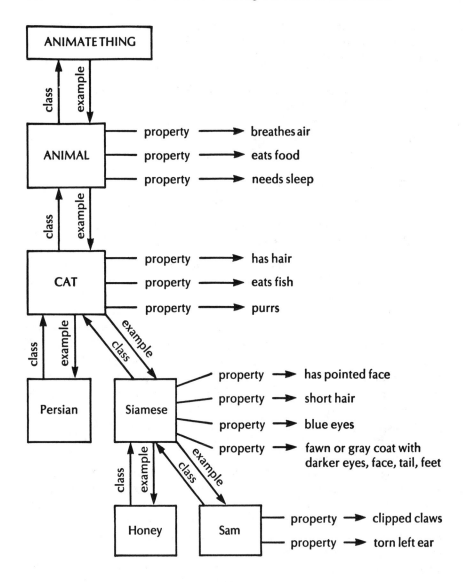

same class) but with a specifically different "property." The medium of exchange, the MONEY, is another form of MERCHANDISE. As in the case of those prepared for objects, semantic maps for actions and events—and sequences of actions and events—present visually the relationships between what students already know and what is new to them.

Semantic mapping is used extensively and successfully in many classrooms. It helps teachers identify possible troublesome points in an assignment, discover appropriate related knowledge students may already have, and make connections between the new and the known. However, some teachers achieve the same goals—when time constraints do not permit development of a full semantic map—by a simple questioning procedure. Once the "new" item is pinpointed and possible familiar ones identified, teachers may ask such questions as

> Have you ever heard of this before? Where? What examples come to your mind? What do you think it means?
>
> In what ways is it like _____? In what ways is it different?
>
> Does it seem to belong in the same general class? What features does it have in common with _____?
>
> What features make it distinctly different from other things in the same class?

Clearly the important goal for teachers is not to have a series of specific questions or to teach a specific terminology (*characteristic* and *defining features;* or *class, example,* and *property* relations). It is certainly not to teach students how to make and use semantic maps. The goal is to encourage them to try—always—to see connections between the new information and ideas they encounter in their reading and all the knowledge they already possess. Those connections account for their texts-in-the-head.

Help Students Make Analogies

Central to all discussion of "relating the new to the known" is analogy-making. Students regularly make analogies on their own, this being one of the main ways schemata are structured and restructured and cognitive learning takes place. Teachers make analogies as they teach, establishing connections between the new material they are trying to teach and the prior knowledge of their students. Efforts to improve reading comprehension must highlight analogy-making.

As Hayes and Tierney (1982, p. 258) point out,

> Much of what is expected to be learned in school must be learned by reading and studying textual materials. Quite often, however, students lack the background knowledge necessary to profit from their reading experiences. When they do, teachers must somehow face the challenge of providing it. Many teachers believe that an effective way to meet this challenge is to provide an interpretive bridge between the unfamiliar material and the knowledge which students do have.

In their study (briefly described in Chapter 2) they asked American high school students (eleventh- and twelfth-graders from a rural-suburban school in California) to read and recall newspaper articles about cricket matches in Australia. Prior to reading, some of the students were given information about baseball, some about cricket, some about baseball and/or cricket *with specific analogies made between the two games,* and some were given unrelated information. The researchers wanted to discover how much prior knowledge (about cricket) helped students understand the articles (about cricket) and how much the analogies between cricket (a new game to them) and baseball (a game they knew) helped them understand the articles. They discovered that not only did prior knowledge have a significant effect upon comprehension but also that analogies contributed to that comprehension (Hayes and Tierney, 1982, pp. 269-279).

How can teachers use this information in their classrooms? Hayes and Tierney stressed analogies: a *pitch,* they said, "corresponds to the infield in baseball" and *wickets* are "a bit like home plate." They told readers "it is from cricket that the American game of baseball developed" but that "unlike baseball, there are always two batsmen in play at the same time." Most good teachers make analogies like these in the course of their daily teaching. When asking students to read material that may present comprehension difficulties, they need to be especially careful to make useful analogies.

In preparing a reading assignment in a middle school social studies textbook, one teacher went through the section on Japan and found several potentially troublesome words. She listed—in advance—useful analogies for her class:

"a *shogun* is something like a general who rules one part of the country"

"a *samurai* was like a knight"

"the *daimyo* was like a military lord, ruling one section"

"it was a *feudal system,* something like they had in Europe before each country was organized around a single king"

Teachers need to remember always that (1) successful analogies relate the new item to something students already know; and (2) analogies—by definition—are never completely accurate. In the examples noted above, it should be clear that it is useless for the teacher to compare the medieval Japanese feudal system to that of Europe's unless students know something of the European system and know that a samurai was not a knight—only *like* a knight.

Analogies are, as Pearson and Johnson (1978, p. 66) point out, "powerful logical and linguistic organizers and deserve inclusion in a comprehension curriculum at the earliest possible point." They suggest that five-year-old children should be encouraged as often as possible to complete such simple analogies as *dog* is to *puppy* as *cat* is to _____. Once in school, they say, children may be asked to complete an exercise such as the following:

Animal	Sound	Animal	Home
dog	bark	lion	den
cat	meow	bear	cave
horse	neigh	deer	thicket
lion	(roar)	bird	(nest)

Middle school and secondary school students may be introduced to the kinds of sophisticated analogy-finding often used by test-makers. Teachers may create test items such as are frequently found in standardized tests or use practice sheets provided by test publishers. The danger with all printed practice exercises—even the simple one of ANIMAL–SOUND/ANIMAL–HOME—is that students (and teachers!) may lose sight of the value of analogy-making in the classroom: *Teachers may use analogies as bridges between the new and the known, and, in the process, show students how they may continue to understand new information by comparing it with what they know.* Much better than duplicated exercise sheets are regularly posed classroom questions such as: In what ways is *A* like *B?* In what ways is it different? What else is *A* like? How is it different? How is *A* unlike *C?* In what respects? Can you tell what *A* is "really" like by comparing and contrasting it with *B* and *C?*

▪ RECAPPING MAIN POINTS ▪

Students understand their assignments largely in terms of what they already know. Prior knowledge *is* important. To help students make use of what they already know, teachers first of all have to discover the quantity and quality of that knowledge. One way to do this is to talk frequently with students, discussing lessons and assignments as well as their own interests and concerns. More formal ways to assess students' prior knowledge are through inventories, questionnaires, the use of the cloze procedure, and informal concept tests. Once teachers have some idea of what students know and do not know, they need to activate appropriate related knowledge through class discussions, pictures, advance organizers, questions, and semantic mapping. When teachers discover that important knowledge is *not* known, or is poorly understood (that is, when appropriate schemata are lacking), they must extend, refine, and often build that key knowledge. They can do this by providing new information orally or through related readings, by setting up situations in the classroom (if possible) that lead to actual experiences, or by using films, pictures, or realia to show necessary information. Reconstructing schemata is often difficult, because the learner's old, well-established ones get in the way. Teachers therefore need to identify the knowledge necessary for comprehension of assignments and develop it carefully through such techniques as semantic mapping and much analogy-making.

END-OF-CHAPTER ACTIVITIES

1. This chapter began with suggested study questions to guide readers. What are your answers to these questions? Were they all answered to your satisfaction? Why? Why not?

2. George Bernard Shaw is said to have approached an unfamiliar book this way: he read only the title and then, with the book closed, wrote out what he believed its table of contents would contain. If its printed table of contents coincided with his version, he assumed he "knew" its contents and often put it aside. If the two tables were markedly dissimilar, he read to discover what he could learn from the author. Tell why this technique is a valuable prior knowledge assessment device and an effective activator of the reader's prior knowledge.

3. From your reading of the approaches to prior knowledge assessment in this chapter, suggest one of your own that either combines positive features of some of them or is unique as far as you know.

4. Refining and enriching schemata by *accretion* and *tuning* are taking place in your life all the time. Give examples of a particular schema you have "polished up" recently. Give examples of schemata you have observed boys and girls changing in your classroom if you can. What experiences caused the refining and enriching—in your personal example and in those of your students?

5. One way to increase the general knowledge of the world that students bring to their reading is reading itself. Read the chapter "Reading Outside the Content Fields" in Margaret Early's *Reading to Learn in Grades 5 to 12* (1984, pp. 304–329) and list the many kinds of non-curricula reading that may provide vicarious experiences. Which, in your opinion, seems to have the greatest impact on students' general background knowledge?

6. Select a selection from a basal reader or content area textbook. List the information and ideas needed by its readers to comprehend it. Be prepared to explain why the author assumed readers would have this knowledge and why you think younger readers would not have it.

7. From the list in #6, select one concept and note related concepts

readers probably already know, that might help them understand the unfamiliar one. Explain ways in which you could help students understand the "new" concept in terms of what they already understand.

8. Select five words from a textbook or basal reader and show how they may be explained to students in terms of their *characteristic* and *defining features*. Show how the same five words may be explained in terms of *class, example,* and *property relations*.

9. Prepare a semantic map for a basal reader word labeling an object. Prepare one for a word labeling an action or a sequence of actions. Be prepared to show how your map(s) may help learners better understand the word(s).

10. Explain what you think the psychologist Julian Jaynes means when he says that "Understanding a thing is to arrive at a metaphor for that thing by substituting something more familiar to us" (1976, p. 52). How does this relate to the point of view of this chapter?

11. Write a brief paper with the title, "Metaphor: The Key to Comprehension." You may read Julian Jayne's provocative second chapter in *The Origins of Consciousness in the Breakdown of the Bicameral Mind* (1976) or base your paper on your own experiences and reflections. You may agree or disagree with this point of view.

REFERENCES

Ausubel, David P. *Educational Psychology: A Cognitive View.* New York: Holt, Rinehart and Winston, 1968.

Bransford, J. D. *Human Cognition: Learning, Understanding, and Remembering.* Belmont, Calif.: Wadsworth, 1979.

Clymer, Theodore, Richard L. Venezky, and Roselmina Indrisano (Eds.). *Ride the Sunrise.* Lexington, Mass.: Ginn, 1982.

Collins, Allan. "Processes in Acquiring Knowledge." In R. C. Anderson, R. J. Spiro, and W. E. Montague (Eds.), *Schooling and the Acquisition of Knowledge.* Hillsdale, N. J.: Lawrence Erlbaum Associates, 1977.

Devine, Thomas G. *Teaching Study Skills: A Guide for Teachers.* Boston: Allyn and Bacon, 1981.

Early, Margaret. *Reading to Learn in Grades 5 to 12.* New York: Harcourt Brace Jovanovich, 1984.

Emerson, Mary. "From Hornbooks to High Honors." In Theodore Clymer, Richard L. Venezky, and Roselmina Indrisano (Eds.), *Ride the Sunrise.* Lexington, Mass.: Ginn, 1982.

Hayes, David A., and Robert J. Tierney. "Developing Readers' Knowledge through Analogy." *Reading Research Quarterly* 17 (1982): 256–280.

Jaynes, Julian. *The Origin of Consciousness in the Breakdown of the Bicameral Mind.* Boston: Houghton Mifflin, 1976.

Manzo, Anthony V. "The ReQuest Procedure." *Journal of Reading* 13 (1969): 123–126.

Marr, M. B. "Children's Comprehension of Pictorial and Textual Event Sequences." In M. L. Kamil and A. J. Moe (Eds.), *Reading Research: Studies and Applications.* Clemson, S. C.: National Reading Conference, 1979.

McNeil, John D. *Reading Comprehension: New Directions for Classroom Practice.* Glenview, Ill.: Scott, Foresman, 1984.

Pearson, F. David, and Dale D. Johnson. *Teaching Reading Comprehension.* New York: Holt, Rinehart and Winston, 1978.

Potter, Thomas C. *A Taxonomy of Cloze Procedure, Part I, Readability and Reading Comprehension.* Inglewood, Calif.: Southwest Regional Laboratory for Educational Research and Development, 1968.

Rumelhart, David P. "Schemata: The Building Blocks of Cognition." In R. J. Spiro, B. C. Bruce, and W. F. Brewer (Eds.), *Theoretical Issues in Reading Comprehension.* Hillsdale, N. J.: Lawrence Erlbaum Associates, 1980.

Rumelhart, David P., and D. A. Norman. "Accretion, Tuning, and Restructuring: Three Modes of Learning." In J. W. Cotton and R. L. Klatzky (Eds.), *Semantic Factors in Cognition.* Hillsdale, N. J.: Lawrence Erlbaum Associates, 1978.

Samuels, S. J. "Effects of Pictures on Learning to Read, Comprehension and Attitudes." *Review of Educational Research* 40 (1970): 397–407.

Schank, Roger C. *Reading and Understanding: Teaching from the Perspective of Artificial Intelligence.* Hillsdale, N. J.: Lawrence Erlbaum Associates, 1982.

Smith, Frank. *Understanding Reading.* New York: Holt, Rinehart and Winston, 1978.

Stauffer, Russell G. *Directing Reading Maturity as a Cognitive Process.* New York: Harper & Row, 1969.

Thomas, J. L. "The Influence of Pictorial Illustrations with Written Text and Previous Achievement on the Reading Comprehension of Fourth-Grade Science Students." *Journal of Research in Science Teaching* 15 (1978): 401–405.

Tierney, Robert J., and James W. Cunningham. "Research on Teaching Reading Comprehension." In F. David Pearson (Ed.), *Handbook of Reading Research.* New York: Longman, 1984.

From Theory to Practice: Developing Word Meaning Knowledge

▪ INTRODUCTION AND OVERVIEW ▪

Students' prior knowledge affects their comprehension of a writer's text: the more they know about the subject discussed in the text, the more apt they are to understand what is being said. Their specific prior knowledge of word meanings plays an even more definite role in their comprehension: they must share with the writer meanings for words.

Students who come to class with some prior knowledge background in skiing, for example, may be able to use a writer's text on skiing to construct in their heads a text that resembles that in the head of the writer when the printed text was prepared. They use the words they do know to activate appropriate skiing schemata, which allow them to guess at the words they do not know. However, as often happens, a text may center on a specific word unknown to students and unguessable from the context: "He wasn't good at the *slalom*." In such cases comprehension is impeded if students have no meaning for the word.

Which words are most important? Which may be guessed? How can students become better guessers? What must teachers do when students have no meanings at all for a word?

Chapter 5 examines answers to these and other questions. It reviews first the reasons for emphasizing knowledge of word meanings in reading comprehension instruction, then at ways of classifying words students encounter in basal reader selections and content area textbooks, and finally at strategies for helping students build meanings for words.

Chapter 5 includes Suggested Study Questions, Teaching Guidelines, and then discussions on

- The Importance of Word Meaning Knowledge
- Identifying Potential Verbal Trouble Spots

      Matching word labels to known meanings
      Noting the multiple meanings of words
      Linking unfamiliar words with existing knowledge
      Developing fresh schemata
      Identifying potential verbal trouble spots

- Building Word Meanings Independently
      Using structural analysis
      Using contextual analysis
      The SSCD approach
- Building Word Meaning Knowledge from the Ground Up
      Semantic feature analysis
      Semantic mapping
      The Spoken Words Activity
      The Frayer Model
      The context approach

Chapter 5 also includes

- Recapping Main Points
- End-of-Chapter Activities
- References

■ SUGGESTED STUDY QUESTIONS FOR CHAPTER 5 ■

1. Why is knowledge of word meanings so important to reading comprehension?
2. Why are some words more difficult for students than others?
3. How many teachers identify the potentially troublesome words?
4. How may students develop word meanings on their own?
5. Which are more important, words or the schemata they label? Why?
6. How may teachers help students develop knowledge of word meanings?

■ TEACHING GUIDELINES FOR CHAPTER 5 ■

Chapter 5 is organized around the following three teaching guidelines derived from recent research and theory in reading comprehension.

Teaching Guideline #1
      Identify words for which students may not nave meanings.

Teaching Guideline #2
Show students how to build word meanings on their own.

Teaching Guideline #3
Help them build meanings for words they are unable to manage on their own.

THE IMPORTANCE OF WORD MEANING KNOWLEDGE

Of all aspects of prior knowledge, knowledge of word meanings is paramount. Phonetic knowledge may help children sound out *pedantic* in "He is pedantic." Syntactic knowledge may allow them to sense that *pedantic* is an adjective (because of the slot it occupies in the sentence and the suffix *-ic*). General prior knowledge background may allow them to make inferences about the meaning of the word if they are provided with enough other information in the passage. But semantic knowledge (that is, knowledge of word meanings) is necessary if they are to comprehend the sentence.

Many studies of vocabulary and vocabulary development support this belief (Deighton, 1959; Dale and O'Rourke, 1971; Graves, 1984). Correlational studies of reading comprehension, too, regularly find that word meaning knowledge is the most important single factor in the comprehension process (Davis, 1968, 1972; Spearritt, 1972). Some contend that students who score highly on vocabulary tests do so because of their "mental agility" and that this agility is what enables them to score highly on reading comprehension tests. However, the research evidence continues to suggest that knowledge of word meanings is the factor influencing success on both types of measures (Graves, 1984). Some research (see, for example, Anderson and Freebody, 1979) seems to suggest that direct instruction in vocabulary may not promote comprehension, but other research (for example, Graves and Bender, 1980) finds that it does. Observation in the classroom certainly supports the belief that students need to know the meanings of the words they read in order to comprehend passages. A sentence such as "All are experienced spelunkers" cannot be comprehended by children—even those with adequate phonological, syntactic, and general world knowledge—unless they have a meaning for *spelunkers* (Durkin, 1983, p. 236).

In their efforts to help students develop meanings for words, reading teachers should recall the generalizations about words and vocabulary development discussed in Chapter 2:

Words get their meanings from language users. Few are created with meanings attached (*polaroid* and *radar*); most have meanings given to them over time by speakers, listeners, writers, and readers. Thus, *nice* to language users of Chaucer's time meant "precise, exact"; through the years people have used it to mean "good, pleasant." *Book* generally meant printed pages bound together, but, because the names of prisoners were written in a book, policemen—and, in time, the general public—began to use it as a verb meaning to list or register (as in a book). (And, because bets were similarly registered in a book, gamblers used it to mean "accept bets.") Meanings, then, are not in the symbols but in the heads of those who employ the symbols.

Children (and adults) connect meanings with these verbal symbols through experience. Over a period of time children connect the word *cat* with a specific pet. *Their* meaning for that word is derived from all their experiences (visual, tactile, etc.) with cats. As they grow older, a specific meaning for *book* becomes extended—through experience—to include related meanings associated with concert attendance, opera librettos, law enforcement,—even horse racing. As individual and social experiences change, word meanings shift—for individuals and for groups of people using the same words.

Words label schemata. One's schema for cat or book are recalled and shared with others by the use of the word, or verbal symbol. When a child "has no meaning" for *slalom* or *spelunkers,* he or she has yet to develop a schema for *slalom* or one for *spelunkers.*

IDENTIFYING POTENTIAL VERBAL TROUBLE SPOTS

Must teachers help students develop meanings for every word in every basal reader selection? in every content area textbook assignment? Surely they "know" many words. Many words must already be in their listening vocabularies. They have heard them many times (and have meanings for them) although they have yet to see them in print. Teachers may be aided in their attempts to identify words students need help with by some kind of classifying system. The one suggested here was originally proposed by Goodman (1970) and further developed by Graves (1984). It classifies all words into four types:

> *Type-1 words* are those already in students' speaking-listening vocabularies but which they cannot yet read.
>
> *Type-2 words* are those like *book* which may be in students' reading vocabularies but with only one or two meanings and which are now being used with a "new" meaning.
>
> *Type-3 words* are words in neither their reading or their oral vocabularies but which may easily be explained (usually with synonyms).
>
> *Type-4 words* are the real trouble spots. They are words in neither reading or oral vocabularies which cannot be explained through existing, related schemata. For them, schemata must be built "from the ground up."

This classification system, as Graves points out (1984, p. 247), tends to parallel the difficulty of the teaching and learning task: teaching students to read words already in their speaking-listening vocabularies is relatively simple; teaching them new meanings for words they know with other meanings is a bit more difficult; teaching words that label concepts easily available to them is more difficult; teaching new words that label completely new and often complex schemata is the most difficult task of all. This system too classifies words and related schemata according to each student's prior knowledge; thus one student's Type-1 word may be another's Type-2 word. Fortunately, however, when classes are reasonably homogeneous, the relationship between the word and schema being taught and students' prior knowledge tends to be similar for most students.

The teaching implications associated with each type require further examination.

Matching Word Labels to Known Meanings _____

Type-1 words are, clearly, the central concern in beginning reading instruction. Children come to school already knowing thousands of words. They have heard them spoken repeatedly and have often said them themselves; but, because they have not yet seen them in print, teachers must show how to relate the (new) printed form to the (known) spoken form. Most school teachers accomplish this major goal of the reading program through systematic instruction in sound–letter correspondences (phonics) and in sight-word recognition.

As children's phonics and other word recognition skills develop, teachers need to be less and less concerned with Type-1 words. After a fair degree of automaticity is attained, children can identify most words in their speaking-listening vocabularies when they see them in print. One recent study found that competent fourth-grade readers could read about 96 percent of the words they could understand orally (Graves, 1980). However, instruction in strategies to read known words needs to continue, because readers have to process the majority of Type-1 words they meet in print instantaneously and automatically, without conscious attention, or else comprehension slows down.

How may teachers improve and continue to improve recognition of Type-1 words? They can maintain systematic programs in understanding and using phonics as a word analysis strategy, teaching the sound–letter correspondences children need to decode printed words. They can teach most-often-used words directly through word lists such as the Dale List of 769 Easy Words or the Dolch Basic Sight Vocabulary of 220 Words (both given in Lapp and Flood, 1983, pp. 136–138), as well as appropriate strategies in structural and contextual analysis. Fortunately, approaches such as these are well described in the professional literature on the teaching of reading. (See, for example, Durkin, 1983; Lapp and Flood, 1983; Burmeister, 1983; Alexander, 1983; or Ekwall and Shanker, 1985.)

Three points about Type-1 words may need to be emphasized:

1. Relatively few students in intermediate grades or in secondary school need to be taught these words; most have learned them.
2. The words do need to be taught, however, so that students respond to them *automatically;* continuing analysis in upper grades impedes comprehension.
3. By seventh grade, boys and girls should have mastered most words found in basic word lists, or at least 1,000 words commonly used in printed texts.

Noting the Multiple Meanings of Words

As many as one-third of commonly used words have multiple meanings! Such *polysemous* words clearly affect reading comprehension. As students read basal reader selections and assignments in content area textbooks, they are regularly confronted by two kinds of polysemous words: those that have multiple common meanings (like *run*) and those that have both a common meaning (or meanings) and a specialized one associated with a particular subject area (like *legend,* which may mean "an old story" or, in science and social studies, the key to a map).

The Living Word Vocabulary (Dale and O'Rourke, 1981) indicates 43,000 words linked with one of their meanings, plus the percentage of students at a given grade level who have demonstrated knowledge of the meaning. Thus *line* has four entries: a stretched string, a boundary, ancestry, and a kind of business. Dale and O'Rourke note that 83 percent of fourth-graders know that *line* can be a stretched string, 80 percent of sixth-graders know it can be a boundary, 77 percent of eighth-graders know that it can refer to descent or ancestry, and 72 percent of tenth-graders know it can mean a line of business. Such a list is of enormous value to textbook writers and authors of basal readers. It can also assist teachers as they decide which words need teaching at any given level. However, teachers cannot in their daily teaching refer to *The Living Word Vocabulary* constantly. Rather, they can use it to sensitize themselves to the problem and occasionally check out words that may come up in class.

How can teachers sensitize students to Type 2 words? One way, clearly, is to call attention to examples that occur in assignments and class discussions. Durkin (1983, p. 238) cites the sentence that came up in a third-grade class discussion: "The children were idle." One child said, "It means a statue." She notes too the confusion triggered by "She certainly was a patient person." Another child explained that *patient* means "when you're sick and you go to the doctor and he tells you that you have to go to the hospital" (p. 238). In each instance the teacher had an opportunity to explain about polysemous words! However, teachers cannot wait until opportunities occur. They need to check out assignments carefully in advance and identify words that may cause students trouble. Then, just as they explain unfamiliar words prior to reading (as most basal manuals suggest), they can explain words with multiple meanings, calling particular attention to the meanings the children have and the meaning used by the writer in the passage. Middle and secondary school teachers need to be especially aware of the polysemous words that have one general meaning (probably known to all students in the class) and a specialized one used in the context of the content area. Thus social studies teachers need to call attention to the fact that *legend,* while it does indeed mean ''an old story,'' means something quite different when found under a map. Content area teachers probably need to check out assignments with care just to detect specialized meanings for familiar words.

Linking Unfamiliar Words
with Existing Knowledge

Students frequently encounter unfamiliar words for which they already have, if only they realized it, enough prior knowledge to construct meanings. Thus a fifth-grade student meets *herbivorous* in a science assignment. He says it aloud (using his best phonics skills) and discovers that it is not a word in his speaking-listening vocabulary. He has no problem with multiple meanings because he has no meaning to begin with. He may not realize—until his teacher calls it to his attention—that he does have enough information to figure out a meaning rather readily. The context of the passage (about the eating habits of dinosaurs) indicates that the word may have something to do with *eating.* One type of dinosaur was referred to as *omnivorous* and described in the passage as one who ate both plants and animals. Because the student knew *herbs* were a type of plant his mother grew, he inferred that (maybe) herbivorous dinosaurs ate plants. Putting two and two together, he then guessed that *carnivorous* dinosaurs ate meat. This student was dealing with a Type-3 word—and doing it most successfully. He took information from his general knowledge background and used it to arrive at a meaning for a new word.

Type-3 words, such as *herbivorous* and countless others, label available or easily taught schemata. They constitute the largest group of words that middle school and secondary school students need to learn. Fortunately they are identifiable and teachable. Just as teachers can spot words with troublesome multiple meanings as they preview reading assignments, so too can they identify words that may be unfamiliar to their students but readily taught. The strategies for teaching and learning have been used and refined for decades in the reading class: using structural clues, or word parts, and using contextual clues in the texts. (Further discussion of specific strategies will be found in the next major section of this chapter.)

Developing Fresh Schemata

Type-4 words label schemata *students do not yet have!* When such words appear in selections and assignments, teachers must do more than advise students to say them aloud, call attention to a second meaning, or point to links with related prior knowledge. Now, teachers must start from the ground up and build a new schemata. *Logarithm* and *chromosome* are such words. They are not in the everyday speaking-listening vocabularies of most secondary school students, so saying them aloud does not reveal meaning. They cannot be readily explained in terms of prior knowledge available to typical students. In each case a schema must be developed for which the word may serve as a label. Graves (1984) uses the word *mores* as an example of a troublesome Type-4 word. Sounding it out is good only if the student already knows the concept. (It may throw him off!) Structural and even contextual analyses will not reveal its meaning to readers. They either know what it means to begin with—or they don't. A teacher could define *mores* as "customs," thus helping students understand it in terms of knowledge they already possess. However, mores are more than simple customs: they are the customs in a society that are regarded by general agreement as highly important and *obligatory*—as shown by strong feelings against deviation and by severe punishment for violations. Not only are mores not customs but, as those who regularly use the word will testify, the definition given here does not fully define the concept. Full understanding comes only after readers have experienced many instances of mores in operation. When they can distinguish among many specific examples of mores and between the concept and related concepts, they may begin to develop meanings for the word itself.

How may teachers treat Type-4 words in assignments? Many of the strategies suggested in the previous chapter on prior knowledge are useful, as are approaches described in the final section of this chapter. The points to note here are that Type-4 words present special teaching problems and that teachers need to make special provisions for instruction in dealing with them.

Identifying Words That May Cause Trouble

As implied here, teachers need to preview assignments carefully to identify words that may impede comprehension. They need to locate words that students may hear and even say regularly but that they have yet to meet in print. They need to watch for words that, while they may be unfamiliar to readers, may be explained easily with synonyms or reference to related knowledge students possess. Teachers especially need to be on the lookout for words that label schemata students have yet to develop. These latter words require teaching. They tend to constitute the major concepts in content area textbook assignments; upper-grade-level teachers need to be particularly aware of such words.

To which words should class teaching time be devoted? A simple plan is suggested here.

1. If students need a meaning for a word in order to understand the selection or assignment, stop and teach it. If comprehension is contingent upon having meanings for *slalom, spelunker, mores,* or *polysemous,* class time must be given to developing, as well as possible within that time, appropriate schemata.
2. If transfer possibilities exist, take class time. When, for example, a teacher judges that *herbivorous* and *polysemous* provide worthwhile opportunities to review structural and contextual analyses skills, time may justifiably be spent on these words.
3. If a word seems useful to know in itself, take time to teach it. Often assignments include words not crucial to comprehension nor rich in transfer possibilities but widely used in and out of school. A teacher may decide to devote class time to teaching them.

BUILDING WORD MEANINGS INDEPENDENTLY

The following summary of the discussion to this point leads to an important observation and a key question for teachers of reading comprehension:

- When students cannot understand a text without an appropriate schema for *mores* (a Type-4 word for them at this time in their lives), teachers need to work on schema development.
- When they are unable to build their own texts-in-the head for a selection without a meaning for *herbivorous* (a Type-3 word for them at this time), teachers have to show them how to develop a meaning using knowledge they already possess.
- When they cannot comprehend a text without a meaning for *patient* (a Type-2 word for them at this time), teachers must explain about multiple meanings and show them how to arrive at a second meaning using contextual clues.
- When they cannot comprehend a printed text unless they have a meaning for *television* (a Type-1 word for them at this time), their teachers must review basic phonic skills so that they may sound out the printed version of a word already in their speaking-listening vocabularies.

In each case teachers are involved in the process of developing word meaning knowledge. They must show, explain, demonstrate, stimulate, or set up practice situations. Unfortunately, as even students recognize, teachers are not going to be available at readers' elbows forever! Somewhere along the way students must become reasonably independent in developing word meaning knowledge.

At what point does teacher involvement in learning stop and reader independence begin?

Using the above summary as a framework for an answer, it may be said that teachers can

> teach enough basic phonic skills so that children may become competent in dealing with Type-1 words before they leave elementary school;

> teach enough about multiple meaning words and provide enough practice in using contextual clues so that students can deal with Type-2 words by the middle grades;

> teach enough structural and contextual analysis skills so that most students can treat Type-3 words by the middle grades; and

> provide enough practice in schema development so that all students may—at least—have insights into how schemata are built by them (and how to treat Type-4 words) before they leave secondary school.

Because strategies for using structural and contextual analyses are so useful in dealing with Type-2, -3, and even -4 words, this section focuses on such strategies.

Using Structural Analysis

In English (and other languages), words were coined in the past by combining words in use with affixes and other words. Thus the verb *know* was combined with the noun-signaling affix *-ledge* to become the noun *knowledge*, and the adverb *back* with the noun *yard* to become *backyard*. The process continues (and probably will continue in the future); hence, *television* and *microchip*, both combinations of existing elements. Children in early grades have this brought to their attention, as teachers sometimes play games to discover how many separate words children find in *football, ballplayer, ballgame, foulball,* etc. The tendency to make new words from existing words and affixes provides teachers with many opportunities to show students how to find meanings in unfamiliar words. They can teach and call attention to *roots* and *affixes*.

Teaching Word Roots   Once students are aware of how words are sometimes made by combinations, teachers can teach them often-used root words, pointing out that many of these come from Latin, Greek, or other languages, and that many are important to know in order to figure out "new" words. One list for discussion and class activities follows:

Root	Meaning	Examples
agri-	field	agriculture, agronomy
anthro-	man	anthropologist, anthropology
astro-	star	astronaut, astrophysics
bio-	life	biology, biologist
cardio-	heart	cardiac, cardiology
chromo-	color	chronometer, chromotology
demo-	people	democracy, democratic
dermo-	skin	epidermis, dermatology
dyna-	power	dynamic, dynamite
geo-	earth	geology, geography
helio-	sun	heliotrope, heliocentric
hydro-	water	hydroplane, hydroelectric
hypno-	sleep	hypnosis, hypnotic
magni-	great	magnify, magnificent
mono-	one	monolithic, monoplane
ortho-	straight	orthodox, orthodentistry
psycho-	mind	psychology, psychometry
pyro-	fire	pyromaniac, pyrotechnics
terra-	earth	terra firma, terrace
thermo-	heat	thermometer, thermofax

Students in class may be encouraged to add to the examples column, either from memory or by checking their dictionaries. They may too be encouraged to watch for words in their reading that use these common roots and that therefore may be added to the class list. Some teachers create interesting games in which children use the roots to make brand-new words of their own: *pyroastro, magnitherm,* etc.

Lists such as this may be found in dictionaries and books on vocabulary and word building. None is all-inclusive; none can be said to contain *all* the key roots. The important value in using such lists is that they can serve as a springboard into activities for making students more conscious of "words within words."

One of the most provocative—especially for secondary school students—was devised by James Brown (1952). It includes only fourteen roots—but these fourteen roots serve as "springboards into meaning" for more than *14,000* English words!

The Fourteen Words

Word	*Prefix*	*Common Meaning*	*Root*	*Common Meaning*
precept	pre-	before	capere	take, seize
detain	de-	away, from	tenere	hold, have
intermittent	inter-	between	mittere	send
offer	ob-	against	ferre	bear, carry
insist	in-	into	stare	stand
monograph	mono-	alone, one	graphein	write
epilogue	epi-	upon	legein	say, study
aspect	ad-	to, towards	specere	see
uncomplicated	un-	not	plicare	fold
nonextended	non-	not	tendere	stretch
	ex-	out of		
reproduce	re-	back, again	ducere	lead
	pro-	forward		
indisposed	in-	not	ponere	put, place
	dis-	apart from		
oversufficient	over-	above	facere	make, do
	sub-	under		
mistranscribe	mis-	wrong	scribere	write
	trans-	across, beyond		

With lists on the chalkboard, on wall charts, or duplicated for student notebooks, students may be encouraged to produce word "families" or "constellations." One is given here for upper level classes and may serve as a model (suggested by Pauk, 1974):

Root words (also called *stem* or *base* words in some books) are not always derived from Latin and Greek. Those that elementary school children need to watch for include "simple" words such as *agree* (in *agreeable*), *home* (in *homesick*, *sing* (in *singer*), *happy* (in *happiness*), and of course thousands of

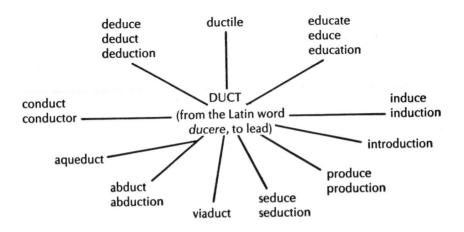

similar words used with affixes to create other words. Teachers may find a comprehensive list of common roots and derived words in *Techniques of Teaching Vocabulary* (Dale and O'Rourke, 1971), as well as an important reminder: Never teach roots and words in isolation, but always give students practice in using the words they discover or produce.

Teaching Affixes　Linguists point out that *morphemes* are the smallest units of meaning in language. Sometimes they may be words (as in *home*) but sometimes they may be roots for other words (as in *homeless*) or affixes attached to other words (as is *less* in *homeless*). Morphemes are classified as "free," meaning that they can stand independently, either as words in themselves or as roots for other words, such as "bound," meaning that they add other meanings to roots by working as *prefixes* or *suffixes* (that is, as *affixes*).

The following chart helps make the distinction:

Bound Morpheme	Free Morpheme	Bound Morpheme
pre-	view	
re-	view	
	view	-er
	view	-ed
	view	-ing
pre-	view	-er
pre-	view	-ed
pre-	view	-ing

Several years ago Russell Stauffer (1942) discovered that fifteen prefixes accounted for 82 percent of the words listed in Thorndike's *A Teacher's Word Book of the Twenty Thousand Words Most Frequently and Widely Used in General Reading for Children and Young People*. They are

ab	ex
ad	in (into)
be	in (not)
com	pre
de	pro
dis	re
en	sub
un	

Teachers can develop a variety of games and exercises to help children remember the meanings these prefixes add to words. For example, they can be given sentences, which are meaningless because wrong prefixes are substituted, and told to rewrite with proper prefixes. They can also create new words using old roots and prefixes of their choice; they can compete to discover who can list the most words with a given prefix. Over a period of time, most students can begin to see that many unfamiliar words can be figured out when one knows prefixes.

Class contests can be developed. Boys and girls see how many words they can find using just one type of prefix. Class lists can be posted. Children can be encouraged to search their school assignments and out-of-class reading to discover more words to add to a class Master List, such as the following:

Prefix	*Meaning*	*Examples*
anti-	against	antitank
auto-	self	automatic
bene-	good	benefit
circum-	around	circumscribe
contra-	against	contradict
hyper-	over	hypertension
hypo-	under	hypotension
inter-	between	interval
macro-	large	macroscopic
micro-	small	microscopic
multi-	many	multimillionaire
neo-	new	neolithic
pan-	all	Pan-American
poly-	many	polygamy
post-	after	postgame
pre-	before	pregame
proto-	first	prototype
pseudo-	false	pseudonym
retro-	backward	retrospect
semi-	half	semiretired
sub-	under	submarine
super-	above	Superman
tele-	far	television
trans-	across	transcontinental

Some prefixes that students need to know before middle school are

anti- (against)	inter- (between)
bi- (two)	ex- (out)
com- (with)	mis- (wrong)
con- (with)	tri- (three)
dis- (not)	super- (over)
em- (in)	sub- (under)
en- (in)	non- (not)
de- (from)	un- (not)
in- (not)	pre- (before)
im- (not)	post- (after)
pro- (in front of)	per- (fully)

Suffixes also modify words, coming at the ends rather than the beginnings. The most common in English are: *-ion* (in *moderation*), *-er* (in *sweeter*), *-ness* (in *hardness*), *-ity* (in *possibility*), *-y* (in *rainy*), *-able* (in *questionable*), and *-ant* (in *pleasant*). One way to teach them is to provide children with common suffixes and their meanings and have them locate examples of each from their reading. One list of common suffixes follows:

-ness (being)	-man (one who)
-ling (little)	-al (pertaining to)
-ty (state)	-y (like a)
-ence (state or quality)	-ness (quality or state of being)
-ous (full of)	-ian, -or, -ist, -er (one who does)
-ious (like or full of)	-en (made of)
-eous (like or full of)	-ly (like)
-et (little)	-ful (full of)
-age (collection)	-ance (state of mind)

Suffixes usually serve grammatical purposes, indicating verbs (*-ed, -s, -ing*), nouns (*-or, -er, -ment*), adjectives (*-er, -est*), adverbs (*-ly*). Some teachers may feel that this grammatical terminology may help learners; others, that it may hinder. In either case, one suggestion stands: it is best to let students make their own generalizations about the purpose the suffix serves by inferring meaning from their own examples. The teacher can start with three or four words students use (*quickness, brightness, sickness*) and build lists, later suggesting the purpose of the suffix (in this case it turns an adjective into a noun).

Some useful suffixes to teach, either directly or inductively, are

-able	meaning	can be done	as in	readable
-ade		thing made		lemonade
-ana		collection of		Americana
-ancy		state of		truancy
-ard		person who		drunkard
-arian		person who		librarian
-ate		to make		fascinate
-ation		process		visitation
-ency		quality of		frequency
-er, -or		person		actor
-esque		in the style of		statuesque
-gram		something written		telegram
-ic		to form nouns		magic
-ical		to form adjectives		comical
-ion		state of		ambition
-ish		to form adjective		clownish
-ism		a belief		realism
-ist		a person who		guitarist
-ize		to make		civilize

-ent	full of	fraudulent
-less	without	fatherless
-ment	state of	puzzlement
-or, -ore	person who	donor, commodore
-ory	place where	laboratory
-ry	collection of	jewelry
-some	like	bothersome
-ster	one belonging to	gangster
-ous	in the nature of	tempestuous
-ward, -wards	course or direction	homeward
-wise	manner	counterclockwise
-wright	workman	playwright
-y	inclined to	dreamy
-yer	person who	lawyer

Lapp and Flood (1983) suggest four rules to guide teachers as they help students build word meanings for themselves using structural analysis:

1. Encourage students to check the endings of words to note tense markers, such as *-ed;* plural markers, such as *-s* and *-es;* and possessive markers, such as *'s.* (Such affixes affect sentence meaning and should be noted.)
2. Encourage them to split words into parts with which they are already familiar (for example, *re-view-ing*). (If they have meanings for the parts, they may use these to construct meanings for the wholes.)
3. Encourage them also to guess the pronunciation of an unfamiliar word by looking at the parts of the word that are familiar to them. (Structural analysis can play a role in decoding through phonics!)
4. Encourage them too to make original compound words. (This may help them better understand how compound words get built.)

Structural analysis—using word roots and affixes—sensitizes students generally to the words they meet in their textbooks and basal readers. It is especially helpful in figuring out Type-3 words, because students build "new" meanings from those they already associate with known roots and familiar prefixes and suffixes. *Transcontinental* does not have to be a "new" word for very long!

Using Contextual Analysis

Readers understand words primarily through context; instruction in the use of context clues is the best way to build students' word power. The seventh-grader who meets *podiatrist* in the sentence, "The policeman's feet hurt, so he went to a podiatrist," will guess the word's meaning from its use; then, if she has learned the use of structure clues, verifies her guess by examining the root and suffix. Context clues do not always work. When faced with a Type-4 word (*spelunker* or *mores*), readers have no prior knowledge to trigger clues.

Fortunately writers (consciously, unconsciously, or because they can't help it) tend to plant context clues in their texts. Some clues need to be called to the attention of students:

1. *Experience clues* (Tom disliked Terry so much that everything Terry did *infuriated* him.)
2. *Comparison-contrast clues* (Tom was lazy but Terry was *diligent.*)
3. *Synonym clues* (The boys yelled, screamed, jumped, danced up and down, and turned cartwheels. Such *animation* was unusual for them.)
4. *Summary clues* (Ted refused to do homework. He lacked respect for his teachers. He was disobedient. He cut school. Finally, the principal had to take *disciplinary* action.)
5. *Association clues* (He studied the front, sides, and back of the new gym and then walked through the front door into the *edifice.*)
6. *Mood or situation clues* (The speed with which he moved across the room, quickly reached the door, and dashed down the steps, showed his great *agility.*)

Other ways of suggesting a word's meaning through context are

1. *Direct statement* (*Glandular fever*, or infectious mononucleosis, is a serious disease.)
2. *Example* (*Methadone* is an example of a synthetic drug.)
3. *Description* (The *griffin* was a mythological monster with an eagle's wings, head, and beak, plus a lion's body, legs, and tail.)

Robinson (1978) notes that in experience clues the experiential background (prior knowledge) readers bring to the sentence becomes the contextual aid, but in mood or situation clues readers infer a feeling that harmonizes with the overall context. He believes that the latter are easier for most readers, because the clues work at the affective level and do not depend on thought.

In addition to these nine kinds of context clues, *syntactic clues* also guide readers. For example, when a student reads "The *corpulent* man sat uncomfortably in the small chair" she knows—because of her built-in sense of the structure of English sentences—that "corpulent" is *adjectival*, not a noun. Her knowledge of inflexional endings (in this case, the suffix *-ent*) tells her that the word is used as a modifier.

How can teachers best help students note context clues? Teachers can preview assignments and selections to discover sentences and passages that provide good context clues for particular words. These may be duplicated or written on the chalkboard before reading so they can be discussed with the group. Also, teachers can prepare brief exercise sheets with clue-laden sentences, such as those in the lists above. They may choose to use commercially prepared materials and workbook exercises, but material written by the teacher for his or her own classes tends to be more timely and pertinent than "canned" material. Examples culled from newspapers, magazines, textbooks, and even school bulletins are more interesting to most classes than the examples in purchased forms. With practice many students can begin to watch for sentences in their reading that include good context clues and can bring these to class for duplication and use.

The SSCD Approach

One way to help students (particularly those in intermediate and middle grades) is the *Sound, Structure, Context, Dictionary Approach* (Devine, 1981). When asked what they should do when they encounter a word unfamiliar to them in an assignment or story, children frequently say, "Look it up in the dictionary." Teachers need to remind them that, before checking their dictionaries, they can use other strategies. Many teachers say, "Let's try these three steps first."

"First, SOUND OUT the problem word. It may be one in your listening vocabulary which you have never happened to see in print. You certainly have heard of the *superintendent* of schools and of *satellites* in *orbit,* but you may never have seen those words printed in a book. Saying them aloud can save you a trip to the dictionary.

"Second, look at the parts of the word, noting its STRUCTURE. Often an unfamiliar word has a prefix, root, or suffix which will help reveal its meaning. You may never have seen *syllabication* or *performance* before, but you can begin to guess their meanings when you see *syllable* and *perform.*

"Third, check for clues in the CONTEXT, that is, the words and sentences surrounding the new word. You may never have heard *anecdotal* before, but when you read 'Abraham Lincoln told little stories and tales, even jokes, to get his points across; he was a master of the anecdotal method of teaching,' you can guess what *anecdotal* probably means.

"Finally, if none of these methods work, you may decide to check out the DICTIONARY, but remember to check the dictionary meanings against the sentence in the book: often words have more than one meaning and you want the one that fits best."

Instruction in the use of structural and contextual analysis helps students (at all levels) to decode unknown words. Such instruction appears to be especially useful with those Type-3 words that can be understood readily through existing prior knowledge. Thus, *anecdote* may be understood in terms of stories and jokes and *transcontinental* in terms of prior knowledge of large land masses and "cross." What happens, however, when students have no prior knowledge of stories, jokes, continents, or even "cross"? Teachers need to discover what students do know to begin to build appropriate schemata.

Idea Box

To teach compound words, one primary grade teacher has the parts of compound words lettered on 3 x 5 cards. She attaches to each a paper clip and has children try to pick up two cards with a horseshoe magnet so that a compound word is created. Children then write these words in their notebooks and continue to make as many new compound words as possible.

Another teacher uses the cards to make a game. Each child has twenty cards face down on his or her desk. At a bell signal, each child is allowed to pick up two cards. If a compound is formed, the child scores a point, and his or her new word goes on the board. The game goes on until all cards are used up.

To give practice in using common affixes, one teacher duplicates short narratives, carefully omitting all prefixes and suffixes. Students are given the missing affixes on a board list and are told to rewrite the story, filling in the appropriate missing parts.

Another teacher gives practice through a simple team game. She writes a root word on the board, and members of opposing teams come to the board individually to add an affix to create a new word. The team that runs out of possible affixes first loses a point.

Another teacher has three coffee cans, each one containing cards with prefixes, roots, or suffixes. As each child's turn comes, he or she takes a card from each can. If a word can be made from the three cards, a point is scored.

To provide practice in the SSCD approach, one teacher has students keep a log in which they enter new words they find outside class. Beside each word they must note the technique they used to unlock its meaning: Were sound clues sufficient? Did structure clues help? Which ones? Was context useful? Did the dictionary help?

Many teachers at all grade levels have students invent new words. They explain how a word like *snide* came about: people took *sneer* and *rude* and created a word for which a need existed. Students need

---

to be reminded that they may take any roots and affixes in the language, but they must be able to define their words and defend them as worthwhile additions to the vocabulary.

To make students aware of the multiple meanings of words, teachers may run informal contests (with or without prizes) to discover who can come up with the most meanings for a given word. Students may be told that *run,* for example, has at least 100 separate meanings, and then be given a common word to start them. (Some good starters are *trip, hit, well, right, field.*)

To teach contextual clues, some teachers have children make up their own! Each child is given a word chosen from the assignment to be read and told to make sure he or she understands the dictionary meaning. Then the child must create an original sentence, which uses the word in such a way that others in the class will get its meaning without going to the dictionary. Students in the group go around the group, each testing out the effectiveness of the made-up context clues.

To help primary grade children begin to see how word meanings are affected by a word's relationships to other words, some teachers use "Relationship Boxes." Shoe boxes or milk cartons serve as nodes of what, in essence, becomes a kind of semantic map. To prepare for a unit on weather, for example, one third-grade teacher labeled boxes "Kinds of Weather," "Causes of Weather," "Predicting Weather," "Peculiar Weather," and so forth. In the days leading up to the unit she had children write their "weather words" on slips of paper and each day insert these in appropriate boxes. As a prereading activity, she copied all contributions on one sheet of paper, using the box labels as category headings, duplicated the sheet, and used it as the basis for class discussion.

To show how important analogies are to meaning, one teacher goes through basal selections and selects words she thinks may cause children difficulties. She then has the children try to give an analogy for each word, telling them that they may ask for help at home or from friends. When the lists of six or eight words-plus-analogies are turned in, she duplicates them for use as a springboard into class prereading discussions. One group had the word "professor": "A professor is like a teacher," "A professor is like an authority," "A professor is like an author," and so forth. Using these comparisons, the teacher was able to help students shape meanings for that word and others on her list, thus increasing understandings of unfamiliar words in the assignment.

Short written comparisons often help students better understand a new term and the concept it stands for. One junior high school teacher discusses a possibly difficult word with the group prior to reading, making analogies he thinks will help them develop meanings of their own. He then has students write a paragraph comparing and contrasting it with similar terms. Thus, because the idea of *barter* was essential to the comprehension of a selection, he discussed it, compared bartering with buying, and had the group write a paragraph with the topic sentence: "Bartering is like buying in many ways but unlike it in certain respects." He gave the students a clear-cut organizational plan to follow and suggested appropriate signal words (such as *however* and *on-the-other-hand*).

Another writing activity helpful to the development of new concepts is *Dictionary Defining*. After discussing important new words to be found in an assignment, many teachers often have boys and girls write out definitions of their own. These are discussed further in the group, reshaped, edited, and then checked against the "official" dictionary definition. Teachers who try this—at all levels—say that it is difficult but rewarding, a valuable activity for thinking through the meanings of words.

BUILDING WORD MEANING KNOWLEDGE FROM THE GROUND UP

Schemata that students already have may be refined and extended through the processes of *tuning* and *accretion* (see Chapter 4). The more experiences students have with an individual schema, the more they sharpen and add to it, polish and tighten it, and generally make it more effective (for remembering, thinking, and, when given a label so that it can be used as a word, communicating). Much of the time spent in school by children is devoted to refining and extending their schemata. Teachers have acquired many strategies for accretion and tuning.

Creating *new* schemata is a more difficult process. When students meet Type-3 words in texts, teachers can point out relationships between knowledge children already have and the new item, thus assisting in the accretion and tuning processes. (An *academy* is like a school; *regulations* are like laws or rules.) Analogies prove useful teaching devices for helping relate the new to the known. When students meet Type-4 words in texts, they tend to have little in the way of appropriate prior knowledge to allow for connection-making. Teachers, now, need to build "from the ground up." But, do they? To explain *mores,* a teacher still must make connections with what students already know: *mores* are like customs. Now, however, more time must be spent on subtleties and distinctions: customs are what people do out of habit (like sending Valentine's Day cards), but *mores* carry an obligation and punishments for violations. The new items must be compared carefully to other knowledge: it is like *this* but only in these ways; it is like A but not B; it resembles C in this respect but not in these others; and so on. Once a new schema is created—essentially by analogy—it continues to be modified by tuning and accretion to bring it more and more in line with the learner's experiences.

Three important inferences may be drawn from these observations:

1. If words are labels for schemata, then it is the development of schemata (through accretion, tuning, and restructuring) that teachers must be primarily concerned with—not simply teaching the labels.
2. If analogy-making plays a role in understanding both Type-3 and Type-4 words, then the two cannot be separated by a sharp line; rather they are on a continuum with more prior knowledge available for Type-3 and less for Type-4.
3. Teachers clearly need to spend more time identifying and trying to teach the schemata underlying Type-4 words.

The remainder of this chapter describes strategies for dealing with Type-4 words and for developing the schemata they label.

Semantic Feature Analysis

Semantic feature analysis grows out of the feature-comparison model first suggested by Smith, Shoben, and Rips (1974), described in Chapter 2. It attempts to account for the meaning of a word by examining the direct and indirect connections it has with related words in a "semantic network." Thus children give the *defining features* of birds ("They have feathers") and then the *characteristic features* ("They fly"), learning as they proceed that bats, for example, are not *true* birds because, although they have the characteristic feature of flying, they lack the defining feature of feathers.

Stieglitz and Stieglitz (1981) describe their use of this kind of analysis in a mathematics lesson: they introduce several content area terms, *triangle, rectangle, parallelogram, circle,* etc. Then they explain such features as "four-

	Four-sided	Curved or rounded	Line segment	All sides equal length	Right angle
triangle	-	-	-	+	+
rectangle	+	-	+	-	+
parallelogram	+	-	+	+	+
circle	-	+	-	-	-
trapezoid	+	-	+	-	-
semicircle	-	+	+	-	-
square	+	-	+	+	+

sided," "curved," "right angle," etc. They then have students complete a Semantic Feature Analysis of Shapes.

Another kind of grid is used by Johnson, Toms-Bronowski, and Pittleman (1981). To help children develop sharper concepts of *shelters*, they list kinds of shelters down one side of the grid and features of shelters across the top. Children then check the features that can be attributed to the kind of shelter.

The grid presented here is only a portion of one children may develop in class. Theirs might include such features as "Cost of Shelters" and "Things You

	large	small	lovely	rustic	simple	spooky	dilapidated	open
cabin				✓				
villa	✓		✓					
palace	✓							
shed		✓		✓	✓		✓	
hovel		✓			✓		✓	
barn				✓				
tent		✓			✓			

Can Find in Shelters'' (freezers, beds, tools, etc.). As children study the emerging patterns of pluses and minuses, they begin to see how schemata are shaped. Thus a shed may be small but it may have a bed in it, or a palace may be large but not have a freezer. The process of building such grids for semantic feature analysis is one way of restructuring students' schemata for words they meet in their reading.

Such analysis may be sophisticated (as the one on geometric shapes) or simple (as the one on shelters); the resulting grids may be elaborately drawn on graph paper or simply sketched in on the chalkboard. All force students to focus in on essential features, characteristic and defining.

Semantic Mapping

Semantic mapping (discussed in Chapter 4) allows students to see relationships in another form. Using nodes and links between nodes, students prepare *maps* rather than grids. Pearson and Johnson (1978) suggest that children look for *class relations, example relations,* and *property relations* (see Chapter 2). Thus they see that dogs are related to animals in that dogs belong to a class of things called animals, that a particular dog named Fido is an example of dogs, and that dogs have certain properties or attributes, such as they bark, have hair, and are loyal. Using this information, children—with their teacher's help—can construct a map for dogs, using class links (is a) and property links (has, is, or does), thus creating a visual representation of complex relationships.

A semantic map for *academy* was drawn in class by a middle school teacher whose students were puzzled that Robert Frost had taught in an *academy*. She quickly sketched in relationships to help them refine, extend, and—in some cases—develop an appropriate schema.

Many teachers always show relationships in chalkboard drawings. By highlighting the relationships (of class, property, and example) they make semantic maps to help students see the shape and contours of the particular concept—and the word that labels it.

As students developed the semantic map for *academy* in class, they began to see the relationships between their own middle school and a college or even the local newspaper. As they filled in the lines at the bottom for specific examples of parochial and private schools, they began to see how their own public middle school related to other schools in the community and to educational institutions in general. After one boy volunteered the entry for day-care centers, they began to debate the question of whether day-care centers should teach little children or simply care for them while their parents worked. When one girl discovered that Pinkerton Academy actually was subsidized by town tax money, they had to further refine their distinction between public and private education.

Refocused semantic maps have been designed to help students understand

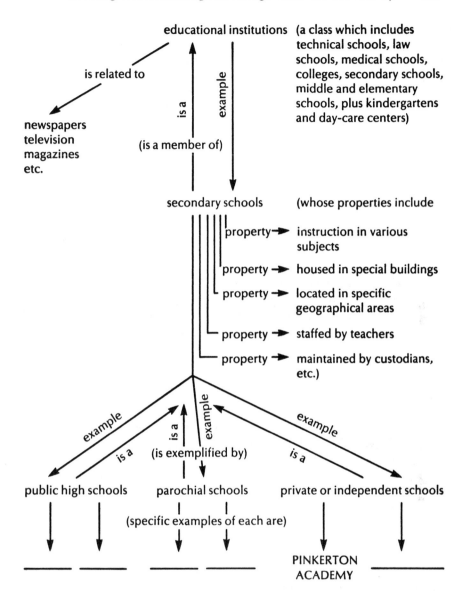

specific words in a text they are reading (Johnson, Toms-Bronowski, and Pit-tleman, 1981). The teacher needs to center on a term that has specific meanings in the text as well as many more common associations. Students draw a map with known examples, properties, and classes, read the passage carefully, and then revise the map to include the "new" meanings. For example, students may not get *boom* in "During a thunderstorm a boom might become dislodged." Their map might look like this:

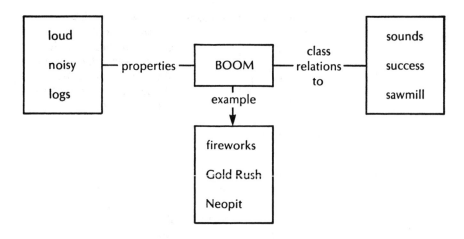

By examining the word in the context of the map, students begin to see some of the problems in assigning specific meanings to the word as it is used in this sentence. Refocused semantic maps are especially valuable in poetry lessons in which teachers want students to be aware of the skill writers use in selecting words.

The Spoken Words Activity

The Spoken Words Activity (Grubaugh, 1985) has students share with the class personal anecdotes and stories suggested by selected words. For example, one girl "explained" *deluge* this way:

> She told of baby-sitting a spirited three-year-old boy who was usually into everything. One evening, the child disappeared from the living room and had been quiet too long. Linda's search led her to the bathroom door from behind which came the sounds of gurgling water. As she opened the door, a deluge of cold water washed over her feet and ran out into the hallway. The child was at the toilet attempting to wash his E. T. doll down the pipes and water was spilling over the bowl in a flash flood.

Linda threw towels on the floor to sop up the water and rescued the doll. She told the class that when she explained the mess to the boy's parents, they gave her an extra three dollars for "combat pay." When she finished her story two other students in the class added their examples of "what deluge meant to them." One told about helping neighbors fortify their homes with sandbags during a real flood in New Orleans; another reported that one of his favorite songs was "Before the Deluge" by Jackson Browne.

Such personal stories related in class can do much to help students shape their meanings for schemata and the words used to label them. In this case, students left the class with meanings for one word considerably refined and extended. As Grubaugh (1985, p. 67) notes, "When youngsters learn new words, they must realize their experience is a resource to probe and question, to build upon, and to be used to form new meaning." The Spoken Words Activity may be used, at all levels, to restructure and build, as well as refine and extend, schemata.

The Frayer Model

McNeil (1984) recommends a model for attaining conceptual meanings of words, developed by Frayer, Frederick, and Klausmeir (1969). It involves seven steps:

1. Discriminating the relevant qualities common to all instances of the concept. The relevant attribute of *globe*, for example, is *spherical*.
2. Discriminating the relevant from the irrelevant properties of instances of the concept. *Large* and *small*, for example, are irrelevant to *globe*.
3. Providing an example, such as the classroom globe.
4. Providing a nonexample, such as a map or chart (both nonspherical).
5. Relating the concept to a subordinate concept, such as *ball*.
6. Relating it to a superordinate concept, such as *global*.
7. Relating it to a coordinate term, such as *map*.

Sometimes, as McNeil points out, a concept cannot be defined by its relevant attributes. In such cases the first two steps are omitted, and a synonym and antonym are substituted for the defining relevant and irrelevant attributes. Thus, for the concept *beautiful,* one may use *pretty* and *lovely*.

How may teachers use this model in the classroom? First, they need to identify words that may cause problems (such as *spelunker, mores,* or *academy*), and then, before students actually read the passages, they discuss them together (suggesting definitions; noting their use in the context of the assignment; looking at possible structural clues; and recalling together—as in the Spoken Words Activity—personal anecdotes). In the case of *academy,* the teacher may say that it is "a kind of school" and then have students pinpoint its relevant qualities ("It's a place where students go to learn"). Students next note together various irrelevant properties ("It may be large or small" or "It doesn't matter whether the building is wood or cement block"). For the third step, the teacher may read aloud a description of the academy in which Robert Frost taught (or tell of one particular academy). For the fourth step, the students may offer nonexamples: "educational television," "the state university," etc. Steps 5, 6, and 7 may include any number of suggestions offered by students and a final summary statement by a volunteer or by the teacher: "An academy is a private school, usually at the secondary level, and often for college preparation."

Academy is easy. When students try to develop the seven steps for a word such as *freedom* or *capitalism*, they need time and considerable teacher guidance. The value of the Frayer Model is that it does provide clearly defined steps. With some preparation most teachers can lead students through the sequence in such a way that the class will begin to develop meanings for words through the appropriate schemata. Teachers who have used the model note that often it is enough to refer to only certain steps. Thus an example, a nonexample, and two or three relevant properties are sometimes enough to give students meanings for words; other times, briefly focusing on steps 1 and then 5, 6, and 7 may be enough.

The Context Approach

Many teachers first use semantic grids and maps, as well as approaches such as Spoken Words, to help students develop meanings for specific words in the text and then supplement such initial guidance with exercises and brief lessons in contextual processing. Realizing that most people share meanings for *boom*, for example, but that it has a "special" meaning in "During a thunderstorm a boom might become dislodged," they come back to the sentence and the passage to make sure students have the contextual meaning.

One effective approach to contextual processing is described by Gipe (1978–1979). She notes that a familiar context often activates a student's relevant prior knowledge, and consequently a "new" meaning may more easily be learned as it relates to "old" knowledge. She gives children three sentences, all of which contain the target word, and has them write what the word means to them after reading the sentences.

One example of an exercise patterned after Gipe's is presented here for the target word *taciturn:*

> Old Harry, as taciturn as ever, sat through the entire discussion without saying a word.
> Charles, certainly the most taciturn boy in the history of our class, managed somehow to go through three years without once opening his mouth in class.
> At our party last week, Sue sat right in the middle of the crowd and, in her taciturn way, never responded to any remarks.
> Give a sample from your experience of a taciturn person: _____.

Variations of the context approach are available in a number of sources (see, for example, McNeil, 1984), but teachers find they can modify or elaborate on them for their own classroom purposes. They may, for example, have students locate sentences and passages, from their school and recreational reading, that illustrate through context the way a particular word is used. They may have volunteers in the class prepare exercises designed to show how certain words may be used. They may also collect examples from their own reading to share with classes.

Like other approaches suggested here, the contextual processing way of developing meaning may best be used in conjunction with other approaches. Thus, for a particularly difficult word (and schema!), a teacher may actually prepare with the class a semantic map *and* have them follow with an exercise in contextual use, or use a semantic feature analysis *plus* an activity such as Spoken Words. For especially troublesome concepts, several approaches may be necessary.

▪ RECAPPING MAIN POINTS ▪

Of all forms of prior knowledge, knowledge of word meanings is the most important for reading comprehension. Students *must* share with writers meanings for words used in texts. Some of these words, however, are already known to students because they are in their speaking and listening vocabularies. Teachers need only provide appropriate instruction in phonetic, structural, and contextual analysis so that the printed forms of the words are recognized. Other words have two or more meanings. Teachers need to make students sensitive to multiple meanings and develop additional ones needed for comprehension of certain texts. Some words unfamiliar to students are easily explained, because students already have related knowledge and can often figure them out through synonyms or by using structural and contextual analysis. Other words, the "really difficult ones," label schemata students have yet to develop. When they are crucial to the comprehension of a text, they demand instruction. Some of the strategies teachers may use with such words include semantic feature analysis, semantic mapping, the Spoken Words technique, the Frayer Model, and the context approach.

END-OF-CHAPTER ACTIVITIES

1. What are your answers to the Suggested Study Questions that began this chapter? Were they answered to your satisfaction? Why? Why not?

2. Select a basal reader selection and locate in it examples of Type-1, -2, -3, and -4 words. Do you find that Type-3 words can be explained

easily by reference to related prior knowledge students have? Explain. Do you find Type-4 words difficult to explain? Explain your answer by citing specific words you found in the selection.

3. Select three Type-3 words from a content area textbook at your grade level. Show how you might teach these words: first, by using synonyms; then, by using structural analysis; and, finally, by using contextual analysis. In the case of these three words, what specific prior knowledge do you think students need to have to develop meanings? Do children you know have appropriate related prior knowledge?

4. Select one Type-4 word and tell how you would teach it. Did you use one of the strategies suggested in the chapter? Why? Why not? If you have a class available to you, take a Type-4 word from a reading assignment and show how you can reach it. Report on the success of the strategy you used.

5. In the section on Identifying Potential Verbal Trouble Spots (pp. 116–121, several recent professional books are noted as including descriptions of ways to use structural and contextual analysis. Check one of these books and summarize the techniques suggested for the group. Do any seem especially effective? Why? Are any new-to-you? Which? Tell about it.

6. If you have a class available, try the SSCD approach suggested in this chapter and report to the group on your success. Why did the approach work for you? How might you modify it?

7. Try the contextual processing approach to developing word meanings by selecting ten words from a basal reader selection or a content area textbook and creating exercises similar to those suggested by Gipe. Have students use these exercises if possible and report on the results to the group. What seem to be the advantages of this approach? the disadvantages?

8. Take a difficult word from a textbook (yours or one of your students') and apply the Frayer Model. Provide: (1) an example, (2) a nonexample, (3) a relevant attribute, (4) an irrelevant attribute, (5) a subordinate term, (6) a superordinate term, and (7) a coordinate term. Tell how the method worked for you or one of your students. Explain how the approach might work as a prereading activity and as a postreading activity.

9. Locate an article on vocabulary development in a professional journal, read it, and explain to the group how it may be understood in terms of the information provided in this chapter. Does its author share the same conceptual framework? In what ways does the basic view of word meaning development differ? How might you synthesize them?

10. Try Grubaugh's Spoken Words Activity on a class of children or with

a group of associates. In what ways does this approach help you re-fine and extend a particular schema? Did you find yourself actually restructuring the schema? Explain what seemed to happen in the ex-periment. Write a brief paper on your experiences using this ap-proach.

REFERENCES

Alexander, J. Estill (Ed.). *Teaching Reading,* 2nd ed. Boston: Little, Brown, 1983.

Anderson, Richard C., and Peter Freebody. *Vocabulary Knowledge and Reading.* Ur-bana, Ill.: Center for the Study of Reading, University of Illinois, 1979.

Brown, James I. *Efficient Reading.* Boston: Houghton Mifflin, 1952.

Burmeister, Lou E. *Foundations and Strategies for Teaching Children to Read.* Reading, Mass.: Addison-Wesley, 1983.

Dale, Edgar, and Joseph O'Rourke. *Techniques of Teaching Vocabulary.* Palo Alto, Calif.: Field Educational Publications, 1971.

Dale, Edgar, and Joseph O'Rourke. *The Living Word Vocabulary,* 3rd ed. Chicago: World Book-Childcraft International, 1981.

Davis, Frederick B. "Research in Comprehension in Reading." *Reading Research Quarterly* 4 (1968): 499–545.

Davis, Frederick B. "Psychometric Research on Comprehension in Reading." *Reading Research Quarterly* 7 (1972): 628–678.

Deighton, Lee C. *Vocabulary Development in the Classroom.* New York: Teachers Col-lege Press, 1959.

Devine, Thomas G. *Teaching Study Skills: A Guide for Teachers.* Boston: Allyn and Bacon, 1981.

Durkin, Dolores. *Teaching Them to Read,* 4th ed. Boston: Allyn and Bacon, 1983.

Ekwall, Eldon E., and James L. Shanker. *Teaching Reading in the Elementary School.* Columbus, Ohio: Charles E. Merrill, 1985.

Frayer, Dorothy A., Wayne C. Frederick, and Herbert J. Klausmeir. *A Schema for Test-ing the Level of Concept Mastery.* (Working Paper No. 16.) Madison: Wis.: Research and Development Center for Cognitive Learning, University of Wiscon-sin, 1969.

Gipe, J. P. "Investigating Techniques for Teaching Word Meanings." *Reading Research Quarterly* 14 (1978–1979): 624–644.

Goodman, Kenneth S. "Behind the Eye: What Happens in Reading." In *Reading: Pro-cess and Program.* Urbana, Ill.: National Council of Teachers of English, 1970.

Graves, Michael F. "Selecting Vocabulary to Teach in the Intermediate and Secondary Grades." In James Flood (Ed.), *Promoting Reading Comprehension.* Newark, Del.: International Reading Association, 1984.

Graves, Michael F., and S. D. Bender. "Preteaching Vocabulary to Secondary Students." *Minnesota English Journal* 10 (1980): 27–34.

Grubaugh, Steven. "Spoken Words: Quality Exposure to Vocabulary Concepts." *En-glish Journal* 74 (1985): 64–67.

Johnson, Dale D., Susan Toms-Bronowski, and Susan D. Pittleman. *An Investigation of the Trends in Vocabulary Research and the Effects of Prior Knowledge on Instructional Strategies for Vocabulary Acquisition.* Madison, Wis.: Wisconsin Center for Educational Research, University of Wisconsin, 1981.

Lapp, Diane, and James Flood. *Teaching Reading to Every Child,* 2nd ed. New York: Macmillan, 1983.

McNeil, John D. *Reading Comprehension: New Directions for Classroom Practice.* Glenview, Ill.: Scott, Foresman, 1984.

Pauk, Walter. *How to Study in College.* Boston: Houghton Mifflin, 1974.

Pearson, P. David, and Dale D. Johnson. *Teaching Reading Comprehension.* New York: Holt, Rinehart and Winston, 1978.

Robinson, H. Alan. *Teaching Reading and Study Strategies.* Boston: Allyn and Bacon, 1978.

Smith, E. E., E. J. Shoben, and L. J. Rips. "Structure and Process in Semantic Memory: A Featural Model for Semantic Decisions." *Psychological Review* 81 (1974): 214–241.

Spearritt, D. "Identification of Subskills of Reading Comprehension by Maximum Likelihood Factor Analysis." *Reading Research Quarterly* 8 (1972): 92–111.

Stauffer, Russell G. "A Study of Prefixes in the Thorndike List to Establish a List of Prefixes That Should Be Taught in the Elementary School." *Journal of Educational Research* 35 (1942): 453–458.

Stieglitz, Ezra L., and V. S. Stieglitz. "Savor the Word to Reinforce Vocabulary in the Content Areas." *Journal of Reading* 25 (1981): 46–51.

From Theory to Practice: Improving Comprehension of School Reading Assignments

■ INTRODUCTION AND OVERVIEW ■

Comprehension as seen here is tricky business. Writers begin with texts-in-the-head and prepare, to the best of their linguistic and rhetorical competence, printed texts, which readers then use as blueprints to develop their own texts-in-the-head. Readers use *their* linguistic and rhetorical competence to interpret those printed texts; but, as noted, their interpretations are affected by their own prior knowledge, particularly their prior knowledge of word meanings.

What can teachers do to help students improve the process of building viable texts-in-their-heads? They can (as described in Chapters 4 and 5) (1) assess students' prior knowledge and help them relate it more effectively to the new ideas and information in printed texts, and (2) teach words in the texts that label schemata important to the writer's message. They can also (as described in Chapters 7 and 8) (3) help students sharpen the cognitive skills they may need to make viable interpretations of printed texts, and (4) show them ways writers organize printed texts, hoping that this knowledge may help them "read the blueprints" more accurately.

However, these are all *general* approaches to comprehension improvement. They involve extending and enriching, refining and restructuring schemata and the words that label them. They involve, too, cognitive skill development and teaching about ways texts are organized. Teachers must follow all these approaches, trusting that students will transfer the outcomes of instruction into their out-of-class and other later experiences as readers.

What can teachers do *immediately* in the classroom to improve students' comprehension? Fortunately many effective strategies have been developed

145

through the years to help students better understand selections in their basal readers and textbook assignments in content area reading. Many of these have been validated to some extent by research findings; many others, not yet researched, have worked for teachers in countless classrooms.

This chapter looks at some of these strategies. They are grouped here under three traditional headings:

the *prereading activities* that can activate students' prior knowledge, while extending, refining, and sometimes building the schemata that comprises that prior knowledge;

the *during-reading activities* that can guide reader–text interactions, while reading is taking place; and

the *postreading activities* that help students remember new ideas and information, while providing teachers with feedback on how well texts have been understood.

The chapter is concerned primarily with *school* reading. The theoretical bases for the teaching strategies described here for school reading assignments underlie *all* reading; the strategies themselves work in reading newspapers, novels, technical reports, and lyric poems. However, because of space constraints, discussion here focuses on school reading assignments. It is assumed that teachers will help students make transfers from basals and school textbooks when they can. It is also assumed that, given the constraints of the typical school and the typical school day, most teachers have influence on only school reading assignments anyway.

Because of this primary focus on school reading, the chapter is also concerned with the transfer possibilities of these "immediate strategies." Do teacher-intervention strategies such as are described here become internalized? Do students use them when their teachers are no longer present? What research evidence supports the belief that young readers will indeed use these "school assignment" strategies when they read magazines, fiction, scientific studies, business reports, and other kinds of reading they will do later in their lives?

Chapter 6 includes Suggested Study Questions, Teaching Guidelines, and then discussions of

- Effective Prereading Comprehension Strategies
  Overviews
  Vocabulary previews
  Structural organizers
  Setting up a purpose for reading
  Student-centered study strategies
  Teacher-directed lesson frameworks

- Effective During-Reading Activities
    Question-answering
    Inserted questions
    Immediate oral feedback
    Time lines and charts
    Listing main ideas
    Outlining
    Paraphrasing
    Summarizing
    Study guides
    Self-monitoring
- Postreading Activities for Comprehension
    Follow up pre- and during-reading activities
    Have students talk about what they read
    Have students write about what they read
    Have students make up tests on their reading
    Encourage students to respond to assignments "creatively"
    Postreading activities and the writing reader
- Teaching Strategies versus Learning Strategies

Chapter 6 also includes

- Recapping Main Points
- End-of-Chapter Activities
- References

▪ SUGGESTED STUDY QUESTIONS
FOR CHAPTER 6 ▪

1. Why are prereading activities important for comprehension?
2. What are some particularly effective prereading comprehension activities?
3. What activities promote active involvement during reading?
4. Why do students need to respond to their reading in some way?
5. In what ways is writing a way of reconstructing meaning?
6. How may teachers help students turn instructional strategies into reading/learning strategies for themselves?

▪ TEACHING GUIDELINES
FOR CHAPTER 6 ▪

Chapter 6 is organized around the following four teaching guidelines, derived from recent research and successful practice in teaching reading comprehension:

Teaching Guideline #1
Show students what to do *before* they begin to read in order to improve their comprehension.

Teaching Guideline #2
Plan appropriate activities to promote active involvement with texts *while* students read.

Teaching Guideline #3
Help students sharpen, develop, and remember their interpretations of a text with appropriate *after*-reading activities.

Teaching Guideline #4
Take steps to help students internalize *instructional* strategies so that they become for them *learning* strategies.

EFFECTIVE PREREADING
COMPREHENSION STRATEGIES

What teachers do in the classroom *before* students begin to read a selection or assignment affects students' eventual comprehension of the printed text. Teachers have known this for years. Teachers' manuals for basal reader series usually include a section on prereading activities in lesson frameworks, and most teachers find that attention to these activities does indeed increase comprehension. The most effective of these instructional strategies are described here.

Overviews

Brief overviews, in which teachers tell students about the selection or assignment prior to reading, serve to activate relevant schemata that students hold in long-term memory and often enrich and refine those schemata. Sometimes an overview may also help students build "new" schemata they will need to better understand the text. Before reading a basal story about sailing, a teacher may discuss her experiences sailing small boats and encourage boys and girls to share their recollections of sailing (either personal experiences or stories remembered from other reading, films, or televiewing). Such simple overviews may take the form of class discussions, brief printed previews, examinations of photographs or illustrations, class viewing of appropriate films, or, in the case of textbook assignments, printed outlines.

Overviews of stories, which included building the prior knowledge important to their understanding, have been used by Graves and others (1980; 1981; 1983). Several experiments support the view that brief previews before reading stories increased learning by an impressive amount. Another experiment by Stevens (1982) indicated that previewing and providing relevant background information helped tenth-grade students better understand passages in a history textbook. Another experiment (Hayes and Tierney, 1982) found that giving students information about the topic treated in the text prior to reading helped readers learn from the text, no matter how the information was presented or how specific or general the information was. These and other studies (reviewed in Pearson, 1984) support teachers' long-held belief that prereading overviews are important. (It is unfortunate that *some* teachers still give reading assignments as preparation for discussion, rather than reversing the order to maximize learning from texts.)

Advance Organizers   Advance organizers (discussed in Chapter 4) are in a sense overviews; they attempt to bridge the gap between where the reader stands when he approaches the assignment and the text itself. While research on advance organizers has not proved conclusive (see Tierney and Cunningham, 1984), many teachers continue to use them in the prereading period. They do provide, as Ausubel posited (1968), an ideational scaffolding for the incorporation of new material. When, for example, a social studies assignment tells of the early days of the clipper ship, it helps students if the teacher presents an overview of ships, sailing, transportation, and specific kinds of ships, thus allowing them to see the new material they will read about in some hierarchical structure (from transportation to sailing to ships to clipper ships, etc.). The process of using an advance organizer in class too may serve, as noted in Chapter 4, to activate prior knowledge students already possess.

Structured Overviews   Structured overviews are spin-offs of advance organizers. They are intended to serve many of the same purposes but also to present a *visual* overview of the concepts and relationships presented in a text. Thus the ideas presented in a text are given to students in advance, arranged in outline form to highlight relationships and any logical order underlying the presentation. Structured overviews (sometimes called *graphic organizers*) display concepts in the text by arranging key technical terms relevant to the concepts to be learned in such a way that the hierarchical nature of the concepts is highlighted. Thus concepts may be categorized as superordinate, coordinate, or subordinate—according to their relationships to other concepts—to achieve a visual structure such as this:

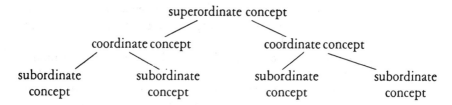

The diagram serves as an organized preview of what the student will read in the assignment and may help him see how terms are used to relate one to the other. (Developing a structured overview for vocabulary previews is described in the next section.)

Vocabulary Previews

Should *all* those words that may present problems to students be taught prior to the students' reading of an assignment? Many teachers' manuals and other sources of lesson frameworks imply that teachers must go through an assignment or selection to identify words that may cause problems, so that these can be explained to students in advance. Such a practice seems to be justified on two grounds: unfamiliar words in general are obstacles to comprehension; and discussing words in class tends to arouse previous associations while providing new ones. Teaching problem words provides "anchors for new information" (Pearson and Johnson, 1978), provides opportunities to relate unfamiliar concepts to familiar ones, and is one aspect of developing the general background knowledge necessary for comprehension.

However, explaining *every* potentially troublesome word in advance is, as many teachers point out, unrealistic. After a teacher presents an overview and establishes a purpose for reading, most students are "ready to go!": time then spent in developing meaning for words postpones the reading experience, and any motivation created by the previous activities diminishes. Two solutions to this problem suggest themselves: teach *only* words whose meanings are crucial to understanding the text, and use a structured overview as a vocabulary activity.

Recent research indicates that it is better to teach key words in the assignment; that these be taught in semantically related sets, so that word meanings and background knowledge improve together; that the key words be taught and learned thoroughly; and that only a few be taught in each reading lesson. As Tierney and Cunningham (1984, pp. 611–612) note in a survey of the relevant research, attempts to teach too many words not crucial to the target passages, without teaching them thoroughly in the context of essential background knowledge, or without teaching only a few words per lesson, are probably "doomed to failure." Preteaching of vocabulary, therefore, seems most justified when a few crucial word meanings are taught with each individual assignment. This leads to a restatement of points made in Chapters 4 and 5:

teachers need to identify those points in an assignment that students probably do not yet know and develop these concepts or schemata in relation to relevant knowledge students do possess. Because such schemata are labeled by Type-3 or -4 words, these should be the focus of the teacher's time and attention in the prereading period.

One way to teach key words in relation to prior knowledge is through the structured overview mentioned earlier. Barron (1969) gives six steps teachers may take to teach key words diagrammatically in a structured overview:

1. Check the assignment and list all words that may be important for students to understand.
2. Arrange these in a schema that shows the interrelationships particular to the learning task.
3. Add to this schema words students probably already understand in order to highlight relationships between the new and the known.
4. Double-check the overview to make sure that major relationships are clearly shown and in a way that students will understand.
5. Share the structured overview with students, telling them why words were placed where they were and asking them to contribute other words.
6. As students read, have them relate other new words and information to the graphic overview.

How does this work in practice? Prior to assigning a passage about an Indian village, a sixth-grade social studies teacher listed the following words as crucial to understanding the text: *compact, castes, hamlet, terrain, dispensary,* and *cremation.* She arranged these words with words children probably did know such as *communities, towns, cities, land, health care, doctors' offices, hospitals, cemeteries, burial,* and others. Her graphic overview showed *communities* as a superordinate; *cities* and *towns* as coordinates; and *villages* and *hamlets* as subordinates. She asked students to give reasons why people clustered together in communities (for access to health services, to be with people like themselves, etc.) and then arranged a vertical column to show how health services, for example, were provided in the types of communities at each level of the chart. In the process of building the overview on the chalkboard she was able to explain other words such as *compact* and *terrain* in the context of *communities,* while also giving meanings for *castes* and *cremation* and other words students had added to the chart. If her focus had been *social classes* rather than *communities,* the board chart would have looked different, but she might have been able to include *hamlet, cremation,* and other words. When encouraged to develop their own structured overviews, individual students will inevitably focus on different key words but many of the same words as well. The point is not to create neat graphics but to help students see relationships between what they know (villages and cities) and hamlets, between cemeteries and crematoria, between dispensaries and hospitals, and so on.

How are structured overviews different from semantic maps? Essentially, both serve the same purpose: to relate the new to the known. Semantic mapping offers the additional dimensions of class, example, and property relations and as such may be more effective for certain items in certain assignments. Teachers must decide on the basis of the reading assignment: some texts include key words that must be treated in mapping exercises; others have terms that may best be explained in terms of structured overviews. In either case, the work in class prepares students for the reading experience to come and is clearly more effective than teaching every "new" word in the text or not providing any prereading preparation. (A somewhat different approach, the Vocabulary Overview Guide, is described in Carr, 1985.)

Structural Organizers

In addition to overviews, which activate prior knowledge, and vocabulary previews designed to clear up problems caused by insufficient word meaning knowledge, some researchers recommend teaching expository text structures with structural organizers as a prereading activity (Slater, 1985). Noting that understanding expository text organization tends to enhance students' reading comprehension, they suggest that teachers use structural organizers to focus attention on the ways passages are organized. Before students read an assignment, they say, teachers should point out the basic rhetorical frameworks underlying the discourse (such as cause–effect, problem–solution, or claim–support–conclusion). Teachers may call attention to specific plans of paragraph organization, signal words, main idea sentences, and the underlying patterns of longer discourse, as well as highlighted phrases and sentences, headings, and subtitles. (See Chapter 7 on ways texts are organized.) As students read they may check through the structure by following an outline prepared in advance by their teacher. In one study Slater found that ninth-graders who received a structural organizer prior to reading and then filled in an outline grid that emphasized passage organization as they were reading outperformed other students (Slater, 1985, pp. 717–718).

Setting Up a Purpose for Reading

Experienced readers tend to read with a purpose. They read to discover answers to specific questions, to verify information, to get a general view of a topic, to discover a writer's point of view, to check predictions they have made, or often simply to enjoy themselves. They find that purpose not only directs their reading toward a goal but focuses their attention. Some students, on the other hand, read school assignments because they have been told to read them. Their purpose for reading is to satisfy a teacher or parent. Because purpose is crucial to comprehension, teachers need to examine ways of assisting students to establish purposes for reading texts. Three general approaches to establishing purpose are described here: questions, predictions, and problems to be solved.

Purposes may come from *questions*. As early as 1926 Pressey noted that questions asked before reading serve a learning producing function. He pointed out that they may increase readers' sensitivity to learning by alerting them to both the nature of the task and its relevance to them, while at the same time offering a means to evaluate, categorize, and generalize (1926). Since then his claim has tended to be supported by research (Levin and Pressley, 1981). Where do such questions come from? They may be generated by teachers who, after reading an assignment, decide that certain questions are answered in the text and who then place these on the chalkboard or distribute them in duplicated form. They may also come from the books themselves; many textbooks in the content area fields and most basal reader manuals provide such "canned" questions for teachers' use. Many teachers, however, believe that the most effective questions come from students. Student-created questions, they say, better direct the focus of activity in reading and encourage both student–teacher and student–student interaction. They say too that questions created by students have the potential to activate inquisitiveness, problem-solving, and the desire to examine ideas and think of alternatives.

Where Do Student Questions Come From?　　Several answers are suggested here:

1. *From the overviews.* Class discussions prior to reading, whether formalized as structured overviews or stimulated informally by pictures or sharing anecdotes and stories, may lead to effective student questions. A teacher may say, "We now know that the assignment is about life in an Indian hamlet. What do *you* want to know about such a community? about the people and their daily lives?" Such questions may be placed on the chalkboard so that, as they read, students can check to see if the text answers their questions. A brief brainstorming session prior to reading can lead to many student questions: "What do we already know about India and its people? What more do we want to learn?" Again, student questions may be listed and serve as guides to the assignment.

2. *From skimming the text.* Teachers may have the class take a few minutes to skim quickly through the pages of the assignment to discover what it is about, and then have them make up questions they want answered: "This seems to be about medical care in isolated Indian villages. Let's go around the group and list questions that you want the author to answer for you about the topic." One value of the SQ3R approach (Survey, Question, Read, Recite, Review) is that each student's reading is done so that he or she can answer personal ques-

tions derived from the initial survey or skimming. Whether an individual or group activity, skimming can lead to questions students themselves want answered.

3. *From titles and headings.* With practice, students can learn to take titles ("Take It or Leave It" or "Henry, Midge, and the Crystal Ball") and headings ("The Food-producing Revolution" or "Earliest Sites of Agriculture") and turn them into specific questions to be answered: Take what? Leave what? Who is Henry? Midge? What have they to do with a crystal ball? What was the food-producing revolution? What were the earliest sites? A heading in a history book that says, "Causes of the Peasant Revolt" naturally leads to "What were the causes of the peasant revolt?" Sometimes such questions may be artificial, but often they do provide students with a purpose for reading an assignment.

4. *From a model such as "5 W's plus H".* Students may be told that newspaper and television reporters are instructed to discover such "basics" about a news story as Who? What? Where? When? Why? and How? They can be asked to read an assignment to discover answers to their own questions based on these key words: "Who is Henry? Midge? What did they do? Where did they do it? When did they do it? Why did they? How did they?" Other models may be based on sequence (What happened first, second, next, finally?), on cause and effect (What caused what effect?), and others. The "5 W's plus H" works on most stories and content area assignments; other models for question making work more effectively on other kinds of texts.

5. *From first sentences.* Sometimes the title is too vague, there are no headings, and the newspaper reporter's model is inappropriate. Students can, in such assignments, take the first sentence from each paragraph and concoct a question from it to guide their reading. One high school student wanted to read a chapter called "Politics in a New Key" for a research project but discovered it had no headings, its title provided no useful questions, and the "5 W's plus H" would not lead to questions for him. Because he wanted to read it, he decided to create questions from each first sentence. Thus "It was too late and Herzl soon realized it" led to "Who was Herzl? Why was it too late? too late for what?" The sentence in the next paragraph (*A strong personal ingredient, more accessible to the psychologist than the historian, unquestionably played a crucial part in his espousal of the redeemer's role*) led to: "What was the 'strong personal ingredient'? Why was it more accessible to psychologists? What part did it play? What does *espousal* mean? *redeemer?* To *whom* does 'his' refer? Herzl?"

Purposes may also come from *predictions*. As Vacca (1981) notes, curiosity and prediction go hand in hand and are the mainstays of prereading instruction: "The more students predict as they read, the more they will read with certainty and confidence; the greater their curiosity, the greater their motivation to read." And it is from their predictions, as many teachers have noted, that come many of the most effective purposes for reading: students read to learn how accurate their predictions are.

How May Predictions Stimulate Purposes?   A variety of suggestions follow.

1. Teachers may read an assignment aloud and stop at a crucial point, asking students to "tell what happens next." Their predictions listed on the board, students then read the rest of the text to discover how well they predicted.

2. After previewing an assignment (by skimming, noting headings, or using a structured overview), the teacher may ask: "What do you think the author will present in these pages?" or "What point of view do you think he will take?" Student answers become their predictions to be checked out.

3. The teacher may write only the first sentence of the assignment on the chalkboard and ask students to write down as many predictions about the assignment as possible. A sentence such as "Highly successful agriculture in the Nile Valley produced a population explosion there" can lead to dozens of student predictions: "Trade increased," "The army became more powerful," "People began to expand and take over new territories," "The rulers became richer," etc. Students then read to verify their individual predictions.

4. Illustrations may stimulate purposes for reading. Just as a first sentence may lead to predictions, so may a good picture. A photograph of two girls in a storm or a drawing of a skier on a steep slope can lead primary-grade children to such predictions as: "They will get wet," "Their mothers will be angry," or "She will fall." Each provides the reader with a reason to read.

5. The teacher may write the first sentence on the board and ask, "How do you think the author will complete this paragraph?" Students then write their own personal versions to be later checked by their reading of the textbook paragraph.

6. Using headings, illustrations, and any overviews presented in class, students either outline or write summaries of the assignment *before they have read it!* Middle school and secondary school students can learn to make "educated guesses" about what authors are going to say and then later read to verify these guesses.

Often (working alone or with students) teachers can set up very specific purposes for reading involving *problems to be solved.* One tenth-grade biology teacher prepared his class for an assignment on heredity by pointing to his head and noting a small bald patch. "My father," he said, "was bald and so was my grandfather. I seem to be developing a bald patch. Will my sons necessarily be bald also?" He then led the class into a discussion of eye color, height and weight, and mathematic ability. He told students that the chapter to be read contained a good deal of information about genes and chromosomes, about the cross breeding of garden peas, and the early experiments of Gregor Mendel, as well as about recent discoveries in genetics. "Some people say," he said, "that girls cannot inherit mathematical ability. Does this mean my daughter cannot be a mathematician? Does it mean that girls in the class should not major in math in college?" The biology teacher then skillfully set up a problem for students: How is it possible to predict on the basis of current genetic knowledge the inheritance of specific human characteristics? The purpose for reading firmly established, his students read the assignment—with, he hoped, increased attention and more comprehension.

Vacca (1981) tells of a class of eighth-graders about to read a selection about African elephants. Their teacher assigned them a hypothetical problem to solve before they read the selection: If you were a Pygmy, alone and with a spear as your only weapon, how would you hunt and kill an elephant? Children offered many possible solutions: "Dig a hole and lure the elephant into it," "Lead the elephant off a cliff." After examining each with the group, the teacher suggested that the answer might be found in the reading assignment. As Vacca notes, "They were off and reading in no time flat" (1981, pp. 93–95).

Purposes for reading that grow out of problems related to the lives of students may be the most effective—but they are not always easy to come by! Many reading assignments do not lead neatly to problems students want to solve. Fortunately teachers can create purposes for reading for most school assignments by using the first two approaches suggested here: students will read to find answers to their own questions and to check out predictions they have made.

Student-Centered Study Strategies

A number of student-centered approaches to school reading assignments provide for previewing, student-created questions, and establishment of purpose, as well as during- and postreading activities.

One of the best known of these approaches to *study* reading (as distinguished from recreational reading of stories and novels) is Robinson's *SQ3R* (1970). Using this approach, students first *survey* the assignment to get a general idea of what the passages are about; then they make up their own *questions* (from headings and subtitles in the text). They next *read* to discover the answers to their own questions, *recite* (in writing or aloud) these answers, and finally *review* by rereading parts of the assignment to verify their answers. Clearly, SQ3R provides students with an overview (obtained from their own survey) plus a purpose for reading (finding answers to their own questions).

Since Francis Robinson first described this approach in the early 1940s, SQ3R has been widely used by teachers and students at all levels and has. stimulated reading teachers to develop many modifications. Because they constitute attractive and effective alternate study-reading approaches, especially for students who have not had success with SQ3R, several are noted here:

PQRST: Preview, Question, Read, State, Test (Staton, 1954)

The Triple S Technique: Scan, Search, Summarize (Farquhar, Krumboltz, and Wrenn, 1960)

OARWET: Overview, Achieve, Read, Write, Evaluate, Test (Norman and Norman, 1968)

OK5R: Overview, Key Idea, Read, Record, Recite, Review, Reflect (Pauk, 1974)

PQ4R: Preview, Question, Read, Reflect, Recite, Review (Thomas and Robinson, 1972)

S4R: Survey, Read, Recite, Record, Review (Stetson, 1981)

PQ5R: Preview, Question, Read, Record, Recite, Review, Reflect (in Graham and Robinson, 1984)

Teachers trying these approaches for the first time should remember that they were not designed for reading narrative fiction; when readers read to discover "what happens next," any preview or overview destroys purpose and pleasure in reading. They should remember too, as Robinson pointed out (1970), that such approaches are not learned by reading about them: they must be practiced under supervision long enough to be internalized.

Teacher-Directed Lesson Frameworks

One of the best-known lesson frameworks was first recommended by Betts (1946). It suggested prequestions prior to reading and the use of the same questions afterward as postquestions, thus providing for both purposeful reading and attention focusing. This general approach has been supported directly and indirectly by research (Anderson and Biddle, 1975; White, 1981; Sachs, 1981). Betts's *Directed Reading Activity* (1955), another version, suggests five stages: exploring students' backgrounds, building students' backgrounds, reading, discussion of the text, and extension of the text. It too has been widely used through the years. (See Donlan, 1985, for a description of its use in a literature lesson.)

A number of other lesson frameworks developed since Betts are recommended for the improvement of reading comprehension. Three are noted here because they provide specifically for important prereading activities.

DR-TA The Directed Reading-Thinking Activity developed by Russell Stauffer (1969) moves students through prediction and verification to considered judgments. It has five steps:

1. First the teacher has students survey an assignment using titles, headings, and pictures to get a general idea of what the author is discussing. While doing this, the teacher regularly asks, "What do you think this section will be about? Why?"
2. Then students read up to a point predetermined by the teacher.
3. The teacher next asks similar questions but posed to reflect the reading; that is, "What was it about? Were you correct? Why did you predict incorrectly?"
4. The group then reads on to the next stopping point, once again reading to find answers to their questions, "What do you think the next section will be about? Why?"
5. The process continues until the completion of the assignment.

DR-TA clearly provides for key aspects of prereading: students do obtain an overview of the assignment and read through it purposefully in order to verify the predictions they have made. Much depends here on the teacher, acting as stimulator and guide, who must stop frequently to ask: "What do you think? Why? Can you support your belief?" DR-TA, as many teachers have noted, is an effective prereading strategy but also an equally effective during-reading activity. Unlike SQ3R and its variants, it is teacher-directed and may or may not have carryover into students' independent reading.

GRP The Guided Reading Procedure, developed by Anthony Manzo (1975), is another structured, teacher-directed activity. It has eight steps:

1. Teachers first prepare students for the assignment by explaining important concepts, building appropriate knowledge background, discovering what students know and do not know, and providing directions for the actual reading.
2. Then students read the assignment, trying to remember all they can.
3. After students have completed the assignment, the teacher tells them to turn their books over on their desks and repeat all they can remember while he or she records this on the chalkboard.
4. The teacher calls attention to information not remembered and suggests that students reread to discover more.

5. Students reread.
6. Their new recollections are now recorded by the teacher on the board but now in outline form.
7. Teacher asks more questions to help students recall more from their reading and tries to synthesize the new information with information obtained by the first reading.
8. Immediate feedback is given to students through a quiz.

Like DR-TA, the Guided Reading Procedure is almost entirely teacher-directed. Students cannot follow either unless they have a skilled teacher to guide them. GRP, however, does provide an overview (Step 1), as well as well-defined purposes for reading. It recognizes the importance of prior knowledge and extending and refining students' schemata, and it also provides the teacher with regular feedback as students proceed through an assignment. Like DR-TA, it focuses on close reading and is an effective during- and postreading activity as well as an effective prereading one.

ReQuest   Although Reciprocal Questioning was originally designed by Manzo (1969) as a remedial procedure, many teachers now use it as both a pre- and during-reading activity. It has seven steps:

1. Teacher and students read together a section of the assignment, usually the first sentence.
2. The teacher closes the book and invites questions from the group.
3. Next the students close their books, and the teacher asks them questions about what they have read.
4. When the teacher believes that students understand that much of the assignment, the next section is read and steps 1 and 2 are repeated.
5. When the teacher thinks students have read enough of the assignment to make predictions about the rest, reciprocal questioning stops and the teacher asks (as in DR-TA), "What do you think the next section will be about? Why?" Students have an opportunity to share their predictions.
6. The group now reads the remaining sections.
7. The teacher checks out the predictions: "Were your guesses right? Where do you think you went wrong? Why?"

ReQuest is less teacher-directed than either DR-TA or GRP, yet it too allows the teacher some control over students as they read assignments. It provides for purpose and attention focusing and seems especially effective with difficult assignments and with students requiring additional guidance. It is clearly a valuable during-reading strategy as well as a technique for setting prereading purposes. (For recommendation for using GRP and ReQuest to improve metacognition, see Manzo, 1985.)

Why Do These Lesson Frameworks Work?   One recent analysis of various lesson frameworks (Cunningham, Moore, Cunningham, and Moore, 1983) suggests that, to be effective, frameworks must

- Establish purposes for comprehending.
- Have students read or listen for the established purposes.
- Have students perform some task that directly reflects and measures accomplishments of each established purpose for comprehending.
- Provide direct informative feedback concerning students' comprehension based on their performance on that task.

They also note that many—but not all—effective frameworks have a preceding phase in which the background knowledge assumed by the text is activated or developed.

The lesson frameworks recommended here do provide the features noted and are regularly used by teachers to promote comprehension. Most give teachers a plan on which they can build lessons; some give students strategies for approaching texts. All seem rooted in a coherent theory of the comprehension process.

Idea Box

One first-grade teacher uses a simple version of a semantic map to prepare children for a basal story on pets. She asks first for different kinds of pets that people have and lists these in circles under the general category "Pets." Then under each separate circle she has children tell if they have such a pet, what names (if any) they give these pets, and some descriptive words to describe the pets. After preliminary discussion she says, "As we read this story, watch to see what pets are mentioned. Did we put these on our chart? Where will we fill them in?"

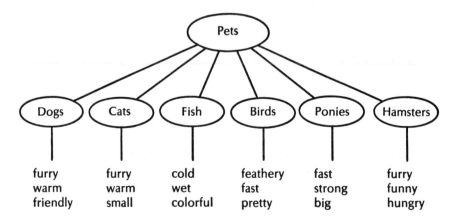

Later, to show that other words may be classified in the same way, she has children tell which of the words in a series would go on top where "Pets" is on the chart and which would go below:

bananas, apples, oranges, fruit
ball, toys, puzzles, truck
penny, nickel, coins, quarters
mother, sister, brother, family

Another primary grade teacher sets up a purpose for reading this way: "Does anyone ever ask you what you learned in school today? As we read this story, be thinking of the new things you learn as you read it. When we finish, tell at least one new thing you have learned from your reading." When all children have had an opportunity to express their "new ideas," she asks them to think about which of these many things may be the most important, thus not only setting up a purpose for reading but also giving practice in thinking about main ideas.

One middle school teacher regularly sets up *Scouting Parties*. He explains that when an expedition is moving into new territory, the leader often sends out scouting parties to check out the new land and report back to the group so that the others will know what to expect in the way of hazards. For new selections in the content area textbook, he has pairs of students read the assignments in advance of the group and prepare advance reports which note Dangerous New Words, Hard Parts, Easy Going, Illustrations to Watch Out For, etc. These volunteers outline their reports the day before for editing and duplication. The reports serve as both overviews and vocabulary previews.

In a sixth-grade social studies class the teacher introduces outlining by explaining that an outline can be a *map* of a new territory. She notes, "Before you go on a hike, you'd like to know what kind of territory you'll be covering. Before you read something new you'd also like a rough idea in advance of what you are getting into." Then she distributes simple outlines of the reading assignments and reads them with the group, explaining that these can give them a look ahead into what they are to study.

A fourth-grade teacher asks children to pretend that they are to be teachers for the coming assignment. She says, "Read it first and decide what you want to emphasize. What are the things you want the students to remember? How can you explain these things so that everyone will really understand them? What questions will you ask?" When children have completed the assignment, she allows opportunities for volunteers to tell how they would teach the lesson.

Many teachers at all levels rely on prediction to help students set a purpose for reading. They read the first pages of a selection aloud with the group and then stop (usually at a carefully chosen spot) to have students predict, "What do you think happens next?" The predictions are written on the chalkboard and students complete the assignment to discover how well they and their friends predicted.

One fifth-grade teacher says she rarely makes tests for her social studies book any more. She tells students that they are to read the assignments in order to make their own tests. As each child reads, he or she jots down possible test questions. After the group has completed the reading, she writes these on the board for discussion and analysis, encouraging students to note which questions are the best. She then duplicates the test questions for her weekly quizzes. She says that she is setting a purpose for reading and also increasing student involvement in reading—while at the same time raising the class level of "test sophistication."

One junior high school teacher has students skim quickly through an assignment, noting headnotes, subtitles, illustrations, and highlighted phrases and sentences; then he has them write a summary of it *before they have actually read it!* Volunteers share some of their summaries before the group reads, and then after everyone has finished reading students individually check their summaries for accuracy. The teacher says that, in addition to providing a good writing activity, such "pre-summarizing" forces boys and girls not only to make predictions but to read carefully to evaluate their predictions.

A high school social studies teacher has students prepare Tables of Contents for books they are about to read. As part of the class's "enrichment reading" program, each student selects one book for each unit to be read in addition to regular textbook assignments. After these books have been selected but before students have had opportunities to examine them closely, each student outlines what he or she thinks the Table of Contents will probably look like. Then students read their books to see how closely their predictions about the book's contents approximates the actual contents. They may check the author's "official" Table of Contents later but not before they have made their own.

EFFECTIVE DURING-READING ACTIVITIES

Must students *do* anything while reading? Why can't they simply sit and read? Sometimes—perhaps—quiet, silent reading may be enough, particularly as students read stories, novels, and certain passages from their content area textbooks. Some consensus exists, however, that much of the time students need to be "active language users thinking their way through a text" (Page, 1982, p. 63). Teachers need to encourage *active involvement* in the reading process; they need to set up activities during reading that will continue to focus attention on the text and provoke students to think about word meanings, possible interpretations, textual organization, and other matters that will affect the texts-in-the-head they develop as they read.

What kinds of activities promote active involvement while reading? Many are suggested in basal reader manuals and in the professional literature. Ten are briefly described here.

Question-Answering

Most of the prereading activities noted in the previous section included questions, either student- or teacher-created. The search for answers provides students with a purpose for reading and tends to focus attention. Sometimes students can read with their questions before them on their desks; as they read through the assignment they note answers or locations of answers on notepaper. The questions may be ones created after an SQ3R-type survey or ones that the teacher has specifically written for the assignment. At other times students may read to find answers to one question ("If you were a Pygmy, alone and with a spear as your only weapon, how would you hunt and kill an elephant?") or to a few related questions ("What did the king do next? Why? Was he right to do this?").

Questions have been called the tools of the teacher's trade (Vacca, 1981, p. 159), but teachers should remember that there are many kinds of questions, some more effective than others. Taxonomies of educational objectives, such as Bloom's (1956), help teachers distinguish among questions that focus on knowledge or on comprehension, on application or on analysis, on synthesis or on evaluation. Clearly questions that can be answered easily with a piece of information from the text are not apt to force active language users to think their way through a text. While teachers may have only a minimum of control over the types of questions students create on their own, they need to think carefully about the questions *they* prepare for students. They need to have in mind, as they make up questions, some taxonomy to guide them.

One useful guide is suggested by Pearson and Johnson (1978, pp. 157–162). Questions may be *textually explicit* (that is, factual recall questions), *textually implicit* (questions that have answers on the page but are not obvious), and *"scriptually" implicit* (questions that require some prior knowledge to be answered). Which kinds of questions should teachers create for lessons? As Pearson and Johnson point out, it is impossible to classify questions in isolation: those that appear to be simple demands on memory for factual details may in fact require a complex set of inferences to answer; those that appear to require high-level thinking may actually be answered from the text. They also note that teachers may not always get the kinds of answers they expect because of the effects of student prior knowledge. The teacher may think the answer is right there on the page, but the student may have already integrated it into the "scripts" or schemata that comprise his or her prior knowledge. What kinds of questions to ask? An answer must be twofold: all kinds, but developed only after considerable thought on the part of the teacher.

Inserted Questions

Giving students questions *while they read* clearly promotes active involvement. Research supports this belief (Hershberger, 1964; Rothkopf, 1966): when students are asked to stop reading and answer a specific question, or are stopped and given a question to be answered in a passage, they outperform students in control groups who "simply read." One recent study found that comprehension was significantly increased when readers were asked to answer questions embedded in the text; such questions appear to stimulate interaction with text for readers who may not otherwise reflect upon what they are reading (Graves and Clark, 1981).

How may such questions be inserted? Many teachers carefully check assignments and, on separate guide sheets, give page and paragraph numbers with questions to be answered. A student, then, may be instructed: "Page 233, first paragraph—Why did the council make this decision?" or "Page 17, last paragraph—Why couldn't the Pygmy frighten the elephant into running over a cliff?". When teachers duplicate short assignments they can type in questions on the master. Going through a four-page assignment, for example, a teacher may see the need to ask ten different questions; rather than type them on one sheet or write them on the chalkboard, she can divide the assignment at appropriate places and insert typed questions.

Vacca (1981, pp. 184–186) suggests *Question Guides.* On these duplicated guide sheets the teacher has arranged, in one column, specific reading directions ("Read page 214, paragraphs 3 and 4"), and in a second column the questions to be answered ("Do the members of the group agree with their leader? What are their suggestions for alternate plans?"). He recommends that teachers draw up a Question Guide Planning Chart in which they spell out (1) the purpose for asking each question, (2) the type of question, and (3) the position of the question. A Planning Guide might look like this:

Purpose	*Type*	*Position*
recall information	factual recall	before reading passage
evaluate information	inferential	after reading passage

Such a guide for the teacher serves the purpose of insuring questions of different types and at all levels. It also assists the teacher as he or she prepares the final Question Guide for students.

A similar guide has been suggested by Cunningham and Shablak (1975). Their *Reading Guide-O-Rama* provides specific directions: "Read page 9 carefully and then tell, 'What exactly did the king say' and 'What were his reasons for saying it?'" or "Next, read pages 10 through 12 and list in your notebook all the evidence you can find to support the opinion that the king's mind had been made up."

Another variation is the *Teacher-Over-My-Shoulder Guide* (Devine, 1981, pp. 167–168) in which student directions are personalized: "Read page 113; everyone tell why the boys ran up that particular hill; Tom and Arthur, who have been in that part of the country, ought to be able to tell us why the hill was different from ones we know around here. Make a note to tell us, boys." Such personalized guides cannot be made for every group, for every reading assignment, but when really active involvement in the reading process is desired, they are worth the teacher's time and effort.

Immediate Oral Feedback

If the goal is maximum, active involvement, the immediate oral feedback provided by various lesson frameworks may be the best way of attaining it. The Directed Reading-Thinking Activity, the Guided Reading Procedure, and the Reciprocal Questioning described in the previous section provide the teacher with opportunities to make students conscious of the text and the ways they are interpreting it. Teacher's questions while reading do indeed seem to stimulate thoughtful, active reading. Students find it difficult to daydream when teacher interrupts regularly to ask: "What do you think this section will be about? Why? What was it about? Did you predict correctly? Why? Why not?" All three frameworks not only provide effective prereading activities but also important during-reading experiences.

One reason many teachers continue oral reading into the intermediate and upper grades is that it does allow for immediate feedback. When students find a particular text difficult, teachers ask them to read aloud. As Tierney and Cunningham note (1984, p. 624), research on oral reading as a comprehension strategy is sparse and equivocal, but it does yield a slight edge in favor of oral reading over silent reading for purposes of comprehension. It may be that oral reading offers the teacher opportunities to interrupt and ask, "What does *that* mean to you? Why do you think the author said that? What do you think will happen next?" It may be that experienced teachers have intuitively sensed the values of immediate oral feedback provided by DR-TA, GRP, and ReQuest and realize that oral reading, punctuated by questions and answers, does indeed promote active involvement and more interaction between text and reader.

Time Lines and Charts

Students may also be encouraged to pay greater attention to the reading process by completing charts and time lines as they read. Many teachers go through an assignment and draw up incomplete charts for students to fill in as they read. For example, while reading about trade in the American Colonies, eighth-graders are asked by their teacher to add information about exports and imports from each colony studied; in the process of reading the chapter they are able to locate important information for the lesson and complete the chart. Many teachers have drawn incomplete time lines for readings in history and for literature selections; as students read, they add data to the lines, using entries made in advance by the teacher to guide them.

One simple time line for the story "Take It or Leave It" by Osmond Molarsky (Clymer, Venezky and Indrisano, 1982) has children completing a sequence that begins with Chester swapping a yo-yo for baseball cards and ending with him swapping a dog for the same yo-yo. In between, he has swapped several items, only two of which the teacher has filled in. Fifth-graders are asked to indicate on the line all the items intervening. Such an activity directs student attention to the sequential order of events in the narrative while also giving them something to *do* while reading, thus increasing interaction between text and reader.

Listing Main Ideas

Main ideas, as will be noted in Chapter 7, are as much in the minds of readers as in the minds of authors. Yet the process of trying to identify main ideas in a text remains a viable learning activity. Teachers can ask students to read an assignment to note what they believe are its main ideas. For example, one teacher regularly says, "I think the author has about eight main points in this chapter; as you read it, jot down those ideas which you think are the key ones." She then has students reread the chapter with their lists in front of them to make "second judgments." They are told at this stage to delete, add, or rephrase. In a third stage of the lesson she asks boys and girls to tell what they finally decided on and encourages them to evaluate one another's lists. A class "master" list is written on the chalkboard and then copied by students into their notebooks.

Teachers who engage students in such an activity are less concerned with the main ideas than with the process of locating and discussing them. The class activity allows them opportunities to examine with students the ways writers use to call attention to what they think are their main ideas: "Are they always in the opening paragraph? Do they always come as first sentences in paragraphs? Are they sometimes highlighted by upper-case letters or italics? What phrases do writers sometimes use to make their main ideas stand out?" Activities such as this also allow teachers to note the tentativeness of so-called main ideas: "Why is John's choice different from Chester's? Why did no one in the group notice this one? Why did everyone notice this one?" The very act of seeking out key points certainly promotes active reading, whether in a primary class or a graduate course in a university!

Outlining

The search for an author's main ideas can lead to a study technique too infrequently used in comprehension lessons. Outlining helps students see main ideas, subordinate information, and interrelationships among them. Although generally inappropriate for responding on paper to narrative fiction, it is a technique useful in content area reading from the earliest grades.

Some teachers prepare duplicated outlines of content area reading assignments and have children follow these outlines as they read, checking items as they come to them. When they seem to perceive that prose is organized in specific ways, teachers prepare similar outlines omitting certain items. (For example, listing four of six main points but leaving blank lines for two; or providing all supporting points but three and telling students to write in the missing lines.) After many lessons of this nature, teachers provide only the Roman numerals, upper-case letters, and, if the outline is more sophisticated, Arabic numbers and lower-case letters. This conventional outlining format may be restrictive to some students, but it does allow for a number of rewards: students given practice in conventional outlining tend to learn the conventional form, they tend to see that expository prose does usually have a basic organizational structure, and they are inclined to be more active as they read.

Various forms of free-form outlining also encourage activity while reading. *Array-outlining* has students identify key points in an assignment, copy these onto small pieces of paper, and arrange the pieces on their desktops in some order. After discussion with other students and teacher, students then copy their arrangement onto a large piece of paper (Hansell, 1978). *Pyramid outlines* are drawings students prepare with key ideas at the top of a pyramid and subordinate ideas arranged appropriately below them (see Walker, 1979). *Mapping*, another free-form, has students copy main and subordinate ideas onto a large sheet and connect these with lines indicating degrees of subordination. In doing such free-form outlines students lose practice in learning about the conventional outline form but do begin to see that expository prose does have structure with key and subordinate ideas arranged in some sequential, organized manner. Most important, in free-form as well as conventional form, students are encouraged to be active while they read. (Chapter 7 includes further discussion of outlining.)

Paraphrasing

It has been said that readers seldom really understand an idea until they can say it themselves in their own words. (See Henry, 1974; Levi-Strauss, 1979; Devine, 1984; and also the following section of this chapter.) Some teachers identify passages they believe present students with comprehension problems and ask students to paraphrase them when they come to them in their reading. For example, a teacher may note that a certain paragraph or sentence in an assignment is crucial to its comprehension; she may therefore spend considerable prereading time discussing that paragraph or sentence. She may also note in the assignment that students should stop when they reach that point and write out a paraphrase: "The sentence at the bottom of page 288 may be difficult to understand. What does it mean to you at this point in your reading? Before you continue reading the assignment, write out in your own words what you think the author means." The paraphrases students write during reading may later be used as the basis for postreading discussion. The actual writing-out *during reading* provides readers with another opportunity to become actively engaged in the reading process.

Summarizing

Brief written summaries offer teachers one of their only means of discovering how much students have comprehended of an assignment; the preparation for summary-writing is one of the most valuable during-reading activities. When readers know that they read to write a summary, they tend to be far more engaged! Many middle and high school teachers particularly have developed summary writing as a reading goal. One teacher, for example, regularly says, "You are going to write brief summaries of the chapter. As you read, you can gather the data you'll need to write." She then shows them that they will need to note main ideas, subordinate details, sequence, and the author's purpose for writing; they will need, in other words, to take notes of some kind in order to remember. As students read she goes from one to another helping them find key points, reminding them to separate main from subordinate ideas, to note sequence, and so forth. The end-product, the summary, is an after-reading activity, but the preparation for it provides for a maximum of active involvement with the text.

Study Guides

Many teachers at all levels prepare study guides to help students move through a reading assignment. Such guides can provide overviews, advance organizers, vocabulary previews, and other prereading activities but can also give students specific tasks to do *while* reading: answering inserted questions, completing time lines and graphs, outlining, and responding to specific items within the text. (The Question Guides, the Reading Guide-O-Rama, and the Teacher-Over-My-Shoulder Guide described above are study guides that focus primarily on during-reading activities.) An effective guide may increase comprehension (Devine, 1981, p. 173) by

defining the purpose for the reading;

explaining difficult words, terms, and concepts;

providing definite questions to answer;

specifying notetaking skills ("List the ten main points," "Outline the first three pages," or "Summarize the main idea on page 42.");

relating the material to previous learnings and the lives of students;

personalizing learnings by speaking directly to individuals and, thus, providing for individual differences;

stimulating creative and divergent thinking through specific questions, activities, and research projects; and

providing students (and their parents!) with a *document* defining all dimensions of the assignment.

Self-Monitoring

The study of metacognition has led in recent years to the development of self-regulatory mechanisms for students to use as they try to comprehend. Some of these may apply particularly to reading comprehension. (See Chapter 8 for a discussion of metacognition and comprehension monitoring mechanisms.) Five "fix-up strategies" seem useful during the time students are actually reading assignments (Pitts, 1983):

1. Students can ignore small problems they encounter in comprehension and move along in the assignment.
2. They can change their rate of reading, slowing down for places that seem especially troublesome or sometimes speeding up to get a larger sample of the text.
3. They can suspend judgment, reading ahead in hope that the writer will fill in gaps, add more information, or clarify points.
4. They can hypothesize, saying to themselves, "I think the author is trying to say this," or "My guess is that he is going to say that," and then read along to test out these guesses.
5. They may reread, checking back to discover if their guesses about word meanings were accurate or their hypotheses about the writer's purposes were reasonable.

How can teachers teach these self-monitoring techniques? First, they need to explain them to students. All students do not realize they can reread, change rate, guess at meanings, and so forth. Prior to reading particular assignments, teachers can take time to review the techniques and show how they work by actually reading passages aloud to the group and demonstrating each. Second, teachers can remind students to self-monitor by asking themselves questions as they read ("What does the writer mean when he says this?") and by often paraphrasing for themselves to check their own understanding. Third, teachers can interrupt silent reading sessions by reminding students that when they are puzzled, they may reread, guess, speed up, slow down, and wait for more information.

Idea Box

What can children do *while* they read? One teacher encourages students to keep "New-to-Me Lists." He points out that many of the ideas in an assignment are going to be familiar to them: they have heard this information before or read it in other books. "It's the new material that we want to watch for," he says, and then he tells them to keep one page in their notebooks for each assignment so that they can keep track of New Ideas. After reading, students share their findings and discuss the importance of the new information.

One middle school teacher outlines most assignments in his science textbook, deliberately folds each page down the middle vertically, and reproduces the half pages. Students are given the half pages and told to complete the outlines as they read. After reading, the teacher distributes the missing halves and students check their outlines to see how closely they came to the teacher's outline. He says that after a few practice sessions, students become supersensitive to the structure of the textbook.

One primary teacher makes children aware of sequence through pictures. She draws simple pictures of events in the basal selection, duplicates these, shuffles them so that they are out of order, and then puts the six or eight pictures on each child's desk. As the children read the story together, they try to place the pictures in proper time sequence.

One fifth-grade teacher has children write out the ideas they think are important in a content area assignment, leaving two spaces between each idea. When they have finished, she quickly cuts these up, separating the ideas. Then she has children exchange their slips of paper and arrange one another's on the desktops so that the most important are at the top and the less important underneath. As she notes, there is seldom complete agreement, but the exercise does force children to begin discriminating between main and "minor" ideas in their reading.

One middle school history class has turned its eighth-grade American history textbook into a digest magazine. As they read each section, the teacher has them isolate the main idea sentences paragraph by paragraph and later string these main idea sentences into "digests" of the section. A chapter with ten subsections of approximately ten paragraphs each becomes, after several lessons, a chapter digest with ten "paragraphs" of ten main idea sentences. The students call their steadily growing opus, "Everything You Wanted to Know about American History at (Practically) a Glance."

To increase active involvement in reading, many teachers do "Mental Pictures." They ask students to stop reading at chosen spots in the assignment and have them tell what they see in their "mind's eye." Students are encouraged to share their own personal pictures and explain why they see what they see.

POSTREADING ACTIVITIES
FOR COMPREHENSION

Teachers' manuals and professional books suggest many postreading activities, such as panel discussions, interviewing, pantomime, model-making, library research, poetry writing, drawing, map-making, and a variety of creative individual and group responses to the assignment. Such activities are often worthwhile and justified on educational grounds. They may help enrich, refine, and restructure students' schemata, heighten interest in the topic of the lesson, and give students opportunities to express themselves. However, the primary goals of postreading activities are to help students (1) further develop and clarify their interpretations of the text, and (2) better remember the texts-in-the-head they have created from the printed texts. As prereading activities should assist readers to find clues to meaning in the text, and as during-reading activities should guide them through the writer's printed version of his or her text-in-the-head, so postreading activities should help them define the interpretations they have created for themselves.

Five suggestions for postreading activities designed to improve comprehension are given here.

Follow Up Pre- and During-Reading Activities

Sometimes teachers set up useful pre- and postreading comprehension strategies and fail to follow up on them! They ask questions to promote purposeful reading; they encourage students to ask questions they want answered; they insert questions into the text of the assignment; they have students predict; they request outlines, time lines, and charts. They provide, in other words, for comprehension to take place by their use of effective strategies. They sometimes—unfortunately—move on to other interesting postreading activities or to the next assignment without providing opportunities for students to share and discuss their answers, predictions, and written responses to the text.

Have Students Talk
about What They Read

Henry (1974, p. 17) points out that most readers deal inadequately with their reading: "We read," he says, "at our own pace, finish with an inchoate lump of meaning unformed by language, and go on to other activity." He suggests that it is not until readers try to communicate the ideas they have read to others that they begin to conceptualize them and discover what meanings they have. Too often students in school are asked to read an assignment, are tested, and are then asked to go on to another assignment. They need to talk about what they have read. They especially need to tell others what they think is the gist, or central idea, of an assignment. Teachers can promote such talk by following up on pre- and during-reading activities, but they need also to provide special opportunities for oral discussions in which readers can sum up what they read.

Teachers can stimulate such summings-up in several ways:

1. They can have students pretend to be television reporters who must sum up a "story" (the reading assignment) in two minutes. After allowing a few minutes for preparation, they can have individuals *tell* the central idea to the group.
2. Students can be encouraged to explain what an in-class reading was all about to another student absent the day it was read.
3. Teachers can ask, "What do you think are the five main ideas of this assignment? Which of these do you think is the number-one main idea under which the others fall?"
4. They can regularly ask, "What was that paragraph all about? Tell us in your own words."
5. Students can be asked to use the "5 W's plus H" model for some selections: "Tell Who did What? Where? When? Why? and How?"

Have Students Write about What They Read

The process of writing about what they have read is one of the most effective means students have of discovering their texts-in-the-head. After completing their reading, most students finish with that "inchoate lump of meaning unformed by language." They need to sit with pen in hand and explore on paper their responses to discover what they really think about the reading. The ideas and information they picked up from the reading remain meaningless to them until they try to tell someone else (or themselves!) their interpretations. And writing, unlike talking, allows more time for the ideas and information to be considered and restructured into contexts meaningful to them. The very process of spelling out on paper one's responses to the reading may be as important as the reading itself. Writing is, indeed, a strategy for "reconstructing meaning" (Hittleman, 1983, pp. 199–200).

What kinds of postreading writing activities encourage conceptualizing, organizing, and restructuring—encourage, in other words, opportunities for students to think through their texts-in-the-head? Three are suggested here: paraphrasing, summarizing, and reporting.

Paraphrasing   Claude Levi-Strauss (1979) noted that, of all the words we use, the word *meaning* is probably the least understood. What, he asked, does *to mean* mean? "It seems to me that the only answer we can give is that *to mean*

means the ability of any kind of data to be translated into a different language."
But, he adds, "I do not mean a different language like German or French, but
different words on a different level. After all, this translation is what a dictionary
is expected to give you—the meaning of words in different words, which on a
slightly different level are isomorphic to the word or expression you are trying to
understand" (p. 12).

Teachers who have tried to explain to others, in writing or in spoken
language, what an article, book, or poem "means" know exactly what Levi-
Strauss is getting at. So often people think they "understand" a selection but,
when put to the test, cannot say what it is about. This is, of course, what Henry
(1974) means when he says that it is not until readers try to communicate the
ideas they have read to others that they themselves begin to conceptualize them
and discover what meanings they have.

Many teachers have sensed this. They say to students, "Tell me in your
own words what the writer is driving at." They have students read a few
paragraphs silently and then tell in their own words the writer's ideas. Some
assume that such an approach is chiefly evaluative: how else can teachers know
what students are comprehending? However, more is involved here than assessment, as many teachers sense: the retelling in their own words—especially in
writing—is an avenue to comprehension.

How can reading teachers exploit paraphrasing? Simple retelling at the
oral/aural level should permeate every classroom. It is not enough for boys and
girls to "silent read" a selection; they must also tell, in their own words, what
they think authors are trying to say. *Written paraphrases* also allow students to
process new data and discover meanings; they also present several advantages
over spoken paraphrases: (1) they give less-sophisticated students more *time*—to
probe, reread, discover, predict, formulate, synthesize, organize; (2) they give
the less-glib students more chance to pace themselves in a less-competitive
classroom context; (3) they give the "writing reader" chances to change his or
her mind (that is, what is said at first may not in fact be what the student wants
to say at all); and (4) they give teachers time to take the papers off to a quiet
place and reflect upon what the student got out of the assignment.

Summarizing   Summarizing brings to the reading class all the advantages of paraphrasing plus a variety of other values. It encourages students to (1)
identify the writer's main ideas, (2) recognize the purpose or intent of the selection, (3) distinguish between relevant and irrelevant material, (4) note the key
evidence offered in support of a thesis or main idea, (5) see the underlying pattern of organization the writer has chosen, (6) note the transitional, or signal, expressions used in the text, and (7) follow the sequence of the material. Thus, in
writing a summary, students gain additional practice in aspects of both the
reading and composition programs. (For research on the effectiveness of summarizing, see Day, 1980; Taylor, 1982; and Cunningham, 1982.)

What should students know about summary writing? They need to understand that they are presenting the gist, or central idea, of the assignment and that they may not introduce any new ideas, omit key ideas, nor introduce their own personal points of view. They should be reminded too that the language they use must be theirs, not the writer's.

How may summarizing be used as a postreading activity?

- Students may write *Reader's Digest*-type "condensations." After reading content area textbook selections, for example, they can write the material in capsule form as if it were to be published in a magazine for "busy readers." Students' condensations may be duplicated for sharing and test reviews as well as for class discussion.
- They may use news story formats (Who-What-Where-When-Why-How papers). Students can write newspaper stories that express the main ideas of assignments using headlines for one-sentence summary statements.
- They may also write formal summary papers. Such papers require students to note the writer's purpose and plan of organization, the sequence, main points, and point of view. As they write, students must constantly compare their interpretations of the text with the text itself, regularly verifying and reverifying, rereading and rereading again.
- Students can compare summaries. When several people have written brief summaries of a passage or assignment, these may be duplicated for comparison. Discussions often lead to observations about differences in student perceptions and interpretations.

Reporting   Gathering data, organizing it, and communicating it to the group in the form of written reports is another useful postreading activity, one that incorporates many of the values of both paraphrasing and summarizing. Such reports may pull together several related selections in a reader or content area textbook: "Now that you have read these eight selections on aspects of courage, think about a short report on 'Courage in Our Time'" or "When you complete the chapter on Central America, plan a brief report on the topic." Such reports may be highly formal, with attention paid to sources, references, even footnotes; they may also be informal written reports designed to condense related data for later test review.

Some possibilities for report writing include the following:

- Students can be encouraged to write magazine-type articles based on content area reading assignments. For example, after reading the chapter "Elements of Weather" in their fourth-grade science book (Cohen et al., 1984), children identified the questions around which it was organized: What causes different temperatures? How does air move? How do we measure wind? How does water get into air? How do clouds form? How do we measure precipitation? Then they formed groups to write out their answers to the questions. When these had been edited and revised by the groups they were combined into an "article" for publication in the class magazine, *Science Today*, a neatly typed monthly production of the fourth grade.

- Teachers can highlight persuasion! Many teachers note that some of the best writing students do often comes from attempts to persuade. When students know exactly whom they are trying to convince and what they want their readers to do, their writing assumes focus and direction. Thus some high school social studies teachers encourage students to argue positions taken from their reading of assignments: "Benedict Arnold Had a Case," "Pearl Harbor Was Not a Surprise Attack," or "Propaganda May Be Good at Times." From a chapter on "Adaptations to Water," fourth-graders can organize arguments against water pollution. Such writing does much to help students shape their texts-in-the-head.

- Students can report on their reading by writing out "conversations." After reading the section in their American history book about the Bay of Pigs invasion, students can write a conversation between John and Robert Kennedy—or two cabinet members—in which they discuss the pros and cons of the invasion of Cuba the night after the formal deliberations. Fourth-graders can respond (in writing) to a science chapter on "Building and Shaking the Earth" by preparing a conversation between a geologist and the mayor of Los Angeles.

- Teachers can suggest how-to-do-it papers. After certain assignments, students can write out directions. High school English students who have read an assignment on propaganda can write "How to Avoid Being Propagandized" or "How to Propagandize." Fourth-graders can respond to their chapter on "Changes in the Earth's Surface" by writing on "How People Can Help Control Erosion."

Have Students Make Up Tests on Their Reading

One effective way to help students better define and further develop their texts-in-the-head is to have them create their own tests for reading assignments. Predicting possible test questions is both a valuable pre- and during-reading activity; preparing an actual test after reading can help students decide main points, relevant information, and writer's purpose.

Students may be told, "If you had written this chapter and wanted to see how well your readers understood it, what questions might you ask them?" They then need to clarify in their own minds what they think the text was about: What was the writer's chief point? What were the subordinate points? How is the text organized? What is important? unimportant? What may be left out? What must we include?

Some teachers review test-taking strategies while showing students how to make tests. For example, they discuss the differences between essay and multiple-choice tests, the advantages and disadvantages of true-false items, sentence-completion items, and fill-in-the-blanks items, and then point out "tips" for test-takers and various test-taking strategies (see Devine, 1981; Graham and Robinson, 1984). As students develop more and more test sophistication, they show them how to polish up their exercises in test-making so that they may be used in class.

Encourage Students to Respond to Assignments "Creatively"

In addition to talking, writing, and test-making, students can respond in other ways to their assignments. Some that lead to restructuring and refining of student interpretations are described here:

- Teachers can note that many people believe "The best way to learn something is to teach it to someone else" and suggest that individual students try to teach the information and ideas in an assignment to others in the class. Some teachers divide a textbook chapter into six or eight sections and assign one group the task of teaching the entire chapter to the class. Each group member must read the entire chapter but *study* his or her section well enough to teach it. After time has been allowed for preparation, individuals have the opportunity to teach. The activity has many of the values of paraphrasing, summarizing, and reporting while at the same time providing a personal and dramatic dimension to the postreading period.
- For some reading assignments teachers can arrange Show-and-Tell sessions. Fourth-graders, for example, can demonstrate the processes of erosion they have just read about by bringing in a tray of dirt and some water and showing how erosion works. High school students can work together in groups to show how a union-management negotiating team works, how an automobile tire is best changed, or how a public opinion poll is conducted. Every reading assignment does not lend itself to such activities, but those that do can be exploited by teachers to provide for different kinds of postreading responses.
- Students can often "act out" assignments. Many texts, especially in social studies and literature, provide opportunities for students to dramatize their interpretations in small groups. A middle school class that has just read Frost's "The Death of the Hired Man" can easily act

out the narrative with individual students playing the parts of the farmer and his wife. Fifth-graders can act out the story of Miguel in Joseph Krumgold's "The Worst and Best of Things" (Clymer, Venezky, and Indrisano, 1982) with different children playing members of the Chavez family. In social studies class, students can reenact events described in their reading. Such dramatic responses to reading assignments allow students opportunities to think through their interpretations: What really happened? What happened first? next? Who did what? to whom? where?

- Students can also respond to reading with pictures, graphs, and models of various kinds. For example, one middle school class read "The Open Window" by Saki. Instead of writing a summary or telling the story in their own words, they were asked to prepare a collage. Working in groups, they located pictures in magazines and newspapers of a girl to represent the girl in the story and of men and boys to represent the father, brothers, and family visitor. They then arranged these sequentially to show—in pictures pasted on cardboard—their interpretations of the story. Science and social studies teachers can encourage students to respond to reading by drawing charts and graphs or by making models. In all these activities students are thinking about what the assignment meant to them and, in the process, discovering what their interpretations look like. A brief examination can reveal to the teacher how well students understood an assignment.

PostReading Activities and the Writing Reader

The pre- and during-reading activities suggested here should aid students as they develop their own texts-in-the-head. The questions and predictions they use to guide them through their reading tend to structure the interpretations they develop; the responses they make while reading contribute further to their interpretations. However, the postreading activities in which they engage play a powerful role in defining the versions of the printed text they will remember and later use. It is their written reports and summaries, their "newspaper articles" and "magazine digests," that tend to establish what they think the text said and remain with them long after the reading experience itself has been forgotten.

Why is writing so important to comprehension? Written activities (unlike oral discussions, acting-out, peer-teaching, and other valuable postreading activities) allow readers opportunities to see their own thinking develop in front of them, in their own words, on paper. Short-term memory being what it is (short!) permits readers to entertain ideas about the text for only a brief moment. A reader says to himself, "Ah, this is what the author is driving at" or "So this leads to that." But seconds later these realizations have been lost. A writing reader says, "This must mean that" or "That refers to this" and *writes it down,* thus catching her thoughts in her notebook to consider, evaluate, rearrange, change, or delete. *Writing out what one thinks an author is saying becomes one of the single most powerful tools for readers to discover their own meanings.* Writing, as many have pointed out, is a powerful tool for thinking. One's language on paper becomes a detached artifact of one's own mind and, once set before one's self for consideration, can be evaluated and manipulated. What emerges on paper becomes the reader's developing text-in-the-head, accessible and changeable.

An example:

A writing reader (any age—from upper elementary school through graduate school!) reads a text that is not immediately comprehensible. The reader has enough linguistic competence and enough appropriate prior knowledge to make connections between the new material of the text and related schemata held in long-term memory. This reader too has a desire to better understand the text and confidence in his or her ability to make sense of it. The reader may read it, think about it, talk to others about it, and think some more. A personal text-in-the-head will result.

However, given some modicum of writing competence, that same reader, functioning as a *writing reader,* can begin to make notes, jot down so-called main ideas, arrange these in sequence, seek out the author's plan of organization, and so forth. With this information now captured in print, safe from the inevitable brevity of short-term memory, the writing reader may evaluate it, change it, refashion it, rethink it—*always with the original printed text available.* The reader may now ask such questions as, "Is this what I *really* think? How can I say that? Does the text really say this? Am I reading too much into the author's words? Is my version sensible? Do I believe what I've written?" The resulting product not only reflects (on paper) the reader's interpretation but allows for rethinking and reinterpretation as the product is being shaped on paper.

All this highlights the value of postreading written activities. Of all strategies teachers may use to help students better comprehend printed texts, thinking-out-on-paper is one of the most effective. Reading lessons need to include summary writing, paraphrasing, written reports, news articles, written responses, and other paper-and-pen activities.

TEACHING STRATEGIES VERSUS LEARNING STRATEGIES

The suggestions made in the chapter for improving comprehension of school reading assignments are largely *teaching,* or *instructional, strategies.* Using advance organizers or structural overviews before reading, incomplete outlines or inserted questions during reading, and written responses to the text after reading all assume teacher effort and control. In each case an informed adult reader guides students through the comprehension process—often in a step-by-step procedure designed to lead student readers to texts-in-the-head similar to the teacher's (and presumably the writer's!). Most of these teaching strategies have been used for years and their use supported by research.

A crucial question for the teaching of comprehension remains: Do students internalize these strategies so that they can carry them into their out-of-class reading? or, as Tierney and Cunningham put it, "Can students be taught knowledge, skills, or strategies that will transfer to their reading of passages with which teachers have not helped them?" (1984, p. 629).

One example may help clarify this question. Many middle, secondary, and college teachers through the years have taught SQ3R—as an *instructional* strategy. They have students survey an assignment and write down questions to be answered by the reading; then they have them read, recite, and review; all of this in the classroom under the direction of the teacher. Many students *internalize* the procedure and use it on their own outside of class. Many, however, do not. The same holds true of other techniques and approaches. Some students learn, under teacher guidance, to establish their purpose for reading by turning headings into questions; listing main ideas, drawing time lines, or making outlines as they read; and to follow up their reading by writing out brief summaries. They then transfer these skills into other classes and actually use them in their reading of magazine articles and books selected for recreational reading. Other students fail to make the transfer. Once deprived of the guidance of a teacher, they fall back into purposeless, passive reading, reading without the active involvement conducive to comprehension.

Why do some students internalize the strategies and transfer the skills? turn teaching into learning strategies? The question is central to comprehension instruction, but little research has been conducted in this area. In their review of research in the teaching of reading comprehension, Tierney and Cunningham (1984, p. 630) found only a few attempts to develop deliberate use of these strategies by readers.

What can teachers do to foster transfer? Two suggestions are made here.

1. Continue regular instruction of the teaching strategies over a long period of time. It is not enough to show, once or ten times, how SQ3R works, how headings may be turned into questions, or how outlines may be developed. Students need opportunities to practice these skills weekly (even daily) over a period of several years, and not only in reading lessons but in all content area study. It may be that many (if not most) American students have been shown these techniques once or twice in their school careers, but it is doubtful whether many have had regular instruction from elementary school through college in all their subject-matter classes. Internalization cannot take place after only a few isolated experiences with a strategy.

2. Deliberate efforts must be made for transfer. Instruction now tends to

take place in class with school assignments, thus minimizing the possibilities of applying strategies to nonassigned reading. Teachers need frequently to have students use specific strategies with out-of-class material. For example, after reminding students to predict on the basis of heading or illustrations or to write one-sentence summaries of assignments, teachers need to say: "Tonight, find a magazine article at home or in the library and read it to discover the accuracy of predictions you made from the pictures" or "For tomorrow's class, bring in one-sentence summaries of five paragraphs from your reading assignment in biology (or another content area class)." Too often transfer fails to take place because too few teachers deliberately plan for it.

■ RECAPPING MAIN POINTS ■

Although teachers cannot intervene in the reading comprehension process when their students are reading outside their classrooms (for recreation, for information, or to fulfill reading requirements in other courses), they do have some control over the ways students approach reading assignments in their own classrooms. They can, for example, provide prereading activities that tend to promote comprehension. Some of these are advance organizers, structured overviews, vocabulary previews, and the establishment of purposes for reading (through the use of prequestions, predictions, and problems to be solved). Teachers can also assure active involvement in the reading of assignments in class by having students answer inserted questions, list main ideas, complete outlines and time lines, summarize and paraphrase, follow study guides, and employ various self-monitoring devices. Teachers can help students better define and remember their interpretations of assignments by having them complete certain activities after reading. Some of these include group discussions, which emphasize paraphrasing and summarizing, written responses involving paraphrasing, summarizing, and reporting, as well as other kinds of responses to reading. Throughout, they need to be aware of the need for students to internalize such teacher-directed instructional strategies, so that these become learning strategies for students to use in reading situations outside their classrooms.

END-OF-CHAPTER ACTIVITIES

1. What are your answers to the Suggested Study Questions at the beginning of the chapter? Did the chapter provide satisfactory answers for you? Why? Why not?
2. Several prereading activities are suggested here, but the time con-

straints of the classroom rarely allow teachers to use more than two or three. How do you decide which to use? In what ways does the nature of the assignment affect your choices?

3. Sometimes students' minds wander away from the assignment! In what ways do some of the recommended pre- and during-reading activities help focus attention? In your experience, what activities work best as attention-focusers?

4. During-reading activities are important not only because they tend to focus attention but also because they promote active involvement. Which of the recommended activities do you favor as a reader? Which do you recommend for classroom use by teachers?

5. Take a basal reader or content area textbook and create possible inserted questions. How would you handle the mechanics of insertion? through guides? by retyping the text or portions of it?

6. Take a selection and create questions students can answer while they read. Try to make some that are textually explicit, the straight factual recall type; try to make some that are textually implicit, that demand inference-making on the part of students. How do these differ from ''scriptually implicit'' questions? Create at least two or three of this latter type. Which are better? Why? Why are they all important?

7. Create a problem situation for a selection or content area assignment. (Remember the Pygmy.) Why are these sometimes difficult to devise? Why are they worth developing?

8. Select a book you or your students are currently studying and show how reader questions may be devised from headings, subtitles, and illustrations. If you have a group of students available, have them try. What are some of the problems students encounter as they create such questions? How can the problems be solved?

9. Use one of the lesson frameworks suggested here (DR-TA, GRP, Re-Quest, or one of the two Betts frameworks) and try it with a class. Why does it work? What problems did you encounter with it? Would you recommend it to others? Why? Why not?

10. Have you ever used SQ3R? If not recently, take a chapter in a textbook or a journal article and try the technique. Does it work for you? Why? Why not? Would you recommend it to others? Why is it not recommended for stories?

11. Why is it so important that students internalize these techniques (take, that is, the teacher's instructional strategies and turn them into personal learning strategies that they can use outside of school)? Some might say students have enough to learn now, that they ought not to be burdened with additional learning chores.

12. Most of the pre-, during-, and postreading activities noted here may be used by primary school children as well as graduate students.

However, some may be more appropriate at certain age and grade levels. Review the activities in the chapter and suggest the age-grade level in which you would introduce and teach each one. Write a brief paper supporting your decisions and, if possible, include in it a chart to make your ideas clearer to your readers.

REFERENCES

Anderson, R. C., and W. B. Biddle. "On Asking People Questions about What They Are Reading." In G. H. Bower (Ed.), *The Psychology of Learning and Motivation* (Vol. 9). New York: Academic Press, 1975.

Ausubel, David P. *Educational Psychology: A Cognitive View.* New York: Holt, Rinehart and Winston, 1968.

Barron, Richard. "The Use of Vocabulary as an Advance Organizer." In H. L. Herber and P. L. Sanders (Eds.), *Research in Reading in the Content Areas: First Report.* Syracuse, N. Y.: Syracuse University Reading and Language Arts Center, 1969.

Betts, Emmett. *Foundations of Reading Instruction.* New York: American Book Company, 1946.

Betts, Emmett. "Reading as a Thinking Process." *The National Elementary Principal* 35 (September 1955): 90–99.

Bloom, Benjamin. *Taxonomy of Educational Objectives.* New York: McKay, 1956.

Carr, Eileen M. "The Vocabulary Overview Guide: A Metacognitive Strategy to Improve Vocabulary Comprehension and Retention." *Journal of Reading* 28 (May 1985): 684–689.

Clymer, Theodore, Richard L. Venezky, and Roselina Indrisano. *Ride the Sunrise.* Lexington, Mass.: Ginn, 1982.

Cohen, Michael, Betty J. Del Giorno, Jean Durgan Harlan, Alan J. McCormack, and John R. Staver. *Science.* Glenview, Ill.: Scott, Foresman, 1984.

Cunningham, J. W. "Generating Interactions between Schemata and Text." In J. A. Niles and L. A. Harris (Eds.), *New Inquiries in Reading Research and Instruction, 31st Yearbook of the National Reading Conference.* Rochester, N. Y.: National Reading Conference, 1982.

Cunningham, P. M., S. A. Moore, J. W. Cunningham, and D. W. Moore. *Reading in Elementary Classrooms: Strategies and Observations.* New York: Longman, 1983.

Cunningham, Richard, and Scott Shablak. "Selective Reading Guide-O-Rama: The Content Teacher's Best Friend." *Journal of Reading* 18 (1975): 380–382.

Day, J. D. *Teaching Summarization Skills: A Comparison of Training Methods.* Unpublished doctoral dissertation, University of Illinois, 1980.

Devine, Thomas G. *Teaching Study Skills: A Guide for Teachers.* Boston: Allyn and Bacon, 1981.

Devine, Thomas G. "Writing to Comprehend." In Donald W. Protheroe (Ed.), *Reading-Writing Connections.* Storrs, Conn.: University of Connecticut, 1984.

Donlan, Dan. "Using the DRA to Teach Literary Comprehension at Three Response Levels." *Journal of Reading* 28 (February 1985): 408–415.

Farquhar, William W., John D. Krumboltz, and C. Gilbert Wrenn. *Learning to Study*. New York: Ronald Press, 1960.

Graham, Kenneth G., and H. Alan Robinson. *Study Skills Handbook: A Guide for All Teachers*. Newark, Del.: International Reading Association, 1984.

Graves, Michael F., and D. L. Clark. "The Effect of Adjunct Questions on High School Low Achievers' Reading Comprehension." *Reading Improvement* 18 (1981): 8–13.

Graves, Michael F., and C. L. Cooke. "Effects of Previewing Difficult Short Stories for High School Students." *Research on Reading in Secondary Schools* 6 (1980): 38–54.

Graves, Michael F., C. L. Cooke, and M. J. La Berge. "Effects of Previewing Difficult Short Stories on Low Ability Junior High School Students' Comprehension, Recall, and Attitudes." *Reading Research Quarterly* 18 (1983): 262–276.

Graves, Michael F., and R. J. Palmer. "Validating Previewing as a Method of Improving Fifth and Sixth Grade Students' Comprehension of Short Stories." *Michigan Reading Journal* 15 (1981): 1–3.

Hansell, T. Stevenson. "Stepping Up to Outlining." *Journal of Reading* 22 (1978): 248–252.

Hayes, D. A., and R. J. Tierney. "Developing Readers' Knowledge through Analogy." *Reading Research Quarterly* 17 (1982): 256–280.

Henry, George. *Teaching Reading as Concept Development: Emphasis on Affective Thinking*. Newark, Del.: International Reading Association, 1974.

Hershberger, W. "Self-evaluational Responding and Typographical Cueing: Techniques for Programming Self-instructional Reading Materials." *Journal of Educational Psychology* 55 (1964): 288–296.

Hittleman, Daniel R. *Developmental Reading, K–8: Teaching from a Psycholinguistic Perspective*, 2nd ed. Boston: Houghton Mifflin, 1983.

Levin, J. R., and M. Pressley. "Improving Children's Prose Comprehension: Selected Strategies That Seem to Succeed." In C. M. Santa and B. L. Hayes (Eds.), *Children's Prose Comprehension: Research and Practice*. Newark, Del.: International Reading Association, 1981.

Levi-Strauss, Claude. *Myth and Meaning*. New York: Schocken Books, 1979.

Manzo, Anthony. "The ReQuest Procedure." *Journal of Reading* 11 (1969): 123–126.

Manzo, Anthony. "Guided Reading Procedure." *Journal of Reading* 18 (1975): 287–291.

Manzo, Anthony V. "Expansion Modules for the ReQuest, CAT, GRP, and REAP Reading/Study Procedures." *Journal of Reading* 28 (March 1985): 498–502.

Norman, Maxwell H., and Enid S. Norman. *Successful Reading*. New York: Holt, Rinehart and Winston, 1968.

Page, William D. "Readers' Strategies." In Allen Burger and H. Alan Robinson (Eds.), *Secondary School Reading*. Urbana, Ill.: ERIC Clearinghouse on Reading and Communications Skills, NCRE, 1982.

Pauk, Walter. *How to Study in College*. Boston: Houghton Mifflin, 1974.

Pearson, P. David (Ed.). *Handbook of Research in Reading*. New York: Longman, 1984.

Pearson, P. David, and Dale D. Johnson. *Teaching Reading Comprehension*. New York: Holt, Rinehart and Winston, 1978.

Pitts, Murray M. "Comprehension Monitoring: Definition and Practice." *Journal of Reading* 26 (March 1983): 516–523.

Pressey, A S. L. A. "A Simple Apparatus Which Gives Tests and Scores—and Teaches." *School and Society* 23 (1926): 373–376.

Robinson, Francis P. *Effective Study*. New York: Harper & Row, 1970.

Rothkopf, E. Z. "Learning from Written Instructive Materials: An Exploration of the Control of Inspection Behavior by Test-like Events." *American Educational Research Journal* 3 (1966): 241–249.

Sachs, A. W. *The Effects of Three Prereading Activities on Learning Disabled Children's Short-term Reading Comprehension*. Unpublished doctoral dissertation, George Peabody College for Teachers, Vanderbilt University, 1981.

Slater, Wayne H. "Teaching Expository Text Structure with Structural Organizers." *Journal of Reading* 28 (May 1985): 712–718.

Staton, Thomas F. *How to Study*. Nashville, Tenn.: McQuiddey Printing Co., 1954.

Stauffer, Russell. *Directing Reading Maturity as a Cognitive Process*. New York: Harper & Row, 1969.

Stetson, E. G. "Improving Textbook Learning with S4R: A Strategy for Teachers, Not Students. *Reading Horizons* 22 (1981): 129–135.

Stevens, K. C. "Can We Improve Reading by Teaching Background Information?" *Journal of Reading* 25 (1982): 326–329.

Taylor, B. "Text Structure and Children's Comprehension and Memory for Expository Material." *Journal of Educational Psychology* 74 (1982): 323–340.

Thomas, Ellen, and H. Alan Robinson. *Improving Reading in Every Classroom*. Boston: Allyn and Bacon, 1972.

Tierney, Robert J., and James W. Cunningham. "Research on Teaching Reading Comprehension." In P. David Pearson (Ed.), *Handbook of Reading Research*. New York: Longman, 1984.

Vacca, Richard T. *Content Area Reading*. Boston: Little, Brown, 1981.

Walker, James. "Squeezing Study Skills (into, out of) Content Areas." In R. T. Vacca and J. A. Meagher (Eds.), *Reading through Content*. Storrs, Conn.: University of Connecticut, 1979.

White, R. E. *The Effects of Organizational Themes and Adjunct Placements on Children's Prose Learning: A Developmental Perspective*. Unpublished doctoral dissertation, Northwestern University, 1981.

From Theory to Practice: Understanding the Ways Texts Are Organized

Writers use their printed texts to try to control and guide the process readers go through as they create for themselves their own personal texts. If writers are good at this, they select and arrange words, sentences, and paragraphs so skillfully that readers may actually form texts in their own minds that are at least somewhat like the texts writers had in theirs while writing.

A writer's printed text becomes a set of signals to help readers make texts-in-their-heads comparable to the text-in-the-head of the writer. Those signals are lexical and semantic—because the writer tries to choose words he or she hopes will stand for the same meanings in readers' minds that are in the writer's. The signals are also syntactic and rhetorical—because the writer tries to arrange these words in sentences and paragraphs in such a way that they will make sense to readers.

This chapter focuses on texts—on how writers put them together and on how readers use the signals within them. It rests upon the belief that readers who understand something of textual construction and organization tend to be better comprehenders. It suggests a variety of strategies for sentence-reading, paragraph-reading, and the reading of longer selections.

Chapter 7 includes Suggested Study Questions, Teaching Guidelines, and then discussions on

- Comprehending Sentences: Problems and Solutions
    Overly complex sentences
    Failure to note punctuation signals

Failure to note signal words
Anaphora
Ellipses or omissions
Unfamiliar rhetorical devices
Specific sentence-reading strategies
- Comprehending Paragraphs: Problems and Solutions
  Teach students to recognize basic paragraph patterns
  Teach signal words
  Teach basic patterns in both reading and writing
  Help students identify main idea sentences
- Comprehending Extended Discourse: Problems and Solutions
  Teach the data pattern
  Make students aware of underlying patterns
  Call attention to paragraph functions
  Review outlining techniques
  Teach previewing techniques
  Show students that stories have structures
- Comprehending Textual Materials: Three Other Considerations

Chapter 7 also includes

- Recapping Main Points
- End-of-Chapter Activities
- References

■ SUGGESTED STUDY QUESTIONS FOR CHAPTER 7   ■

1. What are common causes for failure to understand sentences?
2. What special problems do anaphora and ellipses present as students try to understand sentences?
3. What can teachers do to help students solve common sentence comprehension problems?
4. In what ways are paragraphs usually organized?
5. In what ways are longer pieces of discourse often organized?
6. In what ways are stories organized differently?
7. How may students use knowledge about text organization to increase their comprehension?
8. In what ways does the *external* organization of texts affect comprehension?

▪ TEACHING GUIDELINES
FOR CHAPTER 7 ▪

Chapter 7 is organized around five guidelines, suggested by recent research and observations of successful teaching practices.

- *Teaching Guideline #1*
    Help students perceive and respond to common problems associated with sentence comprehension.
- *Teaching Guideline #2*
    Show students how writers tend to organize paragraphs.
- *Teaching Guideline #3*
    Show them how pieces of longer discourse are commonly arranged.
- *Teaching Guideline #4*
    Show them, too, how stories are often organized.
- *Teaching Guideline #5*
    Give regular practice in using knowledge about textual organization to improve comprehension.

COMPREHENDING SENTENCES:
PROBLEMS AND SOLUTIONS

Students who have some knowledge of the ways writers put their information and ideas into sentences are in a better position to process those sentences than students who do not. To figure out what writers are trying to say in their sentences, readers need to know that each sentence has a *subject* and a *predicate* but may have a *compound subject* and/or *predicate* and may be combined in a variety of ways with other sentences to form *compound sentences* or *complex sentences* with *adjective, adverb,* or *noun clauses.* Readers also need to know, among other things, that sentences may be *declarative* or *interrogative, exclamatory* or *imperative,* that *word order* affects meaning, and that *verbals* may function as *nouns* or *adjectives* (see Durkin, 1983, p. 278).

However, even young readers (as noted in Chapter 1) *know* all this. It is part of their linguistic competence. Children—and even many adults—may not know the terms highlighted in the above paragraph. Such terms are part of the technical terminology used by linguists (particularly grammarians) to describe the grammatical system. All users of the language (who, by definition, have linguistic competence) have acquired knowledge of phonological, syntactic, and semantic operations. Their phonological knowledge allows them to "say" *The goldfish ate the cat;* their semantic knowledge allows meanings for the words

goldfish, ate, and *cat.* Their syntactical knowledge, combined with their semantic knowledge, allows them to puzzle over the sentence: the *goldfish,* as subject
of the sentence, is doing something; *ate,* as predicate, tells what the goldfish is
doing; *cat,* as direct object, completes the action of the transitive verb *ate.* The
youngest child, with semantic knowledge for the meanings of these words, just
knows that something is amiss: goldfish are too small to swallow cats! Very little
of this knowledge is taught to children in school. (Teachers teach technical terms
and a description of how the grammatical system operates, not the system.) This
knowledge—part of each child's linguistic competence—is part of the language
readers bring to the comprehension process. (For more on this topic, see Chomsky, 1968.)

"But," many teachers may ask, "if children know all this already, why do
they sometimes fail to comprehend sentences?" If readers have meanings for
words in a sentence and still have problems comprehending it, the writer of the
sentence may have left something out, is using some rhetorical device unfamiliar
to readers, or has combined several simple sentences into one too complex for
readers to manage at their stage of maturity. These and similar problems with
sentence comprehension need to be examined.

Overly Complex Sentences

Speakers and writers combine simple, or kernel, sentences—each with its
own single subject and single predicate—into often intricate sentences. Thus,
Sally is my friend and *Sally is late for school* are combined into *Sally, who is my
friend, is late for school;* or *The bell rang* and *Sally still isn't here* into *When the
bell rang, she still wasn't here;* or *She's never late* and *Everyone knows
(something)* into *Everyone knows (that) she's never late.* Most students have
enough syntactical knowledge as part of their linguistic competence to process
such sentences easily. However, writers frequently embed several kernel
sentences   into   one   many-layered,   idea-packed   sentence,   forgetting
that—although they feel comfortable with such constructions—their readers
may lose track of the subjects and predicates of the various embedded sentences.
Short-term memory being what it is (short!), readers of scientific papers, certain
literary works, and even high school content area textbooks (whose authors tend
to write highly complex sentences) are unable to process the information
presented. Readers of such sentences—if they are aware of the nature of the
problem—are sometimes forced to put a fingertip under the subject of what appears to be the base, or matrix, sentence and then seek out its predicate,
deciding on the way what purposes are served by the various inserted sentences.
(More on processing complex sentences may be found in Huggins and Adams,
1980, pp. 87–112.)

How can teachers help students comprehend overly complex sentences?
One way is to read each aloud with students and ask such questions as

What is the writer talking about in this sentence?

What seems to be his subject?

What is he saying about his subject?

What words or phrases can we eliminate and still get the basic idea?

How can we cut this sentence up into several shorter sentences?

How might you say this sentence in your own words?

How might an editor for *Reader's Digest* shorten it for that magazine?

Because the ability of students to manage various levels of syntactic complexity is directly related to their age and maturity, teachers need to be sensitive to the syntax of texts they require their students to comprehend. They should remember that, when too many highly complex sentences are found in student reading material, students are being forced to read at their frustrational rather than instructional level. There seems little doubt that the more underlying propositions a sentence contains, the more difficult it will be to understand.

Failure to Note Punctuation Signals

Students sometimes fail to understand sentences because they ignore punctuation signals. They need to be reminded regularly that

a period signals the end of a sentence. It may not mark the end of "a complete thought" as older grammar books say, but it does mark the end of one syntactic string with its own subject, predicate, and modifiers.

an interrogative mark notes a question. Sometimes writers indicate questions by arrangements of words, but generally they use the interrogative mark.

an exclamation point notes an exclamatory remark. For some reason the writer wishes to express an emotional reaction to the statement and so, rather than signal its end with a period, uses an exclamation point.

a colon signals a two-part idea. Usually the first part is an introduction to get the reader's attention and the second an elaboration or summation.

a semicolon indicates that two related ideas are placed side by side. The writer has produced two separate sentences but, for rhetorical reasons, wants them seen by the reader as one on the printed page.

the comma may signal a clause introduced into a sentence, a series of separate items, or some modifier. It tells the reader to slow down, pause,—some interruption in the syntactical arrangement is occurring.

ellipses, dashes, and parentheses indicate asides or less essential additions to the basic sentence. They are often confusing to readers because writers and printers use them interchangeably.

How can these important signals be taught most effectively? Many teachers recommend teaching them in writing lessons as part of the language arts program. Students, they say, will only begin to understand why writers use punctuation marks when they themselves use them *as writers*. It is suggested here that they be taught—and retaught—in both reading and writing classes. Students need to see why writers use colons or parentheses as they themselves write, but they also need to discuss them as they analyze difficult passages together with their teacher. "Why," teachers should ask, "do you think the author set these words off with dashes? Can you write a sentence right now that has some words set off by dashes? Could you have used parentheses? What is the difference? What do they have in common? Why do you think the author used a semicolon rather than a period? a colon? Try writing an original sentence with a semicolon. with a colon. What do these marks indicate to a reader?"

Failure to note punctuation marks is not confined to elementary and middle school students: students in high school and college frequently fail to understand sentences because they disregard these signals. Attention to punctuation signals needs to be a concern of teachers at all grade levels.

Failure to Note Signal Words

Writers (and, of course, speakers) indicate connections and relationships within individual sentences by using certain *signal words*. In addition, they indicate connections and relationships with preceding and following sentences by signaling them with specific words. Students sometimes have problems comprehending sentences because they fail to note these signal words. Teachers need to call attention regularly to them and remind students of their importance.

Some important signal words, according to Durkin (1983, pp. 276–277), are:

What, Who, Why, When, Which, Do, Can, Will (at start of a sentence indicate a possible question)
And (links words, phrases, and sentences)
Or (indicates alternative or appositive)
First, next, while, later, afterward, finally (point up sequence)
The next week, a year later (indicate passing time)
Because, since, so, therefore, consequently (signal cause–effect relationship)
For example (signals illustrations, instances)

Like, as (signal comparison)
Think, probably, believe, possibly (suggest opinion)
For that reason, that is why (refer to previously mentioned idea or event)

How may signal words best be taught in the reading lesson? Three approaches are suggested here:

1. Call attention regularly to signal words that appear in troublesome sentences. When one or more students indicate that a sentence is difficult to comprehend, make sure that the functions of its signals are understood. Ask: Why do you think the author uses *and* or *or* here? Why does she say *because?* What is the point of saying *afterward* or *finally?*

2. Duplicate troublesome sentences from the textbook omitting the signal words; then have students "fill in the blanks." Ask: What kind of word almost *has* to come in this blank? Why? Could the writer have used another word? What might it be?

3. Present series of sentences without signal connectives and have students tell which words they would put in. For example, give a simple sentence that expresses a possible *cause* and a second that expresses a possible *effect.* Ask: What is a good connecting word to link these two in a sensible way? Or give a series of short sentences to be organized in sequence, and ask: What words would you insert to link these in a sensible way? Lead students to see that writers use signal words systematically to serve a definite purpose and that, when readers know the job such signal words usually do, they often can more easily figure out the meaning of sentences.

Anaphora

One troublesome intersentential signal is *anaphora.* Anaphoric expressions include pronouns, pro-verbs, some definite noun phrases, and ellipses:

The book was too difficult. *It* is frustrating him. (Pronoun with the noun *book* as its antecedent.)

She runs every day. *It* is making her feel wonderful. (Pro-verb with *runs* as antecedent.)

The book was easy. His previous one was fun, too. (Noun phrase with *book* as antecedent.)

Her mother graduated from Smith College. Her sister did, too. (Ellipsis, or deletion, with *graduated from Smith College* as the omitted antecedent.)

Anaphoric expressions, as Webber (1980, p. 141) points out, are useful devices for "maxmizing the rate of transfer of meaning." *It,* for example, can evoke in the reader's mind a complex theoretical construct or an entire chain of events leading to some conclusion:

> *It* is frequently referred to as "schema theory."

> In the end, *it* drove students mad.

When antecedents are obvious and occur in a nearby sentence, they cause few comprehension problems. When they are obscure and far removed in the text, they puzzle readers.

What can teachers do to help students with anaphoric expressions? They can read troublesome sentences aloud with students and ask such questions as

> What is the *it* that's frustrating him?

> What is the *it* that's making her feel wonderful?

> What single word could be substituted for *His previous one?*

> What did her sister also do?

Strategies for helping students deal with anaphoric relations fall into four categories:

1. Questioning. (What is the *it* that's frustrating him?)
2. Matching. (Number anaphoric items and their antecedents in duplicated passages, and have students draw arrows from one to the other.)
3. Rule making. (After students have examined several examples, encourage them to make up their own rules to explain anaphora. They may, for example, note that a pronoun is always the same gender as its antecedent or that, when a string of possible antecedents is mentioned, the pronoun is usually linked to the last noted.)
4. Awareness. (Often students fail to note anaphoric relationships because they have never been called to their attention. As difficult passages are read together in class, teachers need to regularly call attention to examples and use the questioning technique recommended above.)

One simple approach for elementary school children is to duplicate a passage such as the following and have them write out on a separate sheet the antecedents for the numbered items.

Raccoons have proliferated in <u>our</u>[1] neighborhood this summer. <u>They</u>[2] can be seen at night in <u>our</u>[3] backyards, in driveways, even on porches. <u>Our</u>[4] dog Dandy trees <u>them</u>[5] constantly. <u>We</u>[6] have to go out in the middle of the night and bring <u>him</u>[7] in the kitchen so <u>the poor things</u>[8] can escape. Otherwise, <u>he'd</u>[9] keep <u>us</u>[10] up all night with <u>his</u>[11] barking.

Ellipses or Omissions

As anaphora is a troublesome intersentential signaling device, so ellipses are a troublesome form of anaphora. When writers "leave things out" they invite comprehension problems. At a simple level, as in *Martha can read 500 words per minute, but I can, too,* most students are not puzzled; they know that the writer is really saying, *Martha can read 500 words per minute, but I can read 500 words per minute, too.* Sometimes, however, students encounter examples in their reading material that present major problems. The author of a high school history textbook, for example, discusses a specific economic problem successfully managed in the 1960s and then, several pages later, concludes that *economists today could learn much,* omitting the important *who studied the problem* or *are familiar with the problem.*

Why do writers (and speakers) use ellipses? They assume that readers (and listeners) carry in their minds, as prior knowledge, the same ideas and information they do. "Why," the language producer asks himself, "need I repeat that information? I know what it is. It's all in my mind." Language receivers, however, may not have the information in their minds as part of their indispensable prior knowledge. They may not have known it before and missed catching it when it appeared earlier in the sentence or text. The information may have dropped from their short-term memories.

How can teachers help with the problem of ellipses? They can

explain what an ellipsis is. It occurs when a writer leaves out a chunk of a sentence—to save time, because she thinks readers already know what has been omitted or because she is careless.

call attention to examples in reading materials. When students are having problems comprehending a sentence with an ellipsis, point out what is missing. Ask them to suggest reasons why the writer omitted these parts.

have students tell what parts are missing. Have students say, or write out, sentences with ellipses, filling in what they think are the missing sections.

use written exercises. Identify in advance sentences from school reading material that have parts missing. Duplicate these and have students mark the ellipses and write out what they think is missing.

have students find examples. Suggest that students search for good examples in their recreational reading, as well as in their school textbooks. These may be posted and/or particularly good examples may be duplicated for class examination.

Unfamiliar Rhetorical Devices

Often writers use specific rhetorical devices to enhance the effectiveness of their texts. Students unfamiliar with these devices need assistance. Some of the most common are

Metaphor—a word that usually means one thing is used in place of another to suggest a likeness or analogy between them (as when one says a computer has memory, or Charles is a fish when he gets into the swimming pool).

Simile—two unlike things are compared, usually with the word *as* or *like* (as in Charles swims like a fish).

Hyperbole—extravagant exaggeration (as in Juan eats enough for the whole Little League team).

Children use such figurative language easily. Any adult who listens in to school yard talk will collect many excellent examples of simile, metaphor, and hyperbole. When children—and older secondary school students—encounter adult examples in their reading material, however, they often are puzzled. Sophisticated adult authors sometimes use figurative language and a variety of rhetorical devices (such as inverted word order) in ways that interfere with readers' comprehension. Many authors use some of them—particularly metaphor—as devices for explaining and improving comprehension (see Jaynes, 1976, pp. 52-59), overlooking the inherent difficulties they present to less sophisticated readers.

What can teachers do? They need to help students find appropriate literal meanings for figurative language. (When the author says, "Charles swims like a fish," what do you think he is really trying to say about Charles? When she says, "Juan eats enough for the whole team," what is she trying to say about Juan?) They also need to help students perceive the differences between the literal interpretation and the figurative one. (When she says, "Juan eats enough for the whole team," what *else* is she saying? When he says, "Charles is a fish," what other things is the author saying about Charles?) Teachers need to provide much direct instruction in both reading and language arts classes over a long period of time. They need to give students practice identifying and creating their own similes, metaphors, and examples of hyperbole. They need to provide students with many examples, not only from basal reader selections and content area textbooks but from poetry and even commercial advertising. In the short term (for today's reading assignment!), teachers need to go through the text, note each figure of speech or rhetorical device that may cause problems in comprehension, and explain it in literal terms, indicating what it is called, why the author probably used it, and why it may bother readers.

Specific Sentence-Reading Strategies

Here are specific steps teachers may take when their students encounter individual sentences they do not understand:

1. Ask students to tell *what* or *who* the sentence is about. (What is its subject?)
2. Ask them to indicate what is being done by the *who* or *what* of the sentence, if possible. (What is the predicate?)
3. Have them tell *where* the sentence takes place. (What words signal location? In, behind, in back of, etc.)
4. Have them tell *when* the sentence takes place. (What words signal time? Later, after, in the morning, etc.)
5. Have them tell *how* something is done. (What words signal "how"? Slowly, quickly, like a fish, etc.)
6. Have them find words and phrases that indicate *how long* or *how much* something is. (What words tell you amounts? time? Until next week, big as an elephant, etc.)
7. Have students "unravel" complex and compound sentences. (How many short sentences do you see in this long one? How might you divide it?)
8. Have them identify antecedents for pronouns. (What is *it?* Who is *she?*)
9. Have them tell what information seems to be missing. (What has the author left out that you need to know? Where do you go to find it? What if you cannot find the information?)
10. Have students paraphrase regularly. (How can you say the sentence in your own words? How might you explain what it means to a younger person?)
11. Have students try to locate the sources of their difficulties. (What is it about this sentence that you cannot understand? If the writer were here with us, what information would you ask from her?)
12. Have them read the sentences immediately preceding and following

the troublesome sentence. (Does the author give you more information that helps you figure out the sentence?)

13. Have students read troublesome sentences aloud. (Does the meaning become clear when you hear it? What about the sentence still
bothers you?)

14. Paraphrase difficult sentences for students. (Often sentences in their
reading material remain incomprehensible—even when students
have meanings for all the words. Teachers sometimes do need to paraphrase and explain.)

Idea Box

To help children better understand long complex sentences, one
fifth-grade teacher regularly schedules "Break Downs." When a
group encounters particularly long sentences, she stops for a quick
analysis: "I think I see three small sentences in this one. One tells
when Harold did something, another tells what he did, and another
tells something else about Harold. Can you pick out the three
smaller sentences all included in the longer complex one?"

To show fourth-graders how end punctuation signs work, one
teacher has laminated sheets with several simple sentences—all
without final punctuation marks. She has prepared a spinner with
five sections: horror, question, command, surprise, and disbelief.
One child spins the spinner and the others mark with felt-tipped pens
the appropriate mark for the sentence.

To demonstrate the importance of proper punctuation marks,
another fourth-grade teacher has laminated sheets with unpunc-
tuated sentences. Students use their felt-tipped pens to show different ways the exact same sentence might be punctuated to show
different meanings. Thus, *"Miguel said Pedro loves them"* may
become either, *"Miguel," said Pedro, "loves them"* or *"Miguel said,
"Pedro loves them."*

To teach awareness of anaphoric elements, many teachers place
particularly troublesome words like *it* and *they* on the board and
stop oral reading periodically to ask, "What is the *it*? Who is *they*?"
Over time, children begin to realize that they need to think about
the individual sentences in relation to those that come before: the
antecedent for *they* may have come in a previous sentence.

Some teachers also keep watch for examples of anaphora in their own reading of newspapers, magazines, and books. When they locate ten examples they duplicate the sentences for class discussion, asking such questions as "Why do we need to know who *they* are? Whatever does the writer refer to here when she says *it*? What has been left out? What more do we need to know?"

To help middle schoolers become aware of common patterns of paragraph organization, one teacher explains generalization, enumeration, time sequence, cause/effect, and comparison/contrast and then divides a back bulletin board into the five categories. Students are encouraged to find examples of each type in their reading of newspapers and magazines, cut out (or recopy) each example, and post it in the proper category on the bulletin board. After two or three weeks enough examples are posted for the teacher to help students see that (1) some types are more common than others and (2) often writers combine types as they write. This search for examples may be done as a contest for groups or individuals.

To teach generalization and the generalization pattern, another middle school teacher uses baseball cards. Each child in the group is given six laminated cards and told to read the information and come up with three generalizations about all six players. Children find it easy to locate specifics for each player but hard to say things that apply to all six. A follow-up activity is to write a paragraph that begins with one of the generalizations and is developed by adding three other sentences referring to all six players.

Paraphrasing "as-you-go" is an activity suggested by many teachers at all levels. Confronted with a troublesome text, students retell it — in writing — as they read. The pace of assignment reading may be slowed but comprehension tends to improve. After students in a group have completed two or three pages (seldom more!) of such written paraphrasing, they are given an opportunity to share with others in the group and discuss their various versions. Such an activity works as effectively with middle schoolers as it does with high school students.

"How Would You Write It?" is another activity that works as well with adults and young adults as with children. After students have read a potentially troublesome paragraph or section of an assignment, they are encouraged to write it over "in their own words." These paragraphs encourage readers to think through carefully the texts they are developing in their heads as they read the author's. Older students may be led through such an activity into discussions of point of view, style, attitude, and tone. One high school teacher uses a variation of "How Would You Write It?" as an introduction to a unit on parody and humor.

COMPREHENDING PARAGRAPHS: PROBLEMS AND SOLUTIONS

Sentences seldom stand alone. They are usually connected with other sentences in some systematic fashion. The problem for scholars of the paragraph—and for teachers who want to teach their students how to read paragraphs better—lies in that "systematic fashion." To date, few authorities agree on the basic characteristics of the paragraph—except to say that it is a group of related sentences, usually (but not always) made to stand out on the printed page by indentation.

At least three models of the paragraph may be found in recent studies. Francis Christensen (1965, pp. 144–156) proposed a *"generative"* model in which the first sentence is "nearly always" the topic sentence, the one "whose assertion is supported or whose meaning is explicated or whose parts are detailed by the sentences added to it." Two types of sequence are related to the topic sentence, according to his description: *coordinate* (in which the topic sentence is developed by other sentences using repetition and parallel structures) and *subordinate* (in which it is developed by other sentences at various levels of generality). A. L. Becker (1965) suggested a *tagmemic* model with "slots" nearly identical for all types of paragraphs. His model offers two kinds of "slot arrangements": the TRI pattern (in which the topic is stated in the T or Topic slot, is narrowed down or defined in the R or Restricted slot, and is illustrated or described in the I or Illustration slot); and the IRT model (which works in reverse, with the illustration given first, then the restrictions on it, and finally the T or topic).

A third model has been called by Paul Rodgers a "discourse-centered rhetoric of the paragraph" (Foster, 1983). Rodgers argues that neither the Christensen nor Becker models—both of which are useful to teachers of reading and composition—are flexible or open-ended enough to account for all paragraphs. Rodgers asserts that all we can say of *all* paragraphs is that their writers have marked them off for special consideration as *stadia of discourse* (1966). These stadia—chunks or measures—of discourse are arrived at intuitively by the writer whose criteria for separating them by indentation include such considerations as tone, rhythm, and form, as well as logic. To Rodgers, the topic sentence of a paragraph may not be in the paragraph but in a preceding or following one.

Reading teachers have traditionally approached paragraph organization from the point of view of *patterns*. (See "Text Structure and Comprehension" in Chapter 3.) Herber (1978) notes four patterns that occur regularly in content area textbooks: enumeration, time order, comparison–contrast, and cause–effect. Robinson (1978) notes six: enumeration, generalization, comparison–contrast, sequence, effect–cause, and question–answer. These breakdowns are supported by recent research and theory (see Levin, 1978; Calfee and Curley, 1984; Horowitz, 1985, 1985). Meyer (1975, 1984), for example, notes five basic patterns:

1. *antecedent/consequent*—which notes a causal relation between topics;
2. *comparison* and *contrast*—which points out the differences or similarities between two topics;
3. *collection* or *list*—which shows how a set of topics is bound together on the basis of some commonality;
4. *description*—which gives more information about a topic by attributes, examples, or elaboration; and
5. *response*—which includes the remark-and-reply, question-answer, and problem-solving formats. (See also Meyer, Brandt, and Bluth, 1980.)

For many years reading teachers have based much of their teaching on the belief that students who know the common patterns—no matter what names they are given in the professional literature—are in a better position to comprehend what writers are trying to say.

Paragraph-reading strategies suggested by the three rhetorical models and the organizational patterns noted by reading teachers are discussed below.

Teach Students to Recognize Basic Paragraph Patterns

Certain patterns or variations of patterns tend to be used more by authors of textbooks in certain areas. Authors of mathematics textbooks, for example, tend to use concept development or principle development patterns more than other writers; authors of science textbooks tend to use classification and problem-solving patterns more than writers in history or economics. However, six basic organizational patterns tend to be used by all writers of expository prose (see Robinson, 1978). Teachers need to show students how these work and how to use them as they read.

Generalization   In using this pattern, the writer makes a broad statement (a generalization, an inference, or even an expression of opinion) and then supports it with evidence, examples, explanations, or reasons. This pattern may be the most widely used in expository prose. Students are taught it (directly or indirectly) in reading lessons when they are taught to find *main idea sentences* and supporting details; they learn it in composition classes when they are shown how to develop *topic sentences* with examples, details, and reasons.

Teachers may introduce the pattern to younger students simply by writing a statement on the chalkboard such as "Sally is selfish" and noting that, as it stands, it is like the tip of an iceberg. It tells what the writer believes but gives others no reason for sharing the belief. The teacher then needs to ask students what information may be added to *support* the statement. Students may provide such sentences as: "Although she had two extra sandwiches and knew I forgot my lunch, she wouldn't share with me" or "I didn't have money for the dance ticket and she had plenty, yet she refused to give me any." An introductory lesson may include: (1) small group discussions in which students suggest evidence to support a list of ten prepared generalizations; (2) writing lessons in which students provide evidence or examples to support a given topic/main idea sentence; or (3) assignments which ask students to locate examples of the pattern in newspapers or magazine articles. Older students may be shown that the topic/main idea sentence may be a true generalization ("Democratic presidential candidates in this century have been supported by organized labor"); an inference ("Poetry is verbal music"); or an expression of opinion ("Astrology may be considered a science"). The generalizations-inferences-opinions chosen for class study may extend through a range of maturity, experience, and grade levels; and may be designed to fit the interests of all students (from "Japanese cars are technically superior to American cars" to "Existentialism is reflected in the films of our time"). (See Devine, 1981, pp. 229–231.)

Enumeration   This pattern is the easiest for students to recognize and use themselves at first. Here the writer simply lists related items. Its topic/main idea sentence is frequently a signal calling attention to what follows: "Many kinds of cats have been domesticated." Once the writer has called attention to her plan of organization, she lists and possibly describes the kinds of cats.

Students may be introduced to this pattern through jumbled lists (on the board or on dittoed sheets). Students may be asked to rearrange the items so that "they make sense" (for example, certain school-day activities on the list fall into place under "Lunch-time Activities," others under "English Class" or "School Sports"). Students are then asked to provide a topic sentence that will account for their newly organized lists (such as "Our school day is full of different activities"). Introductory teaching activities may include: (1) small group work in which students organize prepared jumbled lists and try to find appropriate main idea sentences for them; (2) games where individuals create their own jumbled lists for other students to unscramble and to label with appropriate topic sentences; or (3) locating examples in their textbooks and recreational reading of paragraphs organized by the enumeration pattern. Older students may be challenged to investigate the reasons for enumeration used in paragraphs they find in books and articles: Why did the writer choose enumeration? Could she have used another plan? Is enumeration the most appropriate for her purposes? Why? Does simple enumeration tend to bore readers? Why? What can writers do to make it more interesting?

Comparison and Contrast　Frequently one item may be better understood if it is compared and contrasted with another. People tend to know what they know by comparing and contrasting one thing with other similar and dissimilar things. Thus one *knows* if he is short or tall by comparing himself to others, if Dickens is or is not a major novelist by comparing and contrasting him with other novelists, if a particular teacher is effective or ineffective by comparing and contrasting him with all others one has known. Writers often organize their paragraphs according to this principle.

Students may be shown that writers often point out the similarities or dissimilarities between people, ideas, or objects either (1) by telling all about first one, then the other; or (2) by going back and forth from one to the other point by point. After examining many paragraphs that use these approaches, students themselves may be asked to compare and contrast two items (The Rolling Stones and The Beach Boys; English and mathematics; love and hate; etc.). Their written examples may be studied in class to discover which of the basic approaches were used and ways in which their own paragraphs are like and unlike comparison/contrast paragraphs in books and articles.

Sequence　Sequence is like enumeration in that items are presented to the reader within the paragraph. However, in an enumeration pattern the *order* of items presented is not a primary concern of the writer. (In discussing domesticated cats, for example, she does not necessarily need to mention one particular kind before or after the next.) In the sequence pattern the writer is guided by some predetermined order: items occur in order of importance or magnitude, in a temporal order, in dramatic order, and so on. The actual order chosen by the writer influences the intended meaning (the reader's text-in-the-head!).

One way to introduce students to the sequence pattern is to have them prepare how-to-do-it papers. They can explain how to change an automobile tire, how to make pizza, how to complete a laboratory task, or how to put on a coat. In order to write such a paper themselves, students need to identify each separate step and then arrange these in time order. After they have had some experiences reading (and perhaps checking out) one another's directions, they can be encouraged to locate good and poor examples of how-to-do-it paragraphs in articles, books, and especially manuals accompanying home or shop products. From this introduction, students may move into examinations of sequencing found in history textbooks and in narrative fiction. Once they can identify the separate steps or items in the sequence, they may be shown how writers—especially in narratives—often arrange sequences in order to achieve some climax or dramatic effect.

Reader recognition of sequence patterns is contingent to a large degree upon how well readers can *use* sequencing themselves as writers. Teachers need, therefore, to build into reading lessons many opportunities for students to write out procedures (how-to-do-it papers), stories, historical events, anecdotes, and even jokes. Writing according to the pattern helps students when they encounter it in textbooks and out-of-class reading.

Cause and Effect   Cause and effect (and effect–cause) are similar to both the enumeration and sequence patterns in that items are presented to the reader within the paragraph. Here, however, items are given as causes or effects of other items. One item is subordinated to another in a relationship, implying that it is dependent somehow.

Students may be introduced to the pattern through a writing lesson or class discussion. Events are suggested (school happenings, incidents in the community or neighborhood, historical events) and students are asked to list possible reasons to explain them. With younger students the events selected ought to be explainable in simple terms: the school dance was canceled because of rain or the failure to sell enough tickets; with older students, the subtleties of cause and effect may be examined by asking such questions as: How can we be sure D really caused E? Are A, B, and C causes of D just because they come before it? Are they all equally important causes? Because one thing precedes another in time, does that make it a cause? Students—at all levels—need more class discussion of cause–effect patterns than of the other five. They need to be helped to think through alternatives and the merits of options with teacher guidance so that they will not assume the pattern is always cut and dried. Again, much student writing gives them insights into what writers do when they use the pattern and enables them to recognize it more readily when they see it in their textbooks.

Question and Answer   A common pattern used by writers appears simpler than it is. The writer asks a question and then answers it himself. Students sometimes think that the central point of the paragraph lies in the answer—or the question. Actually, both parts are needed by readers. One without the other is never enough.

To give students practice with this pattern, have them incorporate it into a how-to-do-it paper of their own. After they have written (using a sequence pattern) the steps needed to make a pizza or change a tire, suggest that they put themselves in their readers' position and ask for additional help ("But why do I have to do this before that? What might happen if I forget step #3? Why can't I save time by doing step #5 earlier?"). The questions and the writer's answers can be added to the papers, giving students help in both reading and writing simple question-and-answer pattern paragraphs.

Teach Signal Words

Just as writers indicate connections and relationships within individual sentences by using certain signal words (see preceding section), they indicate them within paragraphs by using appropriate transitional devices. Each of the patterns described here has peculiar to it certain devices or signals: when a writer uses a sequence pattern, she tends to signal readers with words such as *first, next, finally;* when she uses a comparison–contrast pattern, she signals readers with expressions such as *on the other hand, yet, in contrast,* and *in comparison.*

Students need to learn the common transitional devices or signal words. Such instruction may be provided in composition lessons or in reading classes but is surely more effective if given in both.

Here are some of the most common:

for GENERALIZATION
  for example
  for instance
  in other words
  as an illustration
  thus
  another example
  in addition
  also

for ENUMERATION
  to begin with
  then
  first, second, third
  next
  finally
  also
  more
  another
  furthermore
  in addition
  at last

for COMPARISON and CONTRAST
  however
  but

nevertheless
unless
similarly
on the one hand
on the other hand
on the contrary
in contrast
although
yet
even though

for SEQUENCE
first, second, third
next
meanwhile
on (date)
not long after
as
meanwhile
today, tomorrow
soon
finally
at last
now
before, after, while
then
later

for CAUSE and EFFECT
as a result
because
this led to
nevertheless
if . . . then
in order that
unless
since
so that
thus
therefore
accordingly
so
consequently

for QUESTION and ANSWER
   who
   what
   why
   which
   where
   when
   how
   in what way(s)

What are the best ways to teach signal words for paragraphs? Some teachers duplicate lists like the one above and ask students to keep them in notebooks to add other words they meet in their reading. Some teachers simply start a list and have students add to it as they read. Many teachers place the most important signal words on the board or on wall charts and refer to them regularly during reading and writing lessons. Many teachers who have tried various approaches to instruction agree that teaching signal words and phrases in *both* reading and writing lessons is effective: students begin to see why writers use them and why they are valuable to readers.

Teach Basic Patterns in Both Reading and Writing

Most reading teachers teach students to recognize the basic organizational patterns used by writers to structure paragraphs. Most composition teachers provide instruction in the same patterns in writing lessons. Students often fail to see the connection between their reading and writing lessons. For example, a reading teacher may teach students to recognize main idea sentences and supporting examples and details; a composition teacher may teach the same students how to develop a paragraph by supporting a topic sentence with appropriate examples and details; yet, in students' minds and—most important—in their behaviors, the two sets of lessons go unrelated. Actually the mental processes underlying the reading and writing lessons are the same, but the classroom activities have been compartmentalized (and departmentalized!).

To help students recognize and make better use of patterns of paragraph organization, teachers need to teach the patterns in writing as well as reading lessons. Thus increased awareness of the sequence pattern may best be taught by having students write out themselves how-to-do-it papers or simple lab reports; to have them understand the structure of a comparison and contrast paragraph, have them write out paragraphs on "Toyotas vs. Ford Tempos" or "Life in Colonial America Compared to Life in an American City Today." The student who has developed a cause and effect paragraph or a generalization pattern himself is in a better position to comprehend such patterns when he meets one in his content area textbook.

Help Students Identify
Main Idea Sentences

No matter which pattern a writer chooses as the underlying structure around which his data are organized, he *probably* has one sentence in the paragraph that (1) suggests the chosen pattern, and (2) sums up the main idea of the paragraph. In composition and rhetoric classes this single sentence is called the *topic sentence;* in reading classes, the *main idea sentence.* Thus "Despite their apparent differences A and B have much in common" and "The reasons for the president's decision are clear" suggest to readers that the writer will most likely follow, in the first instance, a comparison and contrast pattern and, in the second, a cause and effect pattern. A main idea sentence such as "Sally is selfish" suggests that the statement will be supported by examples and details to confirm the writer's viewpoint. In each case the sentences also serve to sum up the writer's purpose and central idea.

Some problems with main idea sentences and the instructional material designed to teach them follow.

They Sometimes Do Not Exist   One would like to say "Nowhere is it written that every paragraph *must* have a main idea sentence." Unfortunately, it is written—in too many school textbooks and student instructional guides. Actually, many writers do assemble sentences together in acceptable, effective paragraphs without main idea sentences (see Braddock, 1974). Sometimes the rhetorical strategy employed by the writer calls for several indented sentence groups (*stadia of discourse,* in Rodgers's phrase, 1966), none of which needs a separate topic or main idea sentence. Sometimes writers are careless or incompetent and produce sloppy, ineffective texts. (See Chapter 1; also Anderson, Armbruster, and Kanter, 1980; and Estes, 1982.) In narrative (and, especially, narrative fiction) main idea sentences are not necessary.

They Are Not Always First   In the Christensen model discussed earlier the sentence "whose assertion is supported or whose meaning is explicated or whose parts are detailed by the sentences added to it"—in other words, the main idea sentence—is "nearly always" first (1965). However, Becker's tagmemic model (also cited above) allows for two slot arrangements, one in which the topic sentence is first (the TRI pattern) and one in which it is last (the IRT pattern). In the first, the writer makes his statement, defines or restricts it, and then gives illustrations or examples; in the second, he works backwards: gives his examples, restricts the idea to come, and finally provides his main idea.

Rodgers, it will be remembered, demonstrated that often a main idea sentence may be found in preceding or later paragraphs (1966). Most reading specialists have regularly noted that students be taught to look for main idea sentences not only at the beginnings of paragraphs but in their middles, at their ends, and at both their beginnings and ends (Burmeister, 1978; Singer and Donlan, 1980; Santeusanio, 1983).

They Are Sometimes Implied   Often writers do not explicitly state their main ideas. They assume that their readers will infer—from the data given and the organizational pattern chosen—what a paragraph's main idea is. Just as often, sophisticated readers can indeed do this. If, in the paragraph immediately preceding this one, the highlighted sentence *They are not always first* were deleted, most teachers would be able to insert it (or one very much like it). The information given, plus the pattern (from the theory of Christensen to that of Becker to that of Rodgers to what reading specialists say), give readers, especially those who already know something about the topic, clues to guess the main idea.

Unfortunately many students lack the reading experience and the necessary prior knowledge. They cannot easily infer main idea sentences and need instructional assistance.

How may teachers help students recognize main idea sentences? Several strategies are suggested here.

1. *Call attention to typographical aids in the book.* Frequently authors, editors, and book designers work together to help students by highlighting main ideas. They do this by using italics, upper-case letters, shading, underscoring, or colors. Sometimes students read paragraphs and pages unaware that they have been given help by the book itself. Teachers need to remind students of the value of such aids and regularly call them to their attention.

2. *Distinguish between topics and main ideas.* The *topic* is what the paragraph is about; the *main idea* is the position or point of view the writer expresses about some aspect of the topic. To help students make this important distinction, provide lists of topics (the school bus, our auditorium, television commercials) and have *them* make up sentences expressing one idea about the topics ("The school bus is always late," "Our school auditorium has excellent acoustics," "Television commercials are often more entertaining than the actual programs"). Later, have them tell what the topics of textbook paragraphs are before locating the actual main idea sentences. In writing lessons, have students suggest topics, then narrow these down to workable paragraph possibilities before creating a topic (main idea) sentence to develop. Thus students may suggest *rock music* as a topic, restrict that to *Like all music and art it reflects its time,* and finally choose a specific topic sentence for development such as *The lyrics of the Beatles' songs expressed the mood of the sixties.*

3. *Have students express main ideas in complete sentences.* Too often exercises to teach recognition of main ideas present students with multiple-choice

items: ''This story is about (a) rock music, (b) the Beatles, (c) music reflecting its time, or (d) Beatles' lyrics expressing the mood of the sixties.'' Such expediencies may serve test makers but are not necessarily effective for teaching. A main idea sentence is just that: a *sentence.* As they search for them in paragraphs, students need to be reminded to look specifically for sentences that they can *say* (with appropriate vocal inflections) or *write* (with a beginning capital letter and a final punctuation mark).

4. *Start with simple practice exercises.* For intermediate grade and middle school students who have problems identifying main idea sentences, some teachers go through the content area textbook in advance and prepare simple exercise sheets, which include for every paragraph: (1) a sentence that has nothing to do with the paragraph's topic, (2) one on a minor detail, (3) one that presents an important detail or example, and (4) the actual main idea expressed in different language. After students become practiced in selecting the correct answers, develop similar exercise sheets, which include (1) a sentence that expresses a minor detail, (2) one that presents an important example or detail, (3) one that expresses only part of the main idea, and (4) the main idea sentence paraphrased.

5. *Try "What Did the Author Say?"* Have students read four or five selected consecutive paragraphs in a content area textbook, then answer the question, in writing, ''What did the author say in each?'' Divide the class into groups to choose the best responses (four or five one- to two-sentence summaries). The selected sentences are duplicated for the next class meeting. At that time, students are also given a scoring scale to help them rate the selected papers:

5 points	if each summary sentence captures the essence of what the reviewer thinks the author was trying to say
4	if four of the summary statements ''hit the nail on the head''
3	if at least three are accurate in the opinion of the reviewer
2	if two are more-or-less accurate
1	if at least one is acceptable
0	if none seems to get the author's main ideas

Such an activity may be varied in many ways for different class levels. Shrauger (1975) suggests a highly sophisticated version for community college students. Many middle school teachers use a simpler version with the scoring scale placed on the chalkboard and children assigning a number score to each paper they listen to in class. The effectiveness of the approach seems to lie in its cooperative aspect: all students are involved in evaluating the quality of the individual summary sentences. (For more information, see Shrauger, 1975, or Santeusanio, 1983, pp. 89–90.)

6. *Try telegram writing.* Have students write one-sentence telegrams, which provide in as few words as possible a paragraph's main idea. Some middle

school teachers make a game of this activity by having children (1) read a specific paragraph from their textbook, (2) write its main idea in one short sentence, and (3) select together the "telegram" that says the most in fewest words. Variations of this activity include *headline writing* (in which children write headlines of paragraphs for newspapers) and *caption writing* (in which they prepare captions for particularly dramatic pictures or photographs).

7. *Encourage summary-sentence writing.* Have students—at all levels—tell in their own words what they think a paragraph says. In writing activities, have them write single-sentence summary statements that capture the main ideas of paragraphs in their texts. Some teachers explain how writers and editors of digest magazines need to eliminate examples and details to present only a paragraph's central thought. Students then write *Reader's Digest*-like condensations of sections of school textbooks or of articles related to their course work.

8. *Use main-idea study guides.* Many teachers in middle school and high school develop study guides specifically designed to help students find main ideas. They go through the assignment in advance and note main idea sentences if present. Then they duplicate a guide for the assignment, which leads students step by step through its paragraphs, calling attention to well-defined main idea sentences, noting paragraphs that contain poorly defined ones, and asking students to write out what they think are the key sentences in other paragraphs. Such guides may also call attention to patterns of organization and signal words used by authors.

Idea Box

One middle school social studies teacher explains to children that main idea sentences may come in different places in a paragraph: sometimes first; sometimes at the end; sometimes in the middle; and sometimes the main idea sentence is suggested, or implied, and not part of the paragraph. He calls attention to examples of each in the reading assignment and then has students label each paragraph in one section of a chapter according to where the main idea sentence is located: T (for Top), E (for End), M (for Middle), or I (for Implied). After reading the assignment, the boys and girls discuss the author's reasons for placing the main idea sentences where they were placed. (The teacher notes that this exercise in Main Idea Placement is valuable, because it makes people look for main idea sentences—but from a new angle.)

Because signal words are so important in revealing organizational patterns, one teacher has children focus just on Signals for several lessons. He explains the simple transitional elements in sequence patterns (*first, second, next,* etc.). Then he sends boys and girls on a Signals Search to find others used in sequence patterns in their content area books. He next moves on to the other commonly used patterns, encouraging the Signals Search. All "findings" are carefully lettered onto a large wall chart, which boasts the title "The World's Most Complete List of Signal Words."

To help students better understand main ideas in written language, one fifth-grade teacher cuts out news stories from the local paper, cuts off the headlines, glues the stories to cardboard, and laminates them. She then gives individuals the stories (minus headlines) and instructs them to write headlines for them. Afterward, the children share their stories and headlines. She then distributes the "correct" headlines and students compare their work with that of the professional headline writers.

To help seventh-graders realize that stories too have patterns, their teacher draws a large chart on the chalkboard:

He explains that a story would not be fun unless the Character had some Goal to achieve. He then adds to the chart:

Next, he explains that if an author simply told how the Character reached the Goal, the story might not hold the reader's interest. Characters, he explains, usually encounter Obstacles on their way to their Goal:

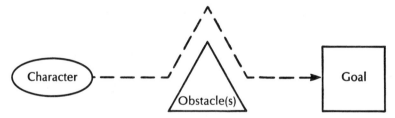

The teacher then reviews several stories the group has read together, pointing out in each the Character, Goal, and Obstacle(s). For their next assignment, students are to read in order to complete a chart showing these three basic ingredients to a story's plan.

As part of a literature lesson, that same teacher uses the Character-Obstacle-Goal Chart to explain that (1) the tension that causes readers to read to a resolution is created as the Character tries to surmount the Obstacle; (2) it is this tension that makes readers turn pages and want to read stories; (3) the apex of the Obstacle triangle is the *high point* or *climax* of the story; and (4) the left side of the triangle may be considered the *rising action* of the plot and the right side, its *falling action*.

Many teachers begin outlining by printing simple outlines of reading assignments on cardboard and laminating them. They try to include at least two main headings with four or five supporting details for each. They then cut these into strips so that they have approximately ten separate strips. These are then given to individuals, jumbled out of order. Children read the assignment and then arrange the strips so that they have an outline of the assignment on their desktops.

Another activity for teaching either outlining or the generalization pattern is to have children work in groups to read assignments in content area textbooks, decide main idea and supporting example sentences for each paragraph, and choose ways of "dramatizing" this information. One fifth-grade group put their sentences on large poster boards and marched across the room in appropriate sequence; another color-coded their outline, with red for main ideas and blue for example sentences.

COMPREHENDING EXTENDED DISCOURSE: PROBLEMS AND SOLUTIONS

Paragraphs rarely appear in isolation: they come to the reader packaged in articles, selections, essays, book chapters, chapter sections,—and in story form. Teachers need to help their students comprehend not only sentences and paragraphs but all forms of *longer discourse* as well. Approaches to longer discourse comprehension improvement are given here.

Teach the Data Pattern

Writers most frequently present their readers with several main ideas in several paragraphs, each related but independent. When they do, they use what some refer to as the *informational pattern* (Sack and Yourman, 1981); others use the *data pattern* (Santeusanio, 1983). They may focus on one major topic for a piece of extended discourse but divide it into parts. Their readers must not only identify the major topic and main ideas related to it but synthesize these, moving from paragraph main ideas to the main idea or ideas of the longer piece. Teachers may explain this to students by comparing a chapter or article to a school or hospital: just as schools or hospitals have separate parts (principal's office, gym, health room, auditorium / admitting office, laboratories, out-patient clinics, operation rooms) so do chapters and articles. When an author writes about a topic (schools), he divides it into its parts (office, gym, classrooms, etc.). Each part he writes about has its own main idea, but each is related to the topic in some way.

One way to introduce the data pattern is to present students with a well-organized article or chapter, calling attention to each subdivision and its main idea and relating these to the topic and main idea of the entire piece. Note the typographical aids included in the book or magazine; point out places where two or three adjoining paragraphs actually constitute a single subdivision; indicate clearly defined signals (*next, in contrast, before*) used by the writer to inform readers of divisions within the piece. Students should also examine poorly organized sections and be shown problems writers present to their readers (fuzzy transitions, lack of signal words, poorly phrased main idea sentences). When students know what to look for, explain the values of *pre-viewing* (or *surveying*) material before they read it. Have them look quickly through a piece of longer discourse and tell (1) what they think the general topic and main idea of the piece is, and (2) what the subdivisions and separate paragraph main ideas may be. Then have them read to discover how well they predicted or guessed. In teaching the data pattern, study guides (which direct student attention to the points the teacher believes important) and guided reading lessons (which allow the teacher to take students sequentially through a selection) are effective.

Make Students Aware
of Underlying Patterns

The six patterns underlying individual paragraphs (see previous section) frequently serve as foundations for longer pieces of discourse. Thus a writer may structure an entire article or chapter around the cause and effect or comparison and contrast pattern; or—as frequently happens—a writer may organize the first subdivisions of a piece according to one pattern and then use others for subsequent paragraphs. Longer pieces of discourse may have several patterns used as organizing devices.

To make students aware of patterns, first review the six common patterns: generalization, enumeration, cause and effect, comparison and contrast, sequence, and question–answer; then point out their use in a carefully selected chapter. Have students read a chapter or article that uses several patterns, asking such questions as: Why did the writer change patterns here? Why is the pattern more appropriate to his subject here rather than there? Is there one single pattern that seems to underlie the whole piece? What is it? Why do you think it was chosen?

Call Attention to Paragraph Functions

When students are able to follow the general plan of a longer piece of discourse (recognize, for example, the way it is divided, the contributions the subdivisions make to the whole, the underlying pattern or patterns), teachers need to help them recognize the *functions* of individual paragraphs. Robinson (1978) notes seven:

Introductory Paragraphs   Usually writers indicate their topic(s) and point of view in a well-defined introductory paragraph. Sometimes they spell out their purposes and set limits on the discussion to follow. In reports and scientific papers, authors will not only say "The purpose of this paper is _____" but will define its scope as well: "It will do the following but not attempt _____." Sometimes writers begin with appropriate anecdotes; sometimes with reviews of previous research. Good writers often provide background to help readers relate the new information to what is known. Teachers can help students become aware of introductory paragraph functions by asking: What is the purpose of this first paragraph? Why did the author begin that way? Can you guess her purpose or plan from the first paragraph? Is it an effective introduction? Why? How might you write it?

Explanatory Paragraphs   These inform, tell about, explain, or provide evidence to support the writer's main idea. They are usually organized by the generalization pattern with a main idea sentence (an inference, statement of opinion, or generalization). Usually they are clearly marked by words and phrases that signal their purpose and relate them to the rest of the discourse. Ask students: What purpose does this paragraph serve? Could it be deleted? Why, or why not? What signal words tell you that it is explanatory?

Narrative Paragraphs   Although narrative paragraphs are most often found in stories, writers sometimes include them in expository discourse—to relate historical events in sequence, to capture reader interest, or to provide explanatory material in anecdotal form. Narrative uses the signal words and phrases found in other types of sequence: *first, next, yesterday, later, soon.* Teachers can help students recognize them and their functions by asking such questions as: What signal words told you this was a story or narrative? Why is the writer inserting a narrative paragraph? What is the purpose of narrative usually? How might you provide this information in some other form?

Descriptive Paragraphs Descriptions of events, persons, or activities—most frequently found in narrative fiction—may be used by writers of expository prose to provide additional information, to give background for an explanation, or to entertain. Writers tend to use special patterns of organization for them: data are presented from one point of view, from left to right, from foreground to background, from unimportant to important, and so on. Students may be helped to understand narrative paragraphs if they can see the writer's pattern, note her signal words (*here, next, behind*), and think about why she uses description in the larger piece. Ask: What plan underlies the paragraph? Why is she asking readers to go from left to right? front to back? What are her signal words? Why is she using description here?

Definitional Paragraphs In a longer piece of discourse, writers sometimes need to define an important term or concept. They may do this by offering a dictionary-type definition, using a system of characteristic and defining features or one of class, example, and property relations (see Chapter 4). They may also give a *stipulative* definition: "By _____, I mean _____." Students may be made aware of definitional paragraphs by asking such questions as: Why does the author stop to tell us that? Could you have continued reading if you did not understand the term? Why? Why not? Does the explanation offered help you to understand the term or concept? In what ways might it be better defined?

Transitional Paragraphs Sometimes a writer needs to let readers know that she is moving in a new direction—into, for example, a subdivision of the main piece or an anecdote. Rather than shift abruptly, she may use a separate paragraph:

> We have examined those parts of the school that serve to educate young minds. Now let us look at those that make life more interesting for many children—the music room, the media center, the library, and the gym.

Or,

> The characteristics of dogs in the wild have been discussed at length. Now we should look at one particular dog, one which came to my attention several years ago.

When such paragraphs appear in articles and chapters, teachers need to call them to students' attention and explain their purposes.

Concluding Paragraphs   A successful article, book, essay, or story provides for the reader a sense of closure. Concluding paragraphs, when well done, give readers a feeling that the writer has achieved his purpose and that they have completed an experience. Usually writers signal their conclusions with expressions such as *finally, in conclusion, the final point,* or *in summary;* sometimes they imply the ending by skillfully pulling together the strands and subdivisions of the piece logically or dramatically. Students need less assistance in understanding the purposes of concluding paragraphs, but teachers may ask: Did this ending ''work'' for you? How would you change the last paragraph? Are there still loose ends hanging? How would you tie them together? Did the writer purposefully leave loose ends? Why?

Teaching students to recognize the various functions of paragraphs in longer discourse will not in itself make them better comprehenders of chapters or articles. It will make them more sensitive to writers' plans and help them realize that, when writers develop a long piece of prose, they usually have an organizing principle or basic design. Students will—at least—begin to look for beginnings, middles, and ends.

Review Outlining Techniques

Many writers follow an outline as they write. Some prepare detailed written ones in advance; others write according to skeletal ones in their heads. Their outlines—written out or in their heads—are their plans of organization and serve to structure their texts. When readers can perceive writers' plans, they are in a better position to comprehend pieces of longer discourse.

One way to help students see a writer's plan is to review (or teach) basic outlining techniques. Many teachers go through a carefully selected article or textbook chapter with their classes, noting main and subordinate points and the transitional devices that signal relationships among them. Then they put an actual outline on the chalkboard: Roman numerals represent the main sections that make up the piece; upper-case letters, the main ideas; Arabic numbers, the supporting examples and details; and so on. Some write the signal words on the board encircled or in colored chalk. Many teachers find this an effective approach to teaching the data pattern (discussed above) and a good introduction to the organization of pieces of longer discourse. As they build outlines with the class, they may ask such questions as: How does the author tell us this is a main, not a subordinate, point? What tells us this is a main idea? Are individual paragraphs organized according to the patterns we have studied? Do you see a sequence pattern? a generalization pattern? What signal words does the author use? Can you see a data pattern underlying this piece? How does it fit together?

What is the introductory paragraph? Where are the descriptive ones? the narrative ones? Why did the author use them in these places? Do you find transitional paragraphs? In what ways might the author have organized this piece differently? more effectively?

After several board lessons of this nature, students can begin to prepare their own outlines of articles and textbook chapters. Some teachers duplicate incomplete outlines, in which some key and subordinate points are printed and others omitted; then have students complete these as they read assignments. Others provide an outline form that resembles the one used by the author; then have their students fill in all main and supporting points. With continued practice most middle and secondary school students are able to begin outlining their own assignments. (If they cannot, those reading assignments may be inappropriate for them!)

To help students better understand how writers get their texts-in-the-head onto paper (and the pitfalls inherent in the process), students need practice in writing from their own outlines. They can (1) outline one section of a textbook chapter and then—with books closed—write their own versions of the book's material; (2) outline a teacher's oral presentation and write it as a possible article or book chapter; or (3) outline information and ideas they already have on a topic and use their own outlines to write short papers. To become better comprehenders, students need insights into the ways writers organize texts. Outlining provides one viable approach to perceiving the structures of longer discourse.

Teach Previewing Techniques

Another approach to the perception of organizational patterns underlying longer discourse is through the use of the previewing strategies discussed in Chapter 6. SQ3R, for example, requires students to make a quick survey of the assignment prior to reading in order to formulate their own purpose-for-reading questions. This survey can also give them a sense of how the writer has organized the text, of where the introduction ends and the main part starts, of what the subordinate sections may be, and where the conclusions, summary statements, and final sections are located.

To make students aware of a writer's organizational plan, many teachers use an approach similar to the following:

What's the Author's Plan?

1. *Preview the assignment.* Take five minutes (now! here in class) and look through the reading material to discover what the author's purpose and general plan might be. Does he spell out his purpose any-

where? Does he give you some idea of the plan of organization? Look carefully to find typographical clues: Does he use boldface? italics? caps or colors? Is the text broken up by lines? white space? Are there clearly defined kinds of paragraphs? introductory? definitional? transitional? Where? Are there signal words or phrases to guide you? What are they? Does the text follow a clear-cut organizational plan? generalization? cause and effect? sequence? question/answer?

2. *Make a rough outline.* In your notebooks, sketch in a rough outline: What are the main sections? the subordinate sections? Where are the chief subdivisions? What words or phrases signal these to you? Can you see breakdowns within paragraphs? within sections? What are they? How are they indicated?

3. *Read to discover how accurate your outline seems to be.* Did you discover the main divisions and subdivisions? Where did you go astray? Why? Does the author seem to have a good plan? What seems to be wrong with it? Why does it work well for you as a reader? What might the author have done to better organize the text? If you were to rewrite this material, what changes would you make?

Show Students That Stories Have Structures

Most selections in basal readers tend to be narrative fiction; much of the material students read later in life will probably be in some narrative form. Readers need to realize that stories, like articles and book chapters, have patterns of organization too. They should see that anecdotes, short stories, novels and plays, as well as television and film scripts, are based on an author's plan, usually some variant of the sequence pattern.

Attention to such patterns has been given new prominence in recent years by research in *story grammar*—defined by Tierney and Mosenthal as "internalized story structures" (1980). Investigators have been studying the "rules" that seem to govern narration, rules which they find in many ways resemble the rules of a phrase grammar (see Prince, 1973; and Rumelhart, 1975). They note that (1) stories have internal structures that may be depicted as hierarchical networks of units of information serving different functions in stories; (2) logical relations exist among these units; and (3) the hierarchical structures correspond to ways readers comprehend and store information found in stories (Stein and Glenn, 1978). One particular story grammar (that of Stein and Glenn) includes three major elements—story, setting, and episode—and five elements within the episodic structure:

1. the initiating event (a change in the environment which prompts a character to respond)

2. an internal response (a character's internal reaction, including goals, effective states, and cognitions)
3. attempts (behaviors motivated by the internal response)
4. consequence (the attainment or nonattainment of the goal, the results of behaviors)
5. a reaction (character's response to the consequence, usually describing feelings and thoughts)

Students do not need to study story grammars, but they do need an awareness of characters, of their goals, of their actions and the consequences of these actions, and of the influence of time and place upon characters and their actions. Just as they are in a better position to comprehend expository prose when they see its pattern of organization, so students may better comprehend a story when they see its underlying structure.

How can teachers develop this sense of structure? Nine suggestions are made here.

Have Students Look for Clues to Time   Often authors tell more or less exactly when a story occurs; many times—particularly in more sophisticated stories—they only hint. As students begin a story in class, encourage them to find words and phrases that signal time. These may be explicit ("Fifteen-year-old Jerry knew that his parents met Mack the year before he was born") or hidden ("They flew into Mexico City in one of the new jets"). Often students need to locate several clues before they can be sure of the approximate time of the narration. Much of this initial learning needs to be done with teacher guidance, with teachers reading aloud the beginnings of stories noting clues with students.

Have Students Find Clues to Place   Again, authors are sometimes explicit as to the story's place, sometimes deliberately obscure. Teachers need, again, to begin stories aloud in class, pointing to specific clues ("Only three cars were in the garage that morning" or "The smog, lack of oxygen, and new smells, combined with the rapidly spoken Spanish all around her, made Isabelle more excited than ever"). Students need to think through their answers to such questions as: What kind of home would have a three-car-plus garage? What kind of a neighborhood must this be? What do you suppose the actual house looks like? What about the grounds and landscaping? What other clues tell you that this is a well-to-do neighborhood?

Have Them Single Out the Main Character(s)   After students read into a story, stop them to discuss the characters. List these on the chalkboard and encourage students to identify those who seem most important. For longer stories, keep with the students a list of characters, main and minor, noting physical and personality characteristics of each.

Help Them See How Authors Reveal Character Traits Authors sometimes say directly, "Bob was tired today." Usually, they reveal a trait or characteristic through the character's actions or speeches. As students read a story together, have them guess traits ("What kind of a person is Mark?") and then tell why they made the guess ("Why do you say he is selfish?"). Lead them to see that usually readers make guesses, based either on the ways characters behave or on their language.

Encourage Students to Specify a Character's Goals Once main characters are identified, ask students to tell what they think are their goals in the story: "What do you think Mark wants most at this time? What motivates him? What are his ambitions?" Lead students to see that characters' goals influence their actions and the ways the story moves ahead.

Encourage Them to Spot Obstacles in the Way of Those Goals Once students note the goals of main characters in the story, have them list the obstacles encountered by the characters as they strive toward those goals. Some teachers make a board chart and, as students read, list and number the obstacles, noting that they serve to maintain suspense and cause readers to continue reading: "Steve wants to graduate from music school but several things get in his way. What first gets in his way? What obstacle does he meet next? What is his greatest obstacle?"

Call Attention to the Chief Parts of a Plot Most stories have an introduction in which the authors provide clues to time and place. Next, they have a series of incidents that show the main character circumventing obstacles to reach his goal. After the goal is reached, they often have another series of incidents leading to some conclusion. Many teachers teach students that stories have (1) an introduction, (2) rising action, (3) a high point, (4) falling action, and (5) a conclusion. Many stories do not conform to this plan; but as students test it out on the stories they read, their awareness to plot structure is sharpened.

Encourage Students to Make Time Lines Most stories are sequenced: one thing happens before the next, in some chronological or dramatic order. One way to help students see structure is to have them make simple time lines on which they mark important events of the story. As they create such charts, they can also indicate considerations like rising and falling actions and the story's high point.

Have Students Answer Key Questions about the Story Often well-phrased questions help direct student attention to the "grammar" of a story. Marshall (1984, p. 85) suggests these:

Setting: Where (or when) did the story happen?
               How would the story change if the setting changed?

Character: What is _____ like?
               What does _____ do and say that makes him/her like _____?
               Why did _____ do _____?

Topic: What is the moral of the story?
               What is the author's opinion about _____?

Conflict: What is the problem _____ faces?
               How might _____ solve this problem?

Reaction I: How does _____ feel about the problem?
               What does _____ think about the problem?

Attempts: What does _____ do first, second, etc.?
               Why does _____ fail to solve the problem?
               What might _____ do next?

Resolution: What did _____ do to solve the problem?
               How was the problem solved?
               Who solved _____'s problem?

Reaction II: How does _____ feel about the solution?
               How do you feel about the solution?
               How would you solve the problem?

COMPREHENDING TEXTUAL MATERIALS: THREE OTHER CONSIDERATIONS

Strategies for comprehending sentences, paragraphs, and pieces of longer discourse are available to students. Several have been suggested here, and others may be found in the professional literature. However, at least three other matters related to reading materials need to be considered by teachers.

External Organization of Texts   Writers, as noted, tend to organize their ideas and information according to some pattern or plan. Their texts thus have an *internal* structure, shaped by the nature of their message, its purpose, its potential readers, and the information and ideas it contains. Another structure, an *external* form of organization, is imposed as it is typed or otherwise readied for publication. Typists, processors, editors, and book or journal designers have to arrange the material to conform to standards and constraints set by the publishing situation—whether these come from large-scale commercial magazine or book publishing or from the duplication of a classroom magazine by ditto masters. In the process of publishing, editors and designers may rearrange and subdivide material, add headings, highlighting, colors, white space, or illustrations. While the basic internal organization remains the same, its appearance may be altered. Usually, when skillfully done, such alterations enhance the readability of the writer's text, but changes may shift emphasis or downplay points the writer considered important.

Type, Illustrations, and Physical Appearance   Related to external organization are matters of type facings, illustrations, and the ways the text appears on the printed page. Research findings in these areas are not clear-cut. Schallert (1980), for example, finds no evidence that illustrations help or hinder comprehension. Researchers, she notes, have come up with "seemingly contradictory conclusions" (p. 503). Most teachers, however, are sensitive to the roles played by good, clear type, white space, and pictures. Such "physical" considerations, they sense, need to be examined as they select reading material for classes. Students certainly consider them when they choose books of their own for recreational reading.

Density   How much information and how many ideas a writer packs into a page clearly affects how easily readers comprehend it. When writers assume readers have necessary prior knowledge they do not have, texts become difficult to comprehend. Too often authors of secondary school content area textbooks squeeze into each printed page a maximum of new data, frequently more than their readers can process. Teachers—at all levels—need to be sensitive to the density problem in school reading materials. Too many new ideas, without the support of illustrative examples and background information, force students to read at their frustrational level in comprehension.

What can teachers do about these matters? They can check and double-check all reading material selected for their classes, not only basal readers and content area textbooks but all supplementary materials, asking themselves such questions as: Does the external organization make sense? Does it appear to coincide with the author's internal organization as I see it? Does the type conform to the expectations of my students? Is it too large? too small? Are the illustrations appropriate? too childish? too adult? Do pictures and graphs obfuscate or clarify? Are there too many new ideas per page? Does the author assume my students know things they have yet to learn?

▪ RECAPPING MAIN POINTS ▪

Readers are more apt to understand a writer's printed text when they have knowledge of the ways texts are organized.

Individual sentences, for example, are organized in systematic ways which most students know. They have problems when they fail to note punctuation or important signal words or when faced with anaphoric elements, ellipses, or unfamiliar complex sentence patterns. Fortunately a variety of sentence-comprehension strategies are available to teachers.

Paragraphs and pieces of longer discourse tend also to be organized according to certain basic plans. Problems in comprehending paragraphs and longer discourse may be lessened for students as they learn widely used organizational patterns. Again, many strategies for comprehending paragraphs and longer pieces are available.

Teachers, trying to improve comprehension by increasing students' knowledge of text organization, also need to be concerned with related matters such as the external structure imposed upon a text by editors and book designers, the type, illustrations, and physical appearance, and the density of information in a text.

END-OF-CHAPTER ACTIVITIES

1. Six stumbling blocks to sentence comprehension are cited here. Give an example of each from your own reading. Can you find other obstacles to sentence comprehension? What are they?

2. Several patterns of paragraph organization are described in this chapter. Select four that are commonly found in textbooks and locate examples of each in your own textbooks. Can you find paragraphs in magazines that follow these patterns? What are they?

3. Many teachers through the years have perhaps overemphasized the teaching of main idea sentences. Much instructional material may have placed too great an emphasis on "Finding the Main Idea." Why? Tell why teachers tend to send students searching for main idea sentences in paragraphs and why this may be futile.

4. A distinction is implied in this chapter between *main idea sentences* and *topic sentences*. What is the difference?

5. Several suggestions are made for teaching students to recognize main idea sentences. Create another approach for a specific grade level.

6. Six types of paragraph functions are described here. Find one example of each in a basal reader or content area textbook.

7. Just how much does awareness of text structure affect comprehension? Read about an actual experiment conducted with third- and fifth-grade students by Lea M. McGee, "Awareness of Text Structure: Effects on Children's Recall of Expository Text" (1982), and write a one-page summary of her findings.

8. Outlining has been recommended as a strategy for better understanding pieces of longer discourse. Test out this recommendation by outlining a chapter in one of your own textbooks. Does it help? hinder? In what ways? Is it worth the effort? Why? Why not?

9. In your own words, explain *story grammar*.

10. Do a reader's expectations shape his or her comprehension of a story? Check out another experiment done by Jill Fitzgerald Whaley (1981) and summarize her findings in a short paper.
11. Select a story from a basal reader or literature anthology and spell out its "grammar." Who is the protagonist? What is his/her motivation or goal? What is the *initiating event?* the time? place? What are the consequences of the protagonist's action(s)? What is the *high point* of the story? its conclusions?
12. Briefly explain the values of story grammar analysis.
13. How does text affect comprehension? Using the information given in Chapter 6, write a one-page paper on the subject.
14. In what ways does this information support a *bottom-up* or *text-based* theory of the comprehension process? (See Chapter 1.) In what ways does it support an *interaction* theory?
15. Write a brief paper on the importance of textual organization to comprehension. *Direct it toward readers who have no background in professional education or psychology.* (How will your work be affected by their lack of appropriate vocabulary? previous knowledge about children? prior knowledge of recent psychological research?)

REFERENCES

Anderson, T. H., B. B. Armbruster, and R. N. Kantor. *How Clearly Written Are Children's Textbooks? Or, of Bladderworts and Alfa.* (Reading Education Report No. 15.) Champaign, Ill.: Center for the Study of Reading, 1980. (ERIC Document Reproduction Service, No. ED 192 275; 63 pp.)

Becker, A. L. "A Tagmemic Approach to Paragraph Analysis." *College Composition and Communication* 16 (October 1965): 144–165.

Braddock, Richard. "The Frequency and Placement of Topic Sentences in Expository Prose." *Research in the Teaching of English* 8 (Winter 1974): 287–304.

Burmeister, Lou E. *Reading Strategies for Middle and Secondary School Teachers,* 2nd ed. Reading, Mass.: Addison-Wesley, 1978.

Calfee, Robert C., and Robert Curley. "Structures of Prose in the Content Areas." In James Flood (Ed.), *Understanding Reading Comprehension.* Newark, Del.: International Reading Association, 1984.

Chomsky, Carol. *The Acquisition of Syntax in Children from 5 to 10.* Cambridge, Mass.: The MIT Press, 1968.

Christensen, Francis. "A Generative Rhetoric of the Sentence." *College Composition and Communication* 14 (October 1965): 155–161.

Devine, Thomas G. *Teaching Study Skills: A Guide for Teachers.* Boston: Allyn and Bacon, 1981.

Durkin, Dolores. *Teaching Them to Read,* 4th ed. Boston: Allyn and Bacon, 1983.

Estes, Thomas H. "The Nature and Structure of Text." In Allen Berger and H. Alan Robinson (Eds.), *Secondary School Reading*. Urbana, Ill.: ERIC Clearinghouse on Reading and Communications Skills, 1982.

Foster, David. *A Primer for Writing Teachers*. Upper Montclair, N. J.: Boynton/Cook Publishers, 1983.

Herber, Harold. *Teaching Reading in the Content Areas*. Englewood Cliffs, N. J.: Prentice-Hall, 1978.

Horowitz, Rosalind. "Text Patterns: Part I." *Journal of Reading* 28 (February 1985): 448–454.

Horowitz, Rosalind. "Text Patterns: Part II." *Journal of Reading* 28 (March 1985): 534–541.

Huggins, A. W. F., and Marilyn Jager Adams. "Syntactic Aspects of Reading Comprehension." In R. J. Spiro, B. C. Bruce, and W. F. Brewer (Eds.), *Theoretical Issues in Reading Comprehension*. Hillsdale, N. J.: Lawrence Erlbaum Associates, 1980.

Jaynes, Julian. *The Origin of Consciousness in the Breakdown of the Bicameral Mind*. Boston: Houghton Mifflin, 1976.

Levin, G. *Prose Models*, 4th ed. New York: Harcourt Brace Jovanovich, 1978.

Marshall, Nancy. "Discourse Analysis as a Guide for Informal Assessment of Comprehension." In James Flood (Ed.), *Promoting Reading Comprehension*. Newark, Del.: International Reading Association, 1984.

McGee, Lea M. "Awareness of Text Structure: Effects on Children's Recall of Expository Text." *Reading Research Quarterly* 17 (1982): 581–595.

Meyer, Bonnie J. F. *The Organization of Prose and Its Effect on Memory*. Amsterdam: North-Holland Publishing Company, 1975.

Meyer, Bonnie J. F. "Organizational Aspects of Text: Effects on Reading Comprehension and Applications in the Classroom." In James Flood (Ed.), *Promoting Reading Comprehension*. Newark, Del.: International Reading Association, 1984.

Meyer, Bonnie J. F., D. M. Brandt, and G. J. Bluth. "Use of Top-level Structure in Text: Key for Reading Comprehension in Ninth Grade Students." *Reading Research Quarterly* 16 (1980): 72–103.

Prince, G. *A Grammar of Stories*. The Hague: Mouton, 1973.

Robinson, H. Alan. *Teaching Reading and Study Strategies: The Content Areas*. Boston: Allyn and Bacon, 1978.

Rodgers, Paul. "A Discourse-centered Rhetoric of the Paragraph." *College Composition and Communication* 17 (February 1966): 2–11.

Rumelhart, David E. "Notes on a Schema for Stories." In D. G. Brown and A. Collins (Eds.), *Representation and Understanding: Studies in Cognitive Science*. New York: Academic Press, 1975.

Sack, Allan, and Jack Yourman. *The Sack-Yourman Developmental Speed Reading Course*. New York: College Skills Center, 1981.

Santeusanio, Richard P. *A Practical Approach to Content Area Reading*. Reading, Mass.: Addison-Wesley, 1983.

Schallert, Diane M. "The Role of Illustrations in Reading Comprehension." In R. J. Spiro, B. C. Bruce, and W. F. Brewer (Eds.), *Theoretical Issues in Reading Comprehension*. Hillsdale, N. J.: Lawrence Erlbaum Associates, 1980.

Shrauger, Virginia Moore. "What Did the Author Say? A Technique for Learning to Organize, Understand and Remember Ideas." In Roy Sugimoto (Ed.), *Pro-*

ceedings of the Eighth Annual Conference of the Western College Reading Association, Whittier, California, 1975.

Singer, Harry, and Dan Donlan. *Reading and Learning from Text.* Boston: Little, Brown, 1980.

Stein, N.L., and C. G. Glenn. "An Analysis of Story Comprehension in Elementary School Children." In R. Freedle (Ed.), *Discourse Processing: Multidisciplinary Perspectives.* Hillsdale, N. J.: Lawrence Erlbaum Associates, 1978.

Tierney, Robert J., and James Mosenthal. *Discourse Comprehension and Production: Analyzing Text Structures and Cohesion.* Champaign, Ill.: Center for the Study of Reading, 1980. (ERIC ED 179 945, January, 1980)

Webber, Bonnie Lynn. "Syntax beyond the Sentence: Anaphora." In R. J. Spiro, B. C. Bruce, and W. F. Brewer (Eds.), *Theoretical Issues in Reading Comprehension.* Hillsdale, N. J.: Lawrence Erlbaum Associates, 1980.

Whaley, Jill Fitzgerald. "Readers' Expectations for Story Structures." *Reading Research Quarterly* 17 (1981): 90–114.

From Theory to Practice:
Thinking about
and beyond the Printed Text

▪ INTRODUCTION AND OVERVIEW ▪

Readers use a variety of cognitive strategies as they try to make sense of texts. They define their own purposes for reading, sample and select information from texts, infer and predict, hypothesize, and check to see if their meanings (their texts-in-the-head) make sense.

This chapter examines three areas in which instruction can have an impact upon the ways students use cognitive strategies to improve their comprehension.

It looks at inferencing and how students may be taught to be better inference makers; then at more advanced reasoning processes such as deductive/inductive reasoning, problem solving, and critical thinking; and finally at comprehension monitoring and specific techniques readers may use to check and double-check the meanings they derive from texts.

Chapter 8 includes Suggested Study Questions, Teaching Guidelines, and then the following discussions:

- Improving Comprehension through Better Inference-Making
    What is inference-making?
    Can inferencing be improved?
    Strategies for better inferencing
- Improving Comprehension through Better Reasoning
    What is deductive reasoning?
    What is inductive reasoning?
    Teaching deductive/inductive reasoning
    Problem solving and reading comprehension
    Critical thinking and critical reading
    Improving critical reading
- Improving Comprehension through Self-monitoring

Which monitoring devices are most important?
How do readers know something is wrong?
Suggested fix-up strategies
Teaching self-monitoring strategies

Chapter 8 also includes

- Recapping Main Points
- End-of-Chapter Activities
- References

■ SUGGESTED STUDY QUESTIONS
FOR CHAPTER 8   ■

1. Must readers always think to comprehend? Why? Why not?
2. What cognitive strategies do readers use as they try to understand texts?
3. Which of these are most important? Why?
4. How may teachers improve students' ability to make better inferences?
5. What is the difference between *forward* and *backward* inferencing? How may students improve their ability to make these kinds of inferences?
6. How may inductive and deductive reasoning be improved?
7. How may critical reading skills be improved?
8. What is metacognition? cognitive monitoring? comprehension monitoring?
9. What self-monitoring devices seem most valuable to readers?
10. What are fix-up strategies? How may teachers teach them?

■ TEACHING GUIDELINES
FOR CHAPTER 8   ●

Chapter 8 is organized around the following teaching guidelines, derived from recent research and observations of successful classroom practices.

- *Teaching Guideline #1*
  Give students practice in inference-making.
- *Teaching Guideline #2*
  Explain and give practice in *forward inferencing* (predicting) and *backward inferencing* (drawing conclusions).

- *Teaching Guideline #3*
  Provide opportunities for students to practice both inductive and deductive reasoning skills in their reading.
- *Teaching Guideline #4*
  Explain and give practice in the critical reading skills they need to be better comprehenders.
- *Teaching Guideline #5*
  Encourage metacognition through comprehension monitoring.
- *Teaching Guideline #6*
  Teach basic self-monitoring devices and fix-up strategies.

IMPROVING COMPREHENSION THROUGH BETTER INFERENCE-MAKING

When a text serves merely to trigger knowledge already in readers' memory, not much thinking takes place. Often—as in the case of a sign like "EXIT"—none takes place. On the other hand, when a text deals with ideas and information readers only partially possess (or with those they do not possess at all!), readers must think. They must begin to actively compare the new material with what they already know, to discriminate more carefully, to hypothesize, to evaluate, check and recheck, look for evidence, draw conclusions, predict, and so on. These mental behaviors are cognitive processes, referred to by some authorities in the past as *higher mental processes* (see Durrell, 1943; or Russell, 1956) or, more recently, as *cognitive skills* (John Anderson, 1980). Many teachers usually call them *thinking skills*.

One seems to predominate in all mental activity: the ability to infer, or to make inferences. Together with such related skills as "recognizing the inferences of others," "evaluating inferences," and "looking for evidence to support inferences," inference-making lies at the center of many other mental processes (such as drawing conclusions, predicting, and hypothesizing). Because it is so important to reading and reading comprehension, teachers need to investigate the process and ways to improve it.

What Is Inference-Making?

Almost all thoughtful teachers have come to recognize that the ability to infer seems paramount in comprehending texts that present unfamiliar material. They know that students have to be able to say at times, "If this is true, and this is true, then maybe I can say this follows." Some teachers base their instruction on a dictionary definition of inference, such as "the act of passing from one proposition, statement, or judgment considered true to another whose truth is believed to follow from that of the former" (Merriam-Webster,

1983, p. 619). Some tell students that an inference is an *educated guess,* the inference-maker observing certain items or events in the environment and guessing that something has occurred or will occur. One teacher explains this by saying, "Imagine a strange man walking into our classroom and looking out our window. He says, *There are black clouds in the sky.* Then, *It will rain soon.* And then, as he stomps out, *This country has terrible weather.* " She explains that the first statement is "factual" in that it can be verified as true or false by another observer. The third is "opinion," because it expresses the speaker's feelings and beliefs. But the second is an "inference." It is the man's guess about what is going to happen and, she points out, is only as good as the man's experience with weather in that part of the country.

Recently cognitive psychologists have offered another explanation of the inference-making process. In developing schema theory they have been interested in accounting for the way new information is meshed with existing knowledge. They believe that, for new information (found, for example, in a reading assignment) to be understood, it must instantiate a schema (that is, a general knowledge structure) held already in the reader's long-term memory. (See Chapter 2.) One researcher (Hansen, 1981, p. 393) offers the following sentence: *The dog became angry when he uncovered a stone instead of his bone.* To understand this, she says, a reader must have prior knowledge of "dogs burying bones" (that is, a dog-burying-bones schema). The reader's understanding may be checked by asking, "How did the dog uncover the bone?" If the answer is "By digging with his front feet" a teacher would know that the student possessed the appropriate schema for understanding this sentence. The cues *dog* and *bone* predisposed the reader to think of dogs burying bones; they instantiated the right schema. However, as Hansen notes, unexpressed, unprinted words are also triggered in the reader's mind by *dog* and *bone*—for example, *digging.* Where does it come from? It is not in the sentence. Rather, it is part of the schema: the reader infers from *dog* and *bone* and the schema that they instantiate that *digging* must be involved.

Inference-making may be seen, according to many recent researchers, as *slot filling.* It occurs when a reader guesses—as in this example—that, if a dog and bone are involved, then digging must be too. The schema includes it. (Imagine, Hansen asks, how confused a reader would be if the next sentence in the text was, "I've just got to get a new shovel,' he murmured to himself.") An inference, then, is a reader's guess that if certain things are "true," then others must be too ("truth" residing in such instances in the fit of those "certain things" with the schema accepted). To go back to the example noted earlier, the strange man saw black clouds through the classroom window. They served for him as cues to instantiate one of his particular weather schemata, one in which black clouds precede rain. One slot in his schema includes black clouds; another, rain. When one slot was filled, he unhesitatingly filled the other. (Imagine if, in his case, the black "clouds" proved to be smoke from a factory or fire. He would have made an incorrect inference—based on an inappropriate schema instantiated by a misreading of the cue.)

Slot filling may be further illustrated by an example of a portion of conversation overheard in an elementary school teachers' lounge:

> I know they'd love to have one. Decorating the box doesn't bother me. Not even exchanging the cards. To tell the truth, I don't even mind the week of emotional build-up leading up to the big event. It's the darn ice cream dripping all over the desks that gets me.

For most elementary school teachers—but not for most engineers, dental hygienists, or even school bus drivers—certain cues here instantiate a party schema, probably a Valentine Party schema. The cues (decorating the box, exchanging cards, the week of emotional build-up, the dripping ice cream) trigger for most a script (see Chapter 2) with several well-defined "slots":

A box is usually decorated to hold the children's cards.

The children exchange cards by putting them in the box and distributing them at the party.

The teacher probably passes out sweets (candy, cakes, ice cream).

The children may play games.

The box will be decorated with hearts.

The ice cream will melt and drip on the desks.

Once a teacher encounters two or three of the cues (the more the better), he or she will be predisposed to think of all the related slots, because they comprise, as a group, the school party script, or schema. Some of these slotted items may not have appeared in the text (in this case, the portion of overheard conversation), but a teacher familiar with school parties will *infer* them. Thus a teacher ought to be able to answer—by inferencing—such questions as *Did the children play games?* and *How was the box decorated?* even though information needed to answer these questions is not provided in the spoken text itself. (Speakers and writers, it should be noted, seldom fill in all slots. Their texts would be excessively long—and boring—if they did. They have to assume that listeners and readers know the appropriate schemata and that they have given enough information to trigger, or instantiate, them.)

Goodman (1984) defines an inference as a general strategy of guessing, on the basis of what is known, what information is needed but is not known. Calling inference guesswork, he notes, does not make it random or mystic: "Our schemata and knowledge structures make it possible on the basis of partial information to make reliable decisions by inferring missing information." "We would be incapable," he adds, "of the decisions we must make if we had to be sure of all the necessary prerequisite information before making each decision" (p. 105).

Can Inferencing Be Improved?

If inferencing is such a necessary component of the comprehension process, then it clearly behooves teachers to try to improve students' inference-making skills. Unfortunately many influential educators have long believed that children's inferencing skills are qualitatively different from adults', and that children are simply not capable of making the same kinds of inferences adults make. (See, for example, Bloom, 1956; or Piaget, Inhelder, and Szeminsho, 1960.) Inferencing competence is held to be contingent upon maturity—or even upon innate intelligence. Thus efforts to provide instruction in this area have not been considered viable. Students, especially younger ones, are believed to need further growth: "They need to be at least twelve years old before they can make good inferences." Some—unhappily—are believed to be (somehow) intellectually handicapped: "Poor Thomas will never be able to infer a thing."

Such beliefs are currently viewed with some degree of doubt (Hansen, 1981). Many psychologists now think that the difference between children's and adults' inferencing may be quantitative rather than qualitative. Recent research suggests that poor inferencing by children may be a consequence of insufficient prior knowledge: children do not lack the ability to draw good inferences; rather, they lack adequate prior knowledge to allow them to draw good inferences in particular situations. (See, for example, Trabasso, Nicholas, Omanson, and Johnson, 1977; and Omanson, Warren, and Trabasso, 1978.) Just as an adult Chinese engineer, raised and schooled in Szechwan in western China, would not be able to infer, from the cues in the teachers' lounge conversation quoted above, that the box was probably decorated with hearts, so children who know nothing about, say, current national monetary policy would be unable to make sensible or acceptable inferences about it. A school administrator, long accustomed to her community's school board meetings, has a schema for school board meetings and is able, on the basis of minimal information, to make inferences about typical school board member behavior. A fifth-grade student only vaguely aware of the existence of such a board cannot be expected to make such inferences, not because of some hypothetical qualitative difference in his inferencing power, but because he has no slots to fill in his school board meeting schema. (He has only a sketchy, undeveloped schema for school boards themselves.)

Other recent research (see, for example, Paris and Lindauer, 1976) suggests that, in addition to lack of prior knowledge, younger students are also handicapped in their inferencing because they have not yet learned to spontaneously integrate new information with old. In cases where children indeed have adequate schemata to make inferences by slot filling, they frequently fail to do so in reading situations because they lack practice. Children do spontaneously draw inferences in their daily lives; in school they fail to make inferences simply because they lack training, practice,—or encouragement. Studies (for example, Hansen, 1981) indicate that instructional techniques designed to induce spontaneity of inferencing are effective.

Strategies for Better Inferencing ────────────────

How can teachers help students become better at inferencing? Clearly prior knowledge serves as the basis for inferencing, and, just as clearly, teachers are limited in what they can do about extending the general knowledge base each student brings into the classroom. However, teachers may give instruction in recognizing inferences and in what some researchers call *spontaneity* in drawing inferences. They can provide training, practice, and encouragement.

Several suggestions for approaches and strategies are given here.

Explain and Discuss Inferences   Children can begin to see that sometimes they make guesses about characters and actions in the stories they read. Teachers need to encourage such "guesswork": "If the boy left the house early and in a great rush, what do you think he was wearing on his feet? Why do you say that? Are there clues in the story? Are you comparing him with yourself? with characters in other stories?" They can point out that these guesses are called *inferences* and that people need to make inferences as they think. They can point out too that inferences are only as good as the knowledge the inference-maker has of the subject: "You can make good inferences about baseball or magic if you know a lot about the subject; when you don't know much about a subject your guesses usually aren't as good." Opportunities need to be provided in class to look at inferences students make and to discuss their validity.

It is important at this stage that teachers provide positive encouragement and support. Inferencing is risky because some inferences may be wrong. Students need to realize that the less they know about a given subject the less apt they are to draw good inferences, but that they nevertheless need to take chances. They should realize that the risk in *not* making inferences may be even greater than the chances they take that theirs may not meet the mark. Teachers certainly—at all levels—should not disparage or negatively criticize inference makers! As Goodman (1984, p. 105) has pointed out, "Level of confidence limits willingness to take risks, which in turn limits inferencing."

Help Students Distinguish Inferences from Facts and Opinions   Most basal readers and school curriculum guides recommend that children learn the difference between statements of fact and of opinion (sometimes called "fact" and "fancy"). Many professional books assist teachers in making the distinction clear for children. (See, for example, Lapp and Flood, 1983, p. 251.) While teaching this important basic distinction, teachers may also begin to teach much about inferences. Teachers may group statements such as these:

I always received an "A" in math.
I received an "A" in algebra.
I will do "A" work in tenth-grade geometry.
I am a good math student.

Susan refused to go to the dance with me.
Janet said she was busy when I asked her.
I'll never get a date for the prom.
I am not popular with girls.

I am in tip-top condition.
I haven't been ill since I was in kindergarten.
When I was four, I had the measles.
I don't need health insurance.

Students may be reminded that factual statements may be verified: another observer may make the same statement ("There are indeed black clouds in the sky," "He did get an 'A' in algebra," or "Susan did refuse to go to the dance"). They may be shown that statements of opinion generally express someone's preferences, feelings, or opinions ("I am a good math student" or "This country has terrible weather"). Within each of the grouped statements one or more neither expresses an opinion nor states a verifiable fact; it may be the speaker's or writer's "educated guess" or inference ("I don't need health insurance").

Such an approach may be followed by student "searches" to discover examples of fact, opinion, and inference in advertising, newspapers, letters-to-the-editor, television, or even textbooks. Students will—and should—argue about the difference between fact and opinion (the distinction is not clear-cut, even for professional logicians); they will often dispute one another about inferences (these are not always clear even to their teachers). The point of such classroom discussions is to help students sensitize themselves to the kinds of statements they encounter and make them aware of the inferences of others.

Give Students Practice in Inference Making   Teachers need to set up situations in class where students can make inferences. They may do this by, for example, noting (1) a white Ford parked in the teacher's parking lot, and (2) today is Tuesday, and then asking, "What do you infer from these two observations?" Because, in this particular school, the music teacher (who drives a white Ford) usually comes on Tuesdays, students will infer that she has come for a visit. Teachers need not explain that the inference is an example of slot filling for a particular music-teacher-visit schema, but they can show, using this situation, how people make inferences. Because the school day and week abound in special scripts or schemata (for lunch, study halls, basketball games, dances, etc.), alert teachers have little trouble setting up such situations.

Middle school and secondary school students can set up their own situations. One teacher, after having given classes practice in making inferences, encourages her students to create "inference-making contests." They list three or more facts or observations on paper, drawing a blank line after them for "contestants" to fill in a reasonable inference. One student created the following:

Mr. Hawkins sat at the table.
He rolled up his sleeves.
He adjusted his slides.
He adjusted his microscope.

Because Mr. Hawkins, a popular school biology teacher, was known to all students in the class, the students were able to fill in the blank line with several possible inferences: "He began to point out the living organisms in the drop of water" or "He was preparing material for his class." Again, the teacher did not need to explain that the blank lines were actually "slots" to be filled in from a biology-teacher schema; she simply wanted students to have additional practice in making—and later defending—their own inferences.

Have Students Make Inferences from Printed Texts   Once students are able to identify inferences and realize when they are making their own, much attention needs to be given to inference-making from printed texts. Newspaper articles and short poems often provide excellent starting points for classroom analysis. One middle school teacher takes brief paragraphs from the daily newspaper and distributes duplicated copies. He encourages his class to list all the inferences they can in their notebooks. From an article about a football game the previous day, students may make ten or more inferences, "things the writer didn't say but which we know are probably true." He uses this approach to show that writers do not need to "say everything" because they sense that their readers already have a great deal of information about his topic. He points out that writers know readers will make inferences and emphasizes the value to readers of constantly making them—and testing them out as they continue reading.

A tenth-grade teacher of literature presents classes with a list of questions which (1) can easily be answered by readers of a poem, but (2) are not answered *in* the poem. For Shelley's "Ozymandias," for example, she asks:

Are there many trees around the piece of sculpture?
Is there much grass?
What kind of a ruler was Ozymandias?
Did his subjects love him?
Did they respect him?
How long ago did he live?

She leads her classes to see that "anyone" can answer such questions: "They're easy!" Then she draws from students the observation that most readers already know much of what Shelley is writing about; the poet did not have to fill in all information because much is already in people's heads. She shows them that, on the basis of what they know about deserts, for example, they are able to *infer* that there are neither grass nor trees; and from what they know about rulers who "sneer" "cold commands," they are able to infer that Ozymandias's subjects did not especially love him.

After practice sessions with short pieces of text, students can move on to textbook assignments where they can be shown that authors of content area schoolbooks operate much the same way as newspaper reporters or poets.

Explain How Inferences Work As Predictors   Often inferences are predictions. When students fill in slots in a time-sequence schema (such as a script), they are making predictions. For example, the schema for eating in the school cafeteria may involve several slots that are chronologically sequenced; some of which include

1st—getting in line

2nd—moving through the line

3rd—selecting food

4th—paying at cash register

5th—finding a table (with friends)

6th—eating

If a text indicated, say, the 1st, 2nd, 5th, and 6th items, a reader familiar with the schema would be able to infer that food was selected and paid for. Such slot filling is typical inference-making. However, if the 1st through the 5th are given and the reader infers "eating," then his inference is a prediction as well. A story that mentioned conversation in the cafeteria line, and later an incident as a character paid for her lunch, would encourage the reader to assume (predict) that later she found a table and ate her lunch. The latter two events (slots) may be seen, in a sense, as the "effects" of the earlier "causes." Indeed, Pearson and Johnson (1978, p. 117) say that predicting outcomes is a type of *future causality*, based on one's prior knowledge about the kinds of effect an explicitly stated cause usually elicits. Borrowing a term from computer science, they call this *forward inferencing* (p. 112).

Such a cognitive operation is indispensable for reading comprehension. Readers need to predict and anticipate what is coming. They must know from the beginning of a story, paragraph, or sentence where it will end; Goodman (1984), among others, notes too that they need to know from the beginning of a clause, phrase, or word where it is likely to end. It is this forward inferencing that makes comprehension flow smoothly as readers develop their own texts-in-the-head.

Kenneth Goodman has also noted that reading comprehension is easier when texts are predictable (1984, p. 106). When readers of stories about, for example, a school Valentine's Day party or "Eating in the School Cafeteria" are familiar with the school-Valentine's Day-party or eating-in-the-school-cafeteria schemata, they may more easily predict what is coming next, fill in missing places, and predict outcomes. It is when readers are not familiar with the appropriate schemata that comprehension may prove troublesome.

What can teachers do to help students become better at making and recognizing predictions? Some suggestions follow:

- *Make students aware of appropriate schemata.* When a class is assigned a specific text, the teacher needs to check what schemata its author assumes readers know. If students know some of these, the teacher may call attention to them: "Notice that the first two pages seem to be about a party." The teacher may want to have a class talk about the party schema to make sure that all are sharing a similar concept: "What was the best party you ever attended? What was it like? What do you remember about it?" When a teacher discovers that students do not share a schema at all, it clearly behooves the teacher to develop it as best he can: "You've never been to a Valentine's Day party! Let me tell you about one the class had last year."

- *Have students make predictions from titles.* Story titles clue readers into stories, providing information for them to predict what may happen. Many teachers provide opportunities, prior to reading, for students to (1) guess what the story may be about, (2) predict the setting, (3) guess what the characters may be like, and so forth. In a sense, the title of a piece hints at a slot in a script or schema.

  Newspaper headlines offer similar opportunities for predicting. Because they often serve to summarize a story in skeleton form, they should give readers a reasonably accurate idea of what is to follow in the article. In one recent study (Watanabe, Hare, and Lomax, 1984) eighth-graders were given such headlines as "Expansion Plans for O'Hare Run into Suburb Flak." It was discovered that students' success in predicting content from headlines alone was influenced (as expected) by prior knowledge, knowledge of specialized vocabulary, and the telegraphic syntax used by headline writers. However, it was also found that practice in prediction-making does work. During the three weeks students were asked to predict the contents of news stories from their headlines, read the articles, and then prove or disprove the accuracy of their predictions from the stories' content. During this time they discussed their reasons for predictions with the teachers who used Stauffer's Directed Reading-Thinking Activity (1970) as the model for the practice. (See later discussion.) Results of this training in prediction-making were highly significant statistically and suggest that teachers who want to improve students' prediction-making try using titles and headlines.

- *Have students make predictions frequently as they read.* Teachers need to stop during both oral and silent reading and ask: "What do you think the boy will do next? Why? What will he probably not do? Why do you say that?
- *Call attention to predictions made in texts.* Often authors will say, "If John forgets again today, he's going to be in trouble," "When Susan finally gets to school, she will be surprised," or "After he finished the book, he was delighted." Such sentences are examples of slot filling, of sequencing based on some schemata, and of causality (the first two of future causality and the last of an item in the past "causing" one in the present). Teachers need to make students aware of predictions made by others.

Explain How Inferences Work As Explanations   The third example cited above leads to an awareness of another type of inference: inferences often explain or account for events occurring previously in a sequence. If the reader of a text about eating in the cafeteria reads that the boy paid for his meal, she infers that the food selected was paid for. Again, good inferencing is contingent upon knowledge of the eating-in-a-school-cafeteria script, or schema. A reader cannot make successful inferences about prior items in a sequence if she is unfamiliar with the script. Pearson and Johnson (1978), again borrowing from computer science, call this process *backward inferencing*.

Unfortunately, because one slot in a sequence occurs before another, one tends to call the earlier one a "cause." Readers often fall into causality traps: because—to use an egregious example—one got in line prior to eating, the assumption may be made that getting into line was the cause of eating!

Backward inferencing needs to be treated carefully at all levels in reading instruction. Readers tend to inference backwards. Rarely have they been taught to distinguish between simple backward inferencing and (1) true causality and (2) drawing conclusions. The first is difficult to pinpoint even in highly controlled laboratory experiments; the second is a matter of reasoning and logical thinking and is therefore several steps removed from basic reading comprehension. (See next section.)

What can teachers do to help students with these kinds of inferences?

- They can present items from a well-known schemata (ordering food in a fast-food establishment or, for older students, changing a flat tire) and have students note relationships: "This happened first, this happened next, and then this happened. Was one the cause of another? Did one just happen before the other? Did one *have* to happen to make the other happen?"
- They can call attention to signal words commonly used by writers to indicate causal relationships. Such words (*because, therefore, so,* etc.)

need to be distinguished from signal words that simply note time sequence (*then, next, finally,* etc.).

- They can also set up situations in the classroom where students may draw conclusions: "If I forget to put John's name on the attendance sheet, what may happen? How do I know it will happen? What previous experiences do we have that lead us to draw that particular conclusion?"
- They can give practice in locating backward inferencing in texts. "The author said Harry fell. What did he say previously that made us think Harry might fall?

Idea Box

How early may cognitive skills be developed in a reading lesson? One kindergarten teacher, Marilyn A. Farina, describes one of her lessons here:

The cognitive skills involved in a reading lesson on the kindergarten level are the same as those involved in a middle or upper grade lesson. After the vocabulary has been mastered a lesson can be prepared that includes elements of the higher mental processes such as drawing conclusions, making inferences, evaluating from what you already know, sensing problems and hypothesizing. The story illustrating this lesson is entitled *The Bee* and is three pages long. Each page has a large picture and a few lines of printed text at the bottom of the page. In pre-primers, the pictures illustrating the text are as important as the text in understanding and evaluating the characters and story line. In most basal pre-primers the same characters, animal or human, follow throughout the series. A few new words are introduced in each story and the text is developed upon the repetition of these words and others that were introduced in earlier stories.

The children are encouraged, with the help of the teacher, to prepare for the story. Before we even open the pre-primer I tell the children that I am going to ask many questions about the story and they are to listen carefully to my questions. They are then to find the answers in the reading of the story. Some sample questions might be "What is the name of the animal in the story," "Is it a sunny day," "How big is the bug," "How many animals . . . people are there in the story."

Even though they are just beginning the reading program, some children already possess many of the cognitive skills necessary to be successful in this program. Young children can be logical, can draw conclusions, enjoy predicting (they don't care whether or not these predictions are true) and can distinguish between real and make-believe.

The following sample lesson involves the above mentioned skills. In discussing the story we look carefully at the picture before we begin the written text. We discuss who or what we think will be in the story, basing our answers on what appears in the illustration. We then read the text and see if our hypothesizing was correct. We try to determine what the main idea may be and then try to predict what will happen next based on what we already know.

The next page brings a new picture and a new character into the story line. Again, we discuss the picture and what we think may happen in the text. We read, discuss, and each child is encouraged to participate in this evaluation before we turn to the final page.

After finishing the story we have a group discussion of the entire story. I ask questions such as "Who did the story tell us about," "Why were the characters important," "Was it a real or an imaginary story." Each question usually brings a flow of answers and it is easy to catch and correct misunderstandings. Another group of questions I find useful are "What happened in the beginning of the story, in the middle of the story and at the end of the story?," "What would you have done if you were part of the story?," "What might happen next if we made the story longer?," "How could we change the story to make a different ending?."

After a usually very lively and informative discussion I ask one or two of the children to tell us the story in her own words and the rest of us agree or disagree as to the logical sequence and/or completeness. This final evaluation is the most important part of the lesson. I re-ask my initial questions and try to elicit answers from all members of the reading group. Most children, this age, enjoy participation in small group oral activities. We are then ready to work in our work books and to go on to the next story.

Following directions involves the use of several cognitive skills. Children have to identify main ideas, note sequence, distinguish between relevant and irrelevant information, and pinpoint their own purposes for reading. Practice may begin in the primary grades with the Hunting Game. Many teachers play this by hiding a small object in the room and placing printed clues around the room: "Walk to the front door," "Take ten steps to the right," "Open the cabinet drawer," and so on. Later, children may be given all the directions at once printed on slips of paper. Some teachers print directions for making a peanut butter and jelly sandwich and allow boys and girls to follow them in class.

One middle school teacher collects printed directions from purchases made by his family. He has directions for assembling bicycles, play swings, lawn furniture, and a variety of items. He duplicates these for students to analyze. He asks, "What is your purpose in reading this? What are the main points? Is order important? Which step seems to come first? second? What prior knowledge do you need to assemble this object? What did the writer assume you know that you don't?" Once in a while he brings an item in for students to study and put together.

To give practice in problem solving, one sixth-grade teacher collects Problems! She has a file of problems that have confronted her and students over a period of years: How to get a cat down from a tree, How to get into your car when the keys are inside it, How to eradicate graffiti from the playground, etc. She outlines the problem, has children suggest hypotheses, has them think through solutions, and, if possible, allows them to test out a hypothesis.

IMPROVING COMPREHENSION THROUGH BETTER REASONING

Often inferencing and predicting are not enough! Readers meet texts that demand more than these regularly used cognitive strategies. Sometimes

- texts are faulty (Writers construct carelessly without providing readers with necessary guidance);
- readers lack appropriate prior knowledge (Writers assume readers have information they do not have, thus forcing them to employ higher-level mental processes if they hope to derive meaning from the text); or
- texts are intended as jumping-off places for reader thinking (Writers have done a good job of crafting their texts and are aware of readers' prior knowledge, but they deliberately design their texts to provoke further reader thinking).

In such cases readers must use several higher mental processes, or cognitive skills, together—as they try to make sense of texts. They need to think both deductively and inductively, to approach meaning-building as problem solving, and to think critically about the meanings they derive from texts.

This section examines ways teachers can improve reading comprehension by teaching certain reasoning processes, particularly deductive/inductive reasoning, problem solving, and critical thinking.

What Is Deductive Reasoning?

Research on deductive reasoning compares reasoning behavior in human beings with the prescriptions of a logical system, one which consists of specific *rules of inference,* which permit true conclusions to be drawn from true premises. Thus, when A *implies* B, and A is given, one may *infer* B. Cognitive psychologist John R. Anderson (1980, p. 298) gives this example:

1. If it rains tomorrow, then the game will be canceled.
2. If the game is canceled, then our team will surely lose the pennant.
3. It will rain tomorrow.
4. The game will be canceled.
From 2 and 4 one may infer 5:
5. Our team will surely lose the pennant.

This is a good example of a valid deduction. But *valid* in deductive reasoning means that all the premises upon which the deduction are based must be true. If one is not, the deduction clearly is not valid. Teachers who intend to teach students something about such reasoning need to remind themselves and their students that deductive reasoning is never concerned with the truth of premises in an argument, only with whether the premises logically imply the conclusions!

Instruction in deductive reasoning eventually takes classes into such topics as *conditional reasoning* (in which deduction involves *if* statements), *sentential logic* (in which it involves *if, and, or,* and *not* statements), and *categorical syllogisms* (which involve quantifiers such as *all, some, no,* and *some not*).

What Is Inductive Reasoning?

When arguments are inductively valid, the conclusion is *probable* if the premises are true (in contrast with deductively valid, in which the conclusion must be certain if the premises are true). A good example is the following argument:

Mary and John live in the same house.
John has the same last name as Mary.
Mary has a picture of John on her desk at work.
Therefore, John and Mary are married.

The conclusion here is not necessarily true but highly probable. It is possible that John and Mary are brother and sister or that they are lovers who happen to have the same name. Many other conclusions may be drawn from the same

premises. However, in inductive reasoning conclusions are valid if they are probable—in contrast to deductive reasoning where conclusions are valid if the
premises are true.

Instruction in inductive reasoning takes classes into discussions of
hypothesis formation and *hypothesis evaluation* and the study of *probability.*

Teaching Deductive/Inductive Reasoning

Logic is traditionally a college-level course (although it has been introduced into some high school programs). Effective instruction in both deductive
and inductive reasoning includes intensive examinations of such matters as the
Venn diagram, modus tollens, and various heuristics, as well as analyses of
logical fallacies. All of this may be more than most reading teachers want to incorporate into their programs. Many psychologists contend that, although
logical thinking can be taught, knowing the principles of logic in the abstract is
not enough anyway. As John Anderson (1980, p. 326) notes, "One needs to
practice the techniques in the situations where they are to be used."

What can teachers do then? Several approaches suggested in the professional literature and by various teachers are noted here.

1. Give students—even younger ones—regular practice in simple
syllogistic reasoning. One teacher takes every opportunity to call attention to examples in the classroom and home: "If the telephone rings, someone is trying to
call us. The telephone is now ringing. Does that mean someone is trying to call
us? Every teacher in our school is a woman. There is a new teacher in the fourth
grade. Can we conclude that the new teacher is a woman?"

2. Provide frequent opportunities to examine such reasoning with
students. "Did you ever pick up a ringing phone only to find there was no one
there? Why do you think this happened? Can we say that ringing telephones do
not necessarily lead to people's voices on the other end? Because every teacher in
our school happens to be a woman, does that mean every teacher has to be a
woman?"

3. Call attention to syllogistic reasoning in schoolbooks. "In the story, it
says all the animals were ferocious. On the next page, we can see a picture of
Ann going to the door to meet what may be an animal. Does that one have to be
ferocious? Why? Why not?" In secondary school textbooks syllogisms are often
spelled out rather clearly. Content area teachers should take advantage of these
examples to point out the reasoning and ways it may go astray.

4. Encourage students to find syllogisms in newspapers, magazines, and
other outside reading. Have them bring these to class and explain how they are
constructed and, if possible, to find weaknesses in the reasoning.

5. After students have become aware of syllogisms, have them note the
"danger words": *if, then, therefore, all, some,* and other quantifiers. Show

them that they must be "supercautious" about these when they read them in sentences. Point out instances in texts where *all* or *some* change the conclusions readers may draw from the reasoning.

6. Introduce high school students to the *sham enthymeme*. Explain that it results when one part of a syllogism—usually the major premise—is left out. Begin with obvious examples, such as "The government controls the use of harmful drugs today; therefore, the government can control the growth of nuclear power plants"; note that, in such a case, the major premise ("Government control is equally effective in drug control and nuclear plant growth") has been omitted. Encourage students to locate similar instances of sham enthymemes in their reading.

7. Introduce secondary school students to the persistent kinds of false argumentation:

Post hoc, ergo propter hoc reasoning ("After this, therefore because of this") occurs when the writer assumes that because A came before B, A must be the cause of B.

Begging the question happens when something is assumed proved, although the proof is not demonstrated. (For example, "The unfair practice of requiring all students to take English should be stopped at once!" assumes without providing proof that the practice is unfair.)

Faulty dilemma presents only two sides of an argument, when actually there are more than two. (For example, before Hitler came to power, he told voters they had to choose between National Socialism and Communism, but they actually had other alternatives.)

Ignoring the question happens when readers are confronted by arguments that ignore the basic issue involved (as when one small child says, "Well, you kicked me" when told "You hurt my arm").

Argumentum ad hominem is found when the speaker or writer sidetracks the argument by making accusations against a person (such as "Don't vote for him no matter what he says about taxes: his wife was an alcoholic!").

After explaining these in class, encourage students to locate examples from their out-of-class reading. (Often the letters-to-the-editor column of the local newspaper provides excellent examples.)

8. Show students how inductive reasoning is used in hypothesis formation. Give them a set of premises and one possible conclusion and lead them to see that from these it is possible to develop a hypothesis for later testing. One good model comes from John Anderson (1980, p. 331):

Fred is allergic to apples.
Fred is not allergic to bananas.

Fred is allergic to plums.
Fred is not allergic to oranges.
Fred is allergic to grapes.
Fred is allergic to cherries.

Therefore, Fred is allergic to the skin of fruits.

The inductive conclusion seems reasonable—assuming that Fred peels his oranges and bananas. Each premise specifies a particular fruit, but the conclusion is general and refers to all fruit. This model can demonstrate to students that induction permits one to proceed from a few examples to a conclusion that will help make predictions about new examples. In other words, the conclusion may be tested out as a hypothesis.

Whenever opportunities arise in the classroom, teachers can encourage students to try this kind of thinking. Students may, after practice, provide models for class practice. One group of high school students developed this:

A togger can be large, red, and square.
A togger can be large, blue, and square.
A togger can be large, yellow, and square.
A togger cannot be large, yellow, and round.
A togger cannot be large, blue, and round.
A togger can be large, orange, and square.
What is a togger?

Students decided that a togger must be a large square. Their conclusion, arrived at by inductive reasoning, became a hypothesis for testing future examples that came their way!

Problem Solving and Reading Comprehension

Some authorities tend to believe that *all* reading comprehension is problem solving. Goodman and Burke (1980) say that all *reading* "is a problem-solving process." Certainly, many texts seem to demand that students use the kind of *goal-directed sequence of cognitive activities* (John Anderson, 1980, p. 257) first codified by John Dewey (1933):

One experiences a "felt difficulty";
then, locates and defines it;
then, searches for possible solutions (hypotheses);
then, reasons to select the best of these; and
finally, tests out the selected solution hypothesis by further observation or experiment.

Recently cognitive psychologists have emphasized the role of prior knowledge in all reasoning—including problem solving. Solving a problem, they say, is not so much a matter of applying certain solving-problem skills as it is of knowing much about the area in which the problem occurs. Rumelhart (1980), for example, stresses the importance of schemata: "Most of our reasoning ability is tied to particular schemata related to particular bodies of knowledge" (p. 55). John Anderson (1980) also notes the importance of expertise: "We cannot become expert problem solvers in all fields" (p. 292).

Should teachers bother, then, to take a problem-solving approach to reading and reading comprehension? Granting the primary role played by prior knowledge, it is still possible to say that problem-solving ability does seem to improve with practice (Anderson, 1980, p. 293). "The issue clearly needs careful research, but it does seem that judicious application of our knowledge about problem solving should lead to better performance" (Anderson, 1980, p. 293). With these words in mind, suggestions are made here for helping students use problem-solving techniques to become better comprehenders.

Call Attention to Problems in the Classroom   During the typical day and week, many situations occur which may be treated as problems to be solved: What to do about graffiti on corridor walls, How to raise money for a school field trip, or Finding more space for student parking in the high school. Note the steps usually taken to solve problems: definition or clarification, possible hypotheses, thinking through hypotheses, testing out the best hypothesis. Allow students time to go through the steps together and actually try to solve "real" problems arising in their lives.

Call Attention to Problem Situations in Class Reading   Good problems for class analysis occur in basal readers and high school content area textbooks. Teachers need to locate these and use them in class to review problem-solving procedures: "Exactly what seems to be the problem here? What possible solutions come to mind? How could we test out these hypotheses? Let's continue reading to discover how the problem is handled in the book."

Recall Real Problems and How They Were Solved   Students may be encouraged to search their memories to recall an instance of problem solving in their own lives. Some may volunteer to share their examples, and note the reasons why the problem came to their attention, the solutions they tried, and the final outcome.

Give "Problem/Solution" Study Guides Before Reading   When appropriate examples of problems are to be found in textbooks, teachers may prepare and distribute special problem/solution study guides, which focus on such questions as

What is the problem discussed in this section?

What is its effect?

What seem to be its causes?

List five possible solutions to the problem.

Which of these seems best to you?

Why do you think this solution has not been tried?

Try Writing Solutions to Problems　Jenkins and Savage (1983, pp. 59–60) suggest that teachers take advantage of the appeal of Dear Abby-type problems. Because letters to ''Dear Abby'' frequently reflect students' own problems, or because they are curious about other people's problems, students will often take typical letters and ''think through'' the problems they present. Selected letters may be duplicated and discussed in class: ''What specifically is wrong here? What solutions do you propose? How could these be tried out?''

Student solutions may be analyzed by the group and then written out as brief ''responses'' from the columnist. Jenkins and Savage recommend that discussions and later written responses be guided by three directions:

Restate the problem so that everyone has a clear understanding.

Relate any experiences that approximate those of the writer.

Explore both sides of the issue explained in the letter.

Use Specific Written Problems for Class and Individual Analysis Teachers can design texts that fit specific groups. For example, a teacher working with high school boys interested in cars distributes exercises like this:

> You are the only mechanic on duty at the shop. A woman brings in a 1978 Plymouth which she says stalls at traffic lights. You check out the car and note that the mileage is normal for its age, that it appears to be well serviced, and that the tank is full. Show how you would go about solving her problem for her. Write your ideas here.
> What do you think the problem is?
> What solutions do you think need be tried?
> Which can be eliminated on the basis of common sense?
> How would you go about testing out your best hypothesis?

Have Students Apply the Problem-Solving Method to Their Textbook Reading　After students are familiar with the five steps of problem solving, encourage them to apply them to a textbook reading assignment:

1. *Recognize the problem.* Have students go through the assignment quickly noting chapter titles, section headings, subheadings, illustrations, and typographical aids. From this search they should be able to—roughly—delineate what "problem" the author deals with in the assignment. They need to write this in their notebooks and teachers need to discuss prior to reading how different individuals have defined the problem, leading the group to share, if possible, a commonly perceived definition.

2. *Collect facts.* Prior to reading, students should discuss what they already know about the problem. Relationships between what they know and what the author deals with may be established and associations between old and new learnings developed.

3. *Form hypotheses.* Again prior to reading, students need to look at the facts and ideas they have collected and begin to make some guesses about the assignment. They may be told that these guesses are working hypotheses or predictions. Some of the hypotheses may be written in notebooks or on the chalkboard as questions, others as statements to be verified.

4. *Test hypotheses.* Now students read—but they read to check their hypotheses. After reading, they need to share their findings and settle disagreements by rereading with the teacher. Predictions may be judged for accuracy and answers to questions verified. To support their findings, students may read appropriate portions of the text to the group.

5. *Form a conclusion.* After the class discussion, students need to summarize the major points of the assignment and prepare a short summary statement of three or four sentences. The summary statement may be copied into notebooks for later review after all agree to its validity and inclusiveness.

This "problem-solving" approach to textbook reading assignments resembles the SQ3R method (see Chapter 1), but it has the additional value of refocusing student attention on problem solving. As they use this, they think in terms of problem solving. Guerra (1984, p. 489) notes that, as they use the five steps, students learn to read not just the content of a specific course but also material from other content areas.

Critical Thinking and Critical Reading

Critical thinking is the kind people do as they scrutinize new ideas and information. As Russell noted many years ago (1956, p. 283), it involves four conditions:

- A knowledge of the field or fields in which the thinking is being done;
- A general attitude of questioning and suspended judgment, a habit of examining before accepting;
- Some application of methods of logical analysis or scientific inquiry; and
- Taking action in light of this analysis or reasoning.

When readers think critically about and with the printed page, they may be said to be reading critically. Through the years, several specific reading skills associated with critical thinking have come to be called *critical reading*. Several of the most important are discussed here with suggestions for teaching them.

Recognizing Purpose   One way to help students learn to recognize a writer's purpose is to (1) present a few paragraphs side-by-side (from a school textbook, a newspaper or magazine article, or even a technical report) and list three or four statements of purpose, only one of which is correct; and (2) discuss in class the reasons why only one is correct. When students begin to see that authors usually have some purpose in communicating, they can bring to class examples they have found in their reading for class analysis. As students read other materials, teachers need to regularly ask such questions as: "Why did the author write this? What were his or her reasons?" Students should be led to realize that in defining purpose they are concerned with three issues: (1) the obvious, "public" purpose of the author; (2) the less-public, sometimes hidden purpose of the author; and (3) the students' own personal purpose for reading. They need to realize, if they are to be good critical readers, that the three are not necessarily the same! Students may be given much practice in applying this skill to letters-to-the-editor, editorials, advertisements, reviews of records and films, stories, and even textbooks.

Distinguishing Relevant from Irrelevant Information   After students are able to recognize an author's purpose, they can begin to distinguish between ideas and information used to support his purpose and irrelevant material that has crept into the text because of careless preparation, sloppy thinking, or the deliberate intention to mislead. Elementary school children can learn to see that if the author's purpose was to explain the causes of the common cold, she should not discuss the energy crisis or the Middle Eastern political situation. They can begin to ask, "Why has this material been introduced? Has the author a hidden purpose?"

One approach to this skill is to give students lists of items, most of which relate to an obvious topic, and have them identify and delete the irrelevant items: "Cross out words that do not belong here—home plate, pitcher, short stop, typewriter, mitt, bat, racket, diamond, outfield, glass, third base." Students may develop their own lists to present to their classes; secondary students may be encouraged to find paragraphs from their reading which contain irrelevancies and share them. High school students may be introduced to the *non sequitur* (an inference or conclusion not based on evidence provided) and search for examples in their reading.

Evaluating Sources   Students need to learn that not all writers are competent to write about the topics they choose. One approach to the skill is to present classes with jumbled lists of topics and "authorities" and have them match person with topic: Mohammed Ali, Michael Jackson, the school nurse, and Bobby Orr on one side, and boxing, hockey, music, and nutrition on the other. Later, students may be given lists with specific jobs (repairing a car, replacing a fuse box, curing a skin rash) in one column and in another the names of people who could best do the jobs, with instructions to connect the right person to the specific task.

Students need to see that an author's credentials are important. Teachers may ask such questions as: "Who would be the best one to write a school health handbook? a homeowners' guide to simple repairs? a manual for an automobile?" They may then be given questions to ask about the authors of materials they read: "What are the person's qualifications? Does she have the appropriate educational background? Does the person have a possible hidden reason for writing?" Classes may be introduced in this way to such reference guides as *Who's Who?*, biographical dictionaries, almanacs, encyclopedias, and so on.

Noting Points of View   To help students recognize conflicting points of view, have them examine actual or teacher-prepared letters-to-the-editor on a specific topic and lead them to see how writers' views differ. Have them later write letters from different points of view: a proposal for a student smoking room from (1) a student who smokes, (2) one who does not, (3) a parent, (4) a physician, (5) a school board member. Ask, "How might the point of view of the fire chief differ? of the football coach? of a lobbyist for the tobacco growers? of the owner of a local store?"

Later students may be encouraged to listen to conflicting viewpoints on television or radio and note (1) the backgrounds of speakers, (2) the "public" and "hidden" purposes they may have, (3) their professions and occupations. Such texts as newspaper articles, printed advertisements, or political appeals may be studied from the same angle: "What is the author's point of view? her purpose? Is there a hidden purpose, do you think? Could the author be biased? How might her background influence her point of view?"

Recognizing Bias and Slanted Language   Explain that a writer often reveals his bias by his language. Note that the writer of the first sentence is probably biased against Johnny, while the writer of the second is neutral: *I saw Johnny slink out of the yard hiding something behind his back;* and *I saw*

Johnny walk out of the yard with the bike tire. Students may be shown that, by choosing certain words rather than others, writers indicate their beliefs and attitudes.

When students are shown that words have connotations and emotional overtones and that the deliberate or unconscious use of certain words in print tends to slant the language and consequently influence readers, they may be asked first to compare passages and then, "What seems to be the purpose of each? the 'public' purpose? the 'hidden' purpose? How should a reader respond to each? Which words are *charged?* Which reveal the author's bias? What do you think is the bias in each?"

The following examples were selected from one seventh-grade teacher's lesson:

1. After Congressman Jones wasted as much time as he could, he stumbled through his speech.

   After Congressman Jones weighed every aspect of the important controversy, he rendered his momentous decision.

   (Which is biased for the Congressman? against him? Which words indicate the writer's bias?)

2. Harry ("Killer") Smith, the notorious gambler, was questioned by the police about a gangland slaying.

   Mr. Harold Smith, well-known in local racing circles, was asked by authorities to comment about the recent events in the city.

   (Which is biased for Smith? which against? Which words are "loaded"? What else may police be called? In what ways do these words show bias?)

3. Danny's shifty eyes darted suspiciously around the room until he located his accomplices.

   Danny's eyes moved brightly across the room until he located his friends.

   (Which is biased for Danny? against him? Which words give away the writer's feelings about Danny?)

Recognizing Emotive Language   Students need to be reminded that language is not always straightforward communication. Sometimes writers express their own emotions or try to arouse the emotions of readers. One way to help students understand emotive language is to tell them about "charged" words. Have them write down all the words they can think of for *police officer;* then group these under the headings, "Favorable," "Neutral," or "Unfavorable." They will see that many words carry an emotional charge; they stimulate certain feelings in readers. Some words, like *mother, snake, kitten, terrorist,* or *church,* arouse feelings in most readers; some in only certain individuals. Write randomly selected words on the chalkboard and have the class discuss which have peculiar significance for them and which seem to be capable of stimulating positive or negative feelings in almost everyone.

Students at all levels should be encouraged to collect and analyze examples of emotive language they encounter. These may be found in advertisements, political speeches, literature, or letters. Lead students to see that emotive language can influence them as they read and that the best way to prevent such influence is to be aware of it.

Improving Critical Reading

Strategies for developing critical reading skills are presented in most professional books for teachers. (See, for example, Burmeister, 1983; Devine, 1981; Early, 1984; Santeusanio, 1983; Zintz and Maggart, 1984). Some suggestions are given here.

1. Have students apply the critical reading skills described in class to social studies textbooks used in school. Have them answer such questions as "Where did the author get the information? Is this source to be trusted? Which statements are clearly facts? opinions? Do you detect any bias? Might an author lie deliberately? unconsciously? Why? What protection do you have, as reader, against misinformation and bias in textbooks?"

2. Teach students the *propaganda devices.* Outline these on the chalkboard and have students find examples in their reading:

Glittering Generality (Noting a vague generality and ignoring the exceptions to it: "Women aren't good in math.")

Name Calling (Giving something a bad label, thus calling attention away from the issue: "That's un-American.")

Transfer (Trying to make the prestige and authority of something transfer over to another: "This must be good cereal, because Michael Jackson uses it.")

Testimonial (Linking the prestige and goodwill of one person to something completely different: "Bobby Orr wears this kind of running shoes.")

Plain Folks (Making a person, especially a star or politician, appear to be just like everyone else: "Did you see the senator? He was carrying his own bags at the airport.")

Card Stacking (Presenting only one side of an argument: "This law will mean lower taxes, more benefits to voters, and less government interference," with no mention of the negative results that may occur.)

Bandwagon (Saying that *everyone* else is doing something; therefore you should do it too: "Nine out of ten athletes use Blotto fountain pens.")

When students locate examples of the devices in their reading, have them note them on pieces of paper and post them on a class bulletin board, arranged under the seven headings. Later, examples may be selected and used as a practice exercise:

Example	*Device*
(1) All us folks down on the farm love Gramma's Sausages.	(Plain Folks)
(2) Everyone in our school's into running. No one bikes anymore.	(Bandwagon)
(3) Successful men smoke X-brand cigars. Smoke them and look like a winner, too.	(Card Stacking; nothing is said about their negative qualities.)

3. Encourage students to follow a *Critical Reading Guide*. Duplicate the following guide for students' notebooks, discuss the questions, and encourage them to use it regularly in their reading.

Has the writer used loaded, or emotionally charged, words? What are they?

Is the author a good source of ideas and information on the subject? Have you checked his or her credentials? What are they?

Which statements are clearly factual? Which are opinions? How can you tell? Which seem to predominate?

Does the writer seem to be deliberately trying to arouse your emotions? What are some examples of emotional language?

Which statements are clearly inferences? Is there evidence to support them?

Has the writer referred to experts by name, or are the references based on hearsay (''They say'' or ''Research proves'')?

Is the writer biased? How do you know?

What assumptions are implied by the author's statements? What are they?

Does the author use any of the propaganda devices? Which? Who do you think is being served here? What emotions are being appealed to?

What is the author's ''public'' purpose? ''hidden'' purpose?

Idea Box

To help children see cause and effect relationships, one primary teacher lists several phrases, all of which could be "causes," on one side of a large piece of cardboard. On the other side she lists phrases that could be related "effects." Beside each cause and effect she punches a hole large enough for a piece of yarn. Children are told to read the phrases and thread the yarn lengths from each cause to its related effect.

To provide further practice in predicting outcomes, one primary teacher has recorded the beginnings of several stories on cassette tapes. Individual children listen to tapes in listening corners and think of ways the stories might end. When several children have heard the same stories, they assemble to tell one another their predictions and then listen to the teacher read the rest of each story.

Using laminated baseball cards, a fifth-grade teacher has children read the information given on each card to make inferences about the players. She explains that an inference is like an "educated guess" and says "You now know a great deal about each person; on the basis of this information you have, what guesses might you make about each player."

To help children discriminate between fact and opinion, one teacher has boys and girls write pairs of sentences, one of which states a fact and the other a related opinion. To get them started, she gives them models such as: Doug Flutie broke three records in one season/He is a fine football player; or Michael Jackson's records have sold more copies than any other recording star in history/Michael Jackson is a fantastic singer. When they have completed a series of pairs, the teacher goes around the group to check the pairs, noting that a fact can be checked by someone else ("Doug Flutie either broke three records or he didn't"/"Michael Jackson either sold more copies or he didn't"), but that opinions express the speaker's or writer's personal feelings about the topic.

To give more practice in inference-making, one fourth-grade teacher finds colored pictures in magazines of various kinds of people (joggers, doctors, construction workers, nurses, executives, and so forth), glues them to cardboard, laminates them, and then cuts off their shoes! She gives each child in the group only a set of shoes cut from the picture, asking, "To what kind of person do you *infer* these shoes belong?" Each child writes his or her inference on a paper with three reasons to support it. After everyone has had an opportunity to discuss the inferences, the teacher distributes the rest of the pictures and children evaluate their own inferences.

To teach more about critical thinking and propaganda techniques, one sixth-grade teacher cuts pictures of merchandise from newspapers and magazines and has children make up television or newspaper advertisements for the merchandise. After each child has presented his or her advertisement, children discuss which (if any) propaganda tricks were used: "Is this an example of the Bandwagon? the Testimonial? Card Stacking?" They then check to see how many statements were factual and how many opinion.

Most writing involves a high degree of careful thinking. Many teachers therefore use the traditional composition lesson as a lesson in the development of thinking skills. One high school teacher selects a controversial issue (such as lowering or raising the state's drinking age) and has students prepare arguments for *both* sides. First, they must think through each position, collect supporting evidence, logically arrange their material, and then focus their arguments for a specific audience; next, they write out first drafts, which they try out on one another to get immediate reader response; finally, students actually write out their papers. She notes that students become more sensitive to reasoning, logic, and the rules of evidence, and therefore better readers as well as better writers.

Another writing activity that promotes better thinking is the *critique*. Students frequently disagree with film, television, or record reviews they encounter in the newspaper. Many teachers have students write their own reviews so that they may become more aware of the thinking needed to evaluate critically, but some teachers have students critique the critiques. Students are encouraged to bring reviews they disagree with to class, share them with others in the group, discuss what they believe is wrong with the reviews, and then write out their criticisms of the reviews. One high school teacher, who does this regularly, says that her students learn more about inferencing, distinguishing fact from opinion, recognizing slanted language and bias, and judging sources of information this way than in lessons where these processes are more formally taught.

IMPROVING COMPREHENSION
THROUGH SELF-MONITORING

Metacognition is the deliberate conscious control of one's own cognitive actions (Brown, 1980). People think—almost incessantly—but are not necessarily always aware of what they are doing. That is, they discriminate and categorize ideas and information, they organize mental data, they hypothesize, infer, predict—all as part of their ongoing mental lives—without being aware of these operations; they often reason syllogistically and try to solve problems without being especially aware of what they are doing. Metacognition occurs when thinkers begin to scrutinize their own thought processes and actively monitor, regulate, and orchestrate these processes in the service of some objective. It occurs, in short, when thinkers think about their own thinking. (For further discussion, see Wagoner, 1983.)

Because metacognition seems to have a positive influence on thinking ability, researchers in recent years have begun to study the relation of metacognition to reading comprehension. They note that metacognition involves not only an awareness of the skills, strategies, and resources used in thinking and learning activities but also the ability to use self-regulatory mechanisms, such as: checking the outcomes of problem-solving attempts, planning subsequent moves, and evaluating the effectiveness of strategies, as well as testing, revising, and remediating (Baker and Brown, 1984). The use of these self-regulatory mechanisms has come to be known as *cognitive monitoring*. When they are used in a reading situation they are called *comprehension monitoring* mechanisms. As Baker and Brown have noted, metacognition, cognitive monitoring, and comprehension monitoring are hierarchically related concepts: comprehension monitoring is one type of cognitive monitoring, and cognitive monitoring is a component of metacognition (1984, p. 22).

Research studies in comprehension monitoring generally use such techniques as *verbal reports* (in which readers are asked questions about their procedures, such as "What do you do if you come across an unfamiliar word?"), *on-line processing measures* (such as photographs of eye movements, direct observations, or analysis of oral reading errors), or *comprehension questions* (such as those asked after reading has been completed). Each technique has advantages and disadvantages; and, because disadvantages tend to outweigh advantages in each case, researchers can never be absolutely sure of what goes on in readers' minds as readers deal with printed texts. It seems fairly certain, however, that good readers are more likely to use various comprehension monitoring devices than poor readers (see Brown, 1980; and Baker and Brown, 1984). As one study notes, "Less experienced and less successful readers tend not to engage in the cognitive monitoring activities characteristic of more proficient readers" (Baker and Brown, 1984, p. 44).

Which Monitoring Devices Are Most Important? _____

Several researchers have tried to pinpoint the specific types of comprehension failures in an attempt to suggest techniques that readers may use to self-monitor. Collins and Smith (1980), for example, have developed a taxonomy of four types of comprehension failures: (1) failure to understand particular words, (2) failure to understand particular sentences, (3) failure to grasp the relationship between sentences, and (4) failure to comprehend how the text fits together as a coherent whole. From this analysis they suggest six "remedies." They say readers may: (1) ignore the obstacle and read on, (2) suspend judgment, (3) form a tentative hypothesis, (4) reread the current sentence, (5) reread the previous context, or (6) go to an expert source for further guidance and information. In a review of the research in this area, Pitts (1983) found certain monitoring devices used frequently. These included rereading, scanning ahead, ignoring confusions, making hypotheses, and changing reading rate (p. 519).

How Do Readers Know Something Is Wrong? _____

Before readers use a monitoring device, they must know that they are not comprehending. But how do they know? The research here does not supply ready answers. Several investigators have tried to alert readers to potential obstacles. Markman (1979), for example, found that, when she told children in advance that texts contained inconsistencies, they tended to locate them; but Baker (1979) discovered that advance warnings about passage anomalies did not seem to improve error detection. She found that, in general, good monitors noted errors with or without being alerted, while poor monitors did not change behavior even when warned in advance. Winograd and Johnston (1980) tried showing children pictures of what texts were about before they read, hoping that if readers had a general idea, or schema, for a text, they would be more apt to detect inconsistencies and violations of the schema. They found, however, that such preparation had little effect; the sixth-grade students in their study did not detect problems any better nor take special actions to make better sense of the passages.

Although the research to date is unclear, there are at least two ways teachers can help students realize when they are having comprehension problems.

1. Teachers can encourage students to regularly check their own comprehension through *self-questioning*. Good comprehenders seem to stop frequently as they read to ask themselves what is happening: "Why did the writer say that? What grounds has he for such a statement? What must have happened before this event? Is that a sensible thing to say? Why not?" Evidently students

may be taught to ask such questions. Andre and Anderson (1978–79), for example, found that, with encouragement, students can learn to ask themselves such questions as "Do I know the meaning of this word? Is this word being used in a new way? Does this sentence have meaning as a whole? What is the main idea?" Thomas Anderson (1980) notes that, when students ask such *understanding questions* (p. 497), they are able to determine the adequacy of their own understanding. Another researcher, Lipson (1982), has used an approach in which students learn to ask understanding questions through bulletin boards and worksheets related to the assigned passages. Collins and Smith (1980) suggest a teacher-modeling technique, in which the teacher regularly demonstrates the kinds of questions a successful reader asks as he or she reads. (More on self-questioning follows in the next section.)

2. Teachers may also encourage much *paraphrasing*. Saying what they think a writer means, in their own words, is one of the best ways readers have of discovering the meaning the writer's text has for them. When readers cannot say what a writer is driving at, clearly something is wrong. As George Henry (1974) has pointed out, "We read at our own pace, finish with an inchoate lump of meaning unformed by language, and go on to other activity." He suggests (as noted in Chapter 6) that it is not until readers try to *tell* the ideas they have read that they begin to conceptualize the ideas and discover what meanings they have for them. Teachers need to encourage students to stop during reading and tell themselves what they have been reading. Paraphrasing is not only a comprehension monitoring device but also a way of assessing one's overall comprehension of passages.

Suggested Fix-Up Strategies

What happens when readers realize that they are not comprehending? Several remedies, or "fix-up" strategies, are suggested in recent research. Most have demonstrated effectiveness (Pitts, 1983).

1. Readers can simply ignore small problems and move on. Because good readers seem to do this regularly, teachers should tell students that this is a legitimate strategy. Several studies have found that successful students skip parts of texts that they do not understand and read ahead to make sense of the section, article, or book. Teachers need to remind students, however, that this trick works only with trivial obstacles; when they fail to understand larger pieces of text, they need to try another strategy.

2. Readers can also change their rate of reading. They may not be getting a large enough sample of the writer's writing to guess his overall plan. Therefore they may deliberately speed up to look ahead or, conversely, slow down for places that appear more difficult. Many students do not realize that changing

pace is "allowed"! Some think that they must read every line at exactly the same speed.

3. Readers can suspend judgment. Good readers often continue to read ahead in hopes that the writer will fill in gaps, add more information, and clarify points in the text. Teachers need to tell students that this too is acceptable reading behavior. "When puzzled by one item," they can say, "read along—maybe increase your rate—and perhaps the writer will explain the item."

4. Readers should hypothesize. When readers are puzzled by individual words, sentences, or even paragraphs, they should make it a habit to hypothesize: "I think the word means _____" or "I think this sentence is supposed to _____." Teachers need to explain that reading is a matter of testing out these hypotheses: "If you think the word means _____, then read along and see if your guess makes sense."

5. Readers may reread. Some students shy away from this obvious fix-up strategy because it is time-consuming and disruptive. They need to be reminded that good readers reread frequently, checking back to discover if their guesses about word meanings were accurate or if their hypotheses about a writer's purposes were reasonable. As several researchers have noted, rereading is especially useful when readers perceive contradictions, irrelevancies, or too many interpretations.

6. Readers can—as a last resort—go to another source. Good readers regularly check outside references; they go to encyclopedias, dictionaries, other books, friends, and teachers. Such a fix-up is also time-consuming and disruptive but often necessary. Teachers need to remind students that, when other strategies fail, it is acceptable for them to check other sources.

Teaching Self-Monitoring Strategies

Teachers may encourage self-questioning and paraphrasing and the subsequent use of fix-up strategies. However, both research and classroom practice (see, for example, Biggam, 1985) suggest other approaches to the development of self-monitoring. Several are noted here.

Discuss with Students the Nature of Reading Students—at all levels—need to be regularly reminded that writers try to communicate messages, that their texts are designed to stimulate readers to figure out these messages, and that readers must be somewhat active mentally as they try to get the writer's messages. In other words, students need to be told, over and over again, that reading is a meaning-getting, meaning-building activity. A first step, therefore, in developing comprehension monitoring is to establish in students the belief that reading is not sounding out print but shaping meanings.

Explain the Obstacles to Comprehension   Readers cannot understand what writers are trying to say unless they have linguistic competence; that is, phonological, syntactical, and semantic knowledge of the language in which the text is written. They cannot understand texts unless they have knowledge of the ways writers organize and structure sentences, paragraphs, and pieces of longer discourse. They need too certain thinking skills (such as the ability to infer, predict, hypothesize). Above all, they need prior knowledge—of the world in general and of the specific subjects of the text—to comprehend. Students need to have all this explained to them, and such explanation should proceed in a systematic and orderly manner. Younger children need to be told that one obstacle to comprehension is lack of the knowledge of word meanings; high school and college students need to be told that they frequently cannot comprehend because writers are careless or unskilled in rhetorical competence. One approach to the development of comprehension monitoring is for the teacher to analyze a reading assignment carefully and list for students as many potential obstacles as possible. A teacher may note, for example, that certain words may cause problems, that the writer has no main idea sentence in a paragraph, that she has no clear-cut plan of organization, that she falsely assumes readers have prior knowledge in a particular area, and so forth. Calling attention to the possible obstacles to comprehension is a vital second step in the development of comprehension monitoring.

Have Students Define Purpose   A writer had a purpose for preparing a text; the reader has his or her purpose for reading it. Self-monitoring is difficult unless readers become aware of these purposes. Teachers need to call students' attention to both. Using headnotes, titles, illustrations, first sentences and paragraphs, and previewing techniques, students need to become accustomed to identifying what they think is the writer's purpose. Teachers need to ask of almost all assignments: "Why do you think the author wrote this? What's its purpose? What's the point?" They need to ask students too to define their own purpose or purposes in reading: "What are you trying to find out? What questions are you trying to answer?" Unless students are aware of their own and the writer's purpose for writing, they are not going to be sensitive to problems in comprehension or the need to cultivate self-monitoring strategies.

Teach Self-Questioning Techniques   Since Francis Robinson (1970) first recommended the SQ3R method many years ago, many reading teachers have told students to first "survey" (skim or preview) an assignment and make up questions they personally want answered *before* they read (and afterward "recite" and "review" their answers). Such an approach to reading becomes a self-monitoring device, because readers are forced to regularly check their answers to their own questions; readers maintain an awareness of what they are doing, why they are doing it, and how well they are succeeding.

A way to develop self-questioning with younger students is the "news reporter's approach.'' Many teachers explain that newspaper reporters try to provide in every story answers to the questions ''Who? What? Why? Where? When? and How?'' They tell children to check as they read to see how well they can answer such questions. For example, a teacher may say ''Read the first page to yourself. Now, make up six questions that a news reporter might ask, such as 'Who is the most important person in the story? What is he or she doing? Why are they doing it? When does this all happen?'''

A self-questioning approach intended both to test comprehension and to increase depth of content learning is suggested by Stewart and Tei (1983). They suggest that more mature students be trained to ask such questions as ''What was the concept introduced? How is it related to the other concepts (if any) in the text? How do these concepts differ? How is this section related to the other sections? How does the author convey the information about the topic?''

One of the most effective approaches to self-questioning is through anticipation of possible test questions. Students are told to skim or quickly read the assignment and then make up questions that a teacher might ask on a test. An alternative is the recommendation to students that they make up test questions as they read. Either way, readers become accustomed to asking questions of a text and checking their own level of comprehension as they read.

Encourage Students to Hypothesize   Once students define their purpose for reading a text and determine what they think the author's purpose is, have them make up a ''theory'' or ''hypothesis'' to account for what they are reading. Good readers seem to do this all the time. They pick up clues in the text and construct for themselves a theory to explain what they think the writer is trying to say. Then they read carefully to see if their theory makes sense. (See Chapter 3.) Students need to be encouraged to do this with guidance in the classroom. Teachers need to point out specific clues in the text that may lead students to a possible ''theory''; and then show students how the theory is tested through their subsequent reading. For example, after agreeing that the author of their science book is probably going to explain sunspots (that seems to be his purpose in these pages), students are told to read the assignment quickly to see if they can construct a theory of sunspots: ''How do you think he is going to explain them?'' The actual reading then becomes a checking-out of student hypotheses. When more than one hypothesis is offered by students, the reading and later discussion tends to be stimulating.

Call Attention to the Text and the Ways It is Organized   Texts are structured by writers. Readers who are aware of ways texts are structured tend to be in a better position to understand what writers are doing. (See Chapter 6.) One approach to developing self-monitoring is continued attention in classroom discussions to patterns of organization, transitional words and phrases, main idea sentences, and other rhetorical means writers use to signal their chosen structures. As students set out to read an assignment, teachers should remind them that is probably has a structure and that it behooves them to be aware of it. A simple monitoring device for high school students (who have learned patterns of organization!) is a set of questions to be asked of troublesome paragraphs:

What pattern is the writer using here? Cause–effect? Sequence? Generalization?

Is there a main idea sentence? What is it?

Are there obvious signaling devices? (*First, next, because, on-the-other-hand*, etc.)

Do successful adult readers do this? Probably only when they are aware of a comprehension breakdown. Most students, however, benefit from regularly watching out for writers' plans of organization, if for no other reason than that it sensitizes them to structure and to possible explanations for noncomprehension. Looking for main idea sentences—whether the reader finds them or not—is a self-monitoring technique.

Encourage Students to Relate What They Are Reading to What They Already Know Relating the new to the known is one of the most effective of all self-monitoring devices. If, while reading, one checks new information and ideas against one's prior knowledge, confirmation of comprehension—or lack of comprehension—is instant. For example, if the successful adult reader becomes aware that most of the printed data are unrelated to what she knows and so are impossible to compare, she concludes at once that she is not comprehending; if the data are "old stuff" to her, then she assumes comprehension. In either case, she is self-monitoring. (See Chapter 4.)

One self-monitoring strategy for students is the preparation of a simple "new-old" list. Some teachers have students draw a line down the center of a page of their notebook, head the left side "New" and the right, "Old"; then, as they read, jot down responses. Thus a middle school student reading about modern Japan might note on the left side that he did not know that Japanese workers worked for only one firm all their lives; and on the right side that he did know that Japan was a democracy. Such a strategy is inherently flawed (How does a reader know what she knows or does not know?), but it does direct readers' attention to their own comprehension of texts, while at the same time forces them to begin to distinguish between the new and the known.

Encourage Much Paraphrasing and Summarizing Paraphrasing, as has been noted, is an important way of discovering if or how well one understands. When teachers ask students to tell in their own words what a paragraph or chapter says, they are able to learn much about the quality of students' comprehension. When students themselves try to tell themselves what a text means, they are using an excellent self-monitoring strategy. Teachers need to encourage as much paraphrasing as possible in reading lessons. As students read in class (silently or orally), teachers should ask them "What does that mean? Tell me in your own words what the author is saying." Students should be encouraged to ask themselves as they read "What does that mean?" and to repeat what they think the author is saying in their own language. As a *self-monitoring* device, paraphrasing may be criticized: the reader may be telling himself, in his own language, an incorrect interpretation. However, paraphrasing remains a valuable tool for the reader, because the inability to paraphrase clearly means one of two things: the author has done an incompetent job, or the reader does not understand the text. The act of paraphrasing, whether used as a self-monitoring device or not, is important to comprehension, because it forces students to conceptualize their ideas and, as Henry (1974) has noted, discover what meanings they have for them.

Summarizing is generally considered a postreading activity. Students are taught to (1) delete trivial information, (2) delete redundant information, (3) think up a blanket term to replace a list of smaller items or actions, and (4) select—or make up—a topic sentence (Brown, Campione, and Day, 1981). However, summarizing may serve as an effective monitoring strategy. When students are instructed in techniques for preparing summaries and have had sufficient practice in writing them, they may be advised—in advance of reading—that a summary-writing exercise will follow. They then read to detect trivial or redundant material, to think of general rather than specific terms, and to watch for possible main idea sentences. Their success—or failure—to achieve these goals as they read indicates to them how well or poorly they are comprehending. (See Chapter 6 for discussion of summarizing.)

Do Much Modeling for Classes   Students, no matter how mature or sophisticated, profit from demonstrations of the above strategies. Many teachers take time to read possibly difficult texts aloud in class and to show students how they themselves check their own comprehension. Thus a middle school teacher may take a poem, read it with the children, and ask himself: What was the author's purpose in writing this? What obstacles may prevent me from understanding it? What words are new to me? used in odd ways? What sentences seem especially strange to me? How do I know if I've understood the poem? What questions might I ask myself? What ideas here are completely new to me? Does it make better sense if I try to explain it in my own words? As the teacher reads the poem and poses the questions, he encourages the children to suggest answers, while he shows how he might answer each.

Davey (1983) recommends a modeling activity called "think-aloud." She reads a passage that contains contradictions, ambiguities, unknown words, and other points of difficulty. As students follow her, reading silently, she shows them how she thinks through "trouble spots" by making predictions, visualizing, verbalizing confusing points, and sharing analogies. She may say

"From the title, I predict that this will tell how fishermen used to catch whales."

"I think this is going to be a description of a computer game."

"I have a picture in my mind now of a car, all alone, on a dark, narrow road."

"This reminds me of the time I drove to Boston and had a flat tire. We were worried and had to walk three miles for help."

"This just doesn't make sense to me."

"This is different from what I expected."

"I had better reread this part."

'Maybe I'll read ahead to see if things get clearer."

Davey notes that, after several such modeling experiences, students can begin to work with partners to practice think-alouds, each child taking turns reading aloud and sharing his or her thinking. The listening partner is encouraged to share thoughts, and both discuss and evaluate one another's ideas about the text and some ways to think about it. As she points out, such activities help students realize not only that reading should make sense but also that "readers can fix things up when reading does not make sense" (1983, p. 46).

Develop Comprehension-Monitoring Study Guides   Many teachers through the years have used study guides to direct student attention to key points in their assignments and to highlight information important to understanding its content (see Devine, 1981, pp. 166–179). Study guides may be designed to assist students as they learn to self-monitor. Teachers may prepare one- or two-page guides that force students to think about their own mental processes as they read. For example, a guide for a specific reading assignment in a content area textbook might ask such questions as

1. From the title, headnote, illustrations, and a quick preview of the section, what do you think is the author's purpose? What is your purpose in reading this?
2. What questions do you want the author to answer for you? (Jot these down in your notebook.)
3. After a first reading, try answering this: What questions about the assignment might a teacher ask on a test?

4. What organizational plan does this author seem to use? Does she deviate from the plan? Where? Why—in your opinion?

Guide items may be more specific and personal:

5. Check—or note in your notebook—those places you had most trouble understanding what the author was saying. Why do you think you had trouble? What might the author have done to help you?
6. Every paragraph has an obvious, well-defined main idea sentence—with three exceptions. Which do not? Why do you think the author omitted them in these places?
7. One sentence on page 17 is extremely complicated. Identify it, and try to explain why most readers would have trouble with it. What seems to be its subject? its main predicate?
8. When did you have to reread? Why?
9. On which occasions did you have to read ahead? Why did you? Were your purposes accomplished?
10. How much guessing did you have to do? (about specific words? about ideas? about new information?)
11. Note the places where you had a comprehension breakdown. Why do you think you had trouble at these spots?
12. Did you get the author's message? Write a one-paragraph summary that organizes his main points in your own words.

Students who have been provided with comprehension-monitoring guides on a regular basis may—in time—internalize the self-monitoring strategies discussed here. Research findings on the values of self-monitoring are as yet not unequivocal nor entirely clear, and, as Baker and Brown (1984, p. 44) note, "instruction aimed at instigating cognitive monitoring should not be regarded as a panacea for reading difficulties." However, teachers may feel fairly confident about developing comprehension-monitoring guides and introducing students to the various approaches mentioned here, because available research evidence does imply that

- Merely making students aware that they should continue studying and self-testing until ready for a test does improve study performance—at least in young children (Brown, Campione, and Barclay, 1979);
- Instructing students in efficient self-questioning is an effective studying procedure (Andre and Anderson, 1978–79);
- Sensitizing readers to the logical structure of a text and the meaning inherent in passages does help the less able reader (Owings, Peterson, Bransford, Morris, and Stein, 1980); and
- Instructing students to evaluate texts for consistency and truthfulness increases the likelihood that they will do so (Markman, 1979).

▪ RECAPPING MAIN POINTS ▪

Often readers immediately comprehend texts; their prior knowledge is such that it allows them to pick up a few clues on the printed page and reconstruct texts-in-their-heads that are the same as the writer's. Most of the time, however, readers have to use cognitive strategies to think through and beyond the printed text before they can arrive at viable interpretations. The most important cognitive process, or skill, they use is inferencing, not only the kind that permits them to hypothesize a missing slot in a script, or schema, but forward inferencing (which allows them to predict) and backward inferencing (which allows them to draw conclusions and explanations).

Readers frequently too must use deductive and inductive reasoning as they develop their interpretations—particularly when they lack adequate prior knowledge or enough clues in the printed text. Almost always they should use critical reading skills to help them evaluate the ideas and information they find in texts.

By thinking about their own thinking processes, readers can learn to use many of these cognitive strategies more effectively. Self-monitoring, for example, allows them to check and recheck their interpretations as they form them in reading; fix-up strategies permit them to pinpoint misunderstandings and take corrective measures.

END-OF-CHAPTER ACTIVITIES

1. Describe an inference you have consciously made recently. In what ways does it fit the description given in the chapter of *slot filling?*
2. Some authorities say that children cannot make good inferences. What arguments might you offer to show that differences between children's and adults' inferencing is quantitative rather than qualitative? Be prepared to explain this difference.
3. What is the difference between *forward inferencing* and *backward inferencing?* Explain the difference and give an example of each.
4. Six strategies for improving inferencing are given in the chapter. Suggest another strategy that you might use in your class.
5. This book contends that readers often comprehend easily and effortlessly without thinking. Give ten examples of texts you have comprehended today without consciously thinking about them.
6. The chapter notes that some texts do demand thinking. What three examples are cited? Give an example of each from your own recent reading.
7. When recently have you done deductive thinking? inductive thinking? problem solving? Be prepared to describe these occasions.

8. In what ways is reading problem solving? In what ways is it not?
9. Seven suggestions are given in the chapter for improving problem solving skills in reading. Suggest another that you might try in your own classes.
10. The chapter discusses the relationship between critical thinking and critical reading. It implies a definition of critical reading without spelling one out. How would you define critical reading? Prepare a brief written definition.
11. Distinguishing fact from opinion is discussed under inferences. What role does fact/opinion awareness play in critical reading?
12. Several recent professional books on reading are cited in the chapter, because they include excellent discussions of critical reading. Locate one of these sources and find in it more strategies for promoting critical reading ability. Be prepared to share these ideas in class.
13. Be prepared to explain the differences between comprehension monitoring, cognitive monitoring, and metacognition.
14. Which monitoring devices are most important? How was an answer to this question obtained?
15. What are fix-up strategies? Name six. Which of these do you find yourself using most frequently?
16. Select one of the research studies cited in the References and write an abstract of it. Be sure to indicate the purpose of the study and the procedures used. Tell why—or why not—it contributes to our understanding of the comprehension process.
17. Write a brief paper on *ways to improve human thinking* based entirely upon what you remember from reading this chapter. (In other words, do not go to other sources nor look back at the chapter.) The completed paper, in addition to being a useful product in itself, should reflect the text-in-the-head you developed as you read.
18. Write a review of this book. In what ways has it helped you better understand reading comprehension? What are the chief insights you derived from reading it? With which points do you agree most strongly? disagree most strongly? Why? If you were to write a similar book, in what ways would it be different?

REFERENCES

Anderson, John R. *Cognitive Psychology and Its Implications*. San Francisco: W. H. Freeman, 1980.
Anderson, Thomas H. "Study Strategies and Adjunct Aids." In R. J. Spiro, B. C. Bruce, and W. H. Brewer (Eds.), *Theoretical Issues in Reading Comprehension*. Hillsdale, N. J.: Lawrence Erlbaum Associates, 1980.

Andre, Marli E. D. A., and Thomas H. Anderson. "The Development and Evaluation of a Self-questioning Study Technique." *Reading Research Quarterly* 14 (1978-79): 605-623.

Baker, Linda. *Comprehension Monitoring: Identifying and Coping with Text Confusion.* (Technical Report No. 145.) Urbana, Ill.: Center for the Study of Reading, 1979.

Baker, Linda, and Ann L. Brown. "Cognitive Monitoring in Reading." In James Flood (Ed.), *Understanding Reading Comprehension.* Newark, Del.: International Reading Association, 1984.

Biggam, Susan Carey. "Preaching What We Practice: Teaching Comprehension Monitoring to Middle-grade Students." *New England Reading Association Journal* 20 (Spring/Summer 1985): 27-34.

Bloom, Benjamin (Ed.). *Taxonomy of Educational Objectives.* New York: David McKay, 1956.

Brown, Ann L. "Metacognitive Development and Reading." In R. J. Spiro, B. C. Bruce, and W. H. Brewer (Eds.), *Theoretical Issues in Reading Comprehension.* Hillsdale, N. J.: Lawrence Erlbaum Associates, 1980.

Brown, Ann L., J. C. Campione, and C. R. Barclay. "Training Self-checking Routines for Estimating Reading Readiness." *Child Development* 50 (1979): 501-512.

Brown, Ann L., J. C. Campione, and J. D. Day. "Learning to Learn: On Training Students to Learn from Texts." *Educational Researcher* 10 (February 1981): 14-21.

Burmeister, Lou E. *Foundations and Strategies for Teaching Children to Read.* Reading, Mass.: Addison-Wesley, 1983.

Collins, Allan, and Edward E. Smith. *Teaching the Process of Reading Comprehension.* (Technical Report No. 182.) Urbana, Ill.: Center for the Study of Reading, 1980.

Davey, Beth. "Think Aloud—Modeling the Cognitive Processes of Reading Comprehension." *Journal of Reading* 27 (October 1983): 44-47.

Devine, Thomas G. *Teaching Study Skills: A Guide for Teachers.* Boston: Allyn and Bacon, 1981.

Dewey, John. *How We Think* (new ed.) Boston: D. C. Heath, 1933.

Durrell, Donald D. "Language and the Higher Mental Processes." *Review of Educational Research* 13 (April 1943): 110-114.

Early, Margaret. *Reading to Learn in Grades 5 to 12.* New York: Harcourt Brace Jovanovich, 1984.

Goodman, Kenneth S. "Unity in Reading." In Alan C. Purvis and Olive Niles (Eds.), *Becoming Readers in a Complex Society, 83rd Yearbook of the National Society for the Study of Education.* Chicago: University of Chicago Press, 1984.

Goodman, Yetta M., and Carolyn Burke. *Reading Strategies: Focus on Comprehension.* New York: Holt, Rinehart and Winston, 1980.

Guerra, Cathy L. "The Scientific Method Helps Secondary Students Read Their Textbooks." *Journal of Reading* 27 (March 1984): 487-489.

Hansen, Jane. "The Effects of Inference Training and Practice on Young Children's Reading Comprehension." *Reading Research Quarterly* 16 (1981): 391-417.

Henry, George H. *Teaching Reading as Concept Development.* Newark, Del.: International Reading Association, 1974.

Jenkins, Carol A., and John F. Savage. *Activities for Integrating the Language Arts.* Englewood Cliffs, N. J.: Prentice-Hall, 1983.

Lapp, Diane, and James Flood. *Teaching Reading to Every Child.* New York: Macmillan, 1983.

Lipson, Marjorie Y. "Promoting Children's Metacognition about Reading through Direct Instruction." Paper presented at the International Reading Association convention, Chicago, Illinois, April, 1982.

Markman, Ellen M. "Reading That You Don't Understand: Elementary School Children's Awareness of Inconsistencies." *Child Development* 50 (September 1979): 643–655.

Merriam-Webster. *Ninth New Collegiate Dictionary.* Springfield, Mass.: Merriam-Webster, 1983.

Omanson, R. C., W. H. Warren, and T. R. Trabasso. "Goals, Themes, Inferences, and Memory: A Developmental Study." Paper presented at the American Educational Research Association convention, Toronto, Canada, 1978.

Owings, R. A., G. A. Peterson, J. D. Bransford, C. D. Morris, and B. S. Stein. "Spontaneous Monitoring and Regulation of Learning: A Comparison of Successful and Less Successful Fifth Graders." *Journal of Educational Psychology* 72 (1980): 250–256.

Paris, S. G., and B. K. Lindauer. "The Role of Inference in Children's Comprehension and Memory for Sentences." *Cognitive Psychology* 8 (1976): 217–227.

Pearson, P. David, and Dale D. Johnson. *Teaching Reading Comprehension.* New York: Holt, Rinehart and Winston, 1978.

Piaget, Jean, B. Inhelder, and A. Szeminsko. *The Child's Conception of Geometry.* New York: Basic Books, 1960.

Pitts, Murray M. "Comprehension Monitoring: Definition and Practice." *Journal of Reading* 26 (March 1983): 516–523.

Robinson, Francis P. *Effective Study,* 4th ed. New York: Harper & Row, 1970.

Rumelhart, David E. "Schemata: The Building Blocks of Cognition." In R. J. Spiro, B. C. Bruce, and W. F. Brewer (Eds.), *Theoretical Issues in Reading Comprehension.* Hillsdale, N. J.: Lawrence Erlbaum Associates, 1980.

Russell, David H. *Children's Thinking.* Waltham, Mass.: Blaisdell Publishing, 1956.

Santeusanio, Richard P. *A Practical Approach to Content Area Reading.* Reading, Mass.: Addison-Wesley, 1983.

Stauffer, Russell G. *The Language-experience Approach to the Teaching of Reading.* New York: Harper & Row, 1970.

Stewart, Oran, and Ebo Tei. "Some Implications of Metacognition for Reading Instruction." *Journal of Reading* 27 (October 1983): 36–43.

Trabasso, T. R., D. A. Nicholas, R. C. Omanson, and L. Johnson. "Inference and Story Comprehension." Paper presented at the Society for Research in Child Development, New Orleans, Louisiana, 1977.

Wagoner, Shirley A. "Comprehension Monitoring: What It Is and What We Know about It." *Reading Research Quarterly* 43 (Spring 1983): 328–346.

Watanabe, Patricia, V. C. Hare, and R. G. Lomax. "Predicting News Story Content from Headlines." *Journal of Reading* 27 (February 1984): 436–442.

Winograd, Peter, and Peter Johnston. *Comprehension Monitoring and the Error Detection Paradigm.* (Technical Report No. 153.) Urbana, Ill.: The Center for the Study of Reading, 1980.

Zintz, Miles V., and Zelda R. Maggart. *The Reading Process: The Teacher and the Learner,* 4th ed. Dubuque, Iowa: Wm. C. Brown Publishers, 1984.

Testing Reading Comprehension

It has always seemed appropriate that teachers do something after teaching to discover to what extent students have profited from their teaching. Reading teachers, probably since the earliest days of formal reading instruction, usually create simple tests, asking questions about passages read or requiring written responses to lessons. When it became apparent that instruction sometimes failed in its purposes, many teachers began to use versions of their tests to improve instruction by identifying the kinds of problems students encounter as well as the students who might have these problems. Later, when administrators, school board members, and others wanted to compare large groups of students, specialists began to develop tests to facilitate such comparison-making, thus allowing for those outside the classroom to compare individual schools, classes, and teachers. Some of the instruments so developed were further refined to permit diagnosis of individual needs, to make predictions, and to serve as a basis not only for comparisons between groups but also for discovering correlations between reading test scores and scores of various other kinds of tests purportedly measuring other student characteristics. In recent decades the development and merchandising of tests has become a relatively large-scale industry in the United States; and in recent years testing—especially in reading—has often seemed to so usurp instructional time in schools that some reading teachers talk of the tail wagging the dog.

What do these many reading tests—and there are now hundreds of them—actually reveal about *reading comprehension?*

Do any of them indicate how students construct their own texts-in-the-head?

Do they tell what those texts-in-the-head may be?

Which tests are possibly helpful? Which may be misleading?

How may teachers discover the effectiveness of their reading comprehension instruction?

The most widely used kinds of tests are described briefly here, with some comments made about their effectiveness as measures of reading comprehension.

Standardized Reading Tests

Standardized tests allow for comparisons to be made between individual students, classes, and schools by establishing *standards* or *norms* to which individual test scores may be compared. Prior to their development, a fourth-grade teacher (for example) could compare Robert or Mary with one another, with other children in the class, or with her memories and/or records (both possibly inaccurate) of previous fourth-grade children. Comparisons tended to be impressionistic: "Robert doesn't do as well as others in his group" or "Mary seems much better than other fourth-graders I've had." By providing a yardstick to compare Robert and Mary with other fourth-graders nationally, test makers eliminate much guesswork (and bias) from the comparison-making process. The yardstick provided by test makers is a set of averages of test scores obtained by administering the test to a large group of similar students throughout the country. After administering the test, test makers may find that—on the average—fourth-graders nationally answered correctly 25 of 45 test items in one area of reading (such as vocabulary), fifth-graders answered 30 of the 45, and sixth-graders, 35. Using this data as a yardstick (or norm), the test maker offers test users charts to compare (often by using percentiles or grade-equivalence scores) raw scores obtained by their students with the "national norm." Thus if Robert gets 27 of the 45 items in the subtest, he may be said to be reading at the 4.2 level (that is, fourth grade, second month); Mary's 35 may put her at the 5.8 level. By combining scores for various subtests (in vocabulary, study skills, comprehension, etc.), test makers can also give a "total" score (in either grade equivalence or percentile scores), which may be used to compare individual students, classes, and schools.

What does all this have to do with *reading comprehension?* especially with reading comprehension when it is defined—as it is in these pages—as the process of building texts-in-readers'-heads? The answer must be "Very little."

In the first place, all information obtained from standardized tests must be interpreted in view of the *limitations* inherent in all such testing:

1. Scores reflect performance at only one short point in students' lives and may thus be affected by fatigue, ill health, emotional strain, and a myriad of other factors detrimental to test-taking.

2. The texts provided by the test maker may not be of interest to the test taker; and, as noted in Chapter 1, comprehenders-to-be must *want* to comprehend a text for comprehension to take place.

3. Test makers, because of the nature of their task, must set time constraints upon test takers; and, as noted in both Chapters 1 and 8, some texts demand the use of cognitive skills and reasoning powers, which often requires considerable time. (This limitation raises an important point: Do such timed tests measure speed of thinking or quality of thinking? This in turn leads to what may be an even more im-

portant point: Should schools be concerned with the quality of students' thinking or its rate and quantity?)

4. Test makers sometimes assume students share a body of information (prior knowledge) that all do not necessarily have, thus handicapping students from groups markedly dissimilar from those in the norm population (particularly those in minority and low socioeconomic groups).

5. Too often tests (or subtests) purportedly measuring reading comprehension actually measure for recall of factual details.

In addition to these general limitations inherent in standardized testing, at least three others need to be considered by teachers trying to promote and measure reading comprehension:

6. The "comprehension" scores provided by such tests are usually based on a few subtest scores, each of which reflects only one *aspect* of the total comprehension process. One such test measures (1) recognizing main ideas, (2) making inferences, (3) word knowledge in context, and (4) getting literal meaning. These separate subtest scores are then combined to give *one* comprehension score. While few dispute that each of these four is involved somehow with the comprehension process, fewer would claim that they constitute the process. Clearly, to take one example, identifying main ideas can help readers understand certain texts; but alone, or in combination with the other three, it is not reading comprehension. The same may be noted of the other three.

7. The comprehension scores seem to rest on the belief that comprehension is an amalgamation of bits and pieces rather than a holistic process. As noted immediately above, one test combines four subtests of four separate and distinct aspects of comprehension to provide a single score (with its appropriate percentile rankings and grade equivalencies). Other tests measure (sometimes with only four or five test items for each) such aspects as drawing conclusions, making predictions, distinguishing fact from opinion, recognizing propaganda techniques, noting bias, following sequence, judging sources, and so forth. They then combine results from such disparate "subtests" into a single total comprehension score! Test users are thus encouraged to believe that comprehension consists of many separate skills and processes—and that these should be taught separately and sequentially. Unfortunately evidence to support this view of comprehension is lacking (see Chapter 3). Readers may indeed use such separate skills and processes as they build their own texts-in-the-head for a printed text, but they do not necessarily use them. Testing to discover how effectively students use them is important, but the

results of such testing do not automatically reveal much about students' comprehension of specific texts.

8. Comprehension scores from standardized reading tests often fail to consider student prior knowledge. At one level, prior knowledge seems to be ignored by test makers. One finds test items that may be answered successfully by students who have not read the test passages. Students already know the answers as part of their general knowledge of the world. Test makers nevertheless ask the questions and interpret the resultant test scores in terms of reading comprehension, when in fact students have not had to comprehend the passages at all. The answers were already stored in their long-term memories. (One egregious example: fourth-graders are asked to read a passage in which is included the information that George Washington was the first president of the United States. Among the test items is one that lists four presidents—George Washington included—and tells them to check the first president!)

At another level, prior knowledge is assumed when it should not be. Thus one finds questions that may be answered successfully only by students who share certain knowledge of the world. Some students—particularly those from low socioeconomic or minority groups—are penalized because they lack the assumed world knowledge.

Many of the most widely used standardized reading tests were initially developed two or more decades ago. Their underlying assumptions reflect little or none of the research and theory in reading comprehension of the past ten years. Although their publishers boast of "up-dating" and constant refinements, those efforts have tended to focus on statistical and technical improvements—not on redesigning the tests so that they are more in accord with contemporary views on the comprehension process.

Criterion-Referenced Tests

Prior to the development of norm-referenced standardized reading tests, Robert and Mary may have been compared (as noted above) to one another, their classmates, or other fourth-graders their teacher remembers; with standardized tests their scores may be compared with the mean grade-level scores of other elementary school children throughout the country. In other words, standardized tests provide a fairly firm standard or norm for comparing Robert and Mary with not only other fourth-graders but other children generally. They allow teachers to say "Robert isn't reading at grade level" and principals to say "Our fourth-graders score above the national norms."

Many educators note, however, that the "fairly firm" standard is in fact rather relative itself: it depends always on how all those other children average out; and they may not perform the same year after year. Is there, many have asked, an even firmer yardstick? Many have suggested *criterion-referenced* tests, which use an individual's ability to perform a certain task as the standard. In such a test, Mary is asked to find the main idea sentence in each of ten passages. If she is successful a certain number of times, say eight, then she is said to have "mastered" that particular operation. Her teacher may then say "Mary's mastered the skill of finding main ideas: she got 8 out of 10."

In constructing such tests, test makers list all important skills associated with—in this case—reading comprehension. (They do the same for decoding, study skills, computation, and other areas to be tested.) Then they prepare pass–fail items, perhaps ten for each skill, set up (arbitrarily) levels for passing (such as 8 out of 10), and sequence the items from easy to hard or low to high. Test makers note various advantages such criterion-referenced tests have over standardized norm-referenced tests. For example,

1. Rather than tell (vaguely) that students read at certain grade levels (not especially valuable information in itself), criterion-referenced tests reveal more-or-less *exactly* which skills have been learned so far.
2. They may be used diagnostically by teachers, because they indicate not only which skills have been learned or need to be learned but also those in which students require further instruction and practice.
3. They thus pinpoint targets for teachers: "Mary needs help in finding main ideas, while Robert can move on to 'predicting outcomes.'"

But how well do these tests measure *reading comprehension?* Clearly they too suffer some of the same disadvantages of standardized tests: they reflect performance at one point in time; they may not interest students sufficiently for them to try to comprehend; and they set arbitrary time constraints upon testees. In addition, criterion-referenced tests present some other problems to teachers trying to measure comprehension:

1. They assume that comprehension is a complex of separate skills. Most standardized reading tests rest on the same assumption, but developers of criterion-referenced tests carry this belief to extremes, sometimes testing as many as thirty discrete skills and implying that the combined scores reflect comprehension.
2. Criterion-referenced tests may provide *too much* information. Standardized tests have been criticized because they focus on too few aspects of comprehension: "What specifically should I teach?" teachers ask. "Which skills do I need to work on?" Criterion-referenced tests, on the other hand, give teachers so many individual skills to think about for each group or class of children that teaching reading comprehension becomes a Herculean task, requiring vast

managerial and engineering skills on the part of already busy classroom teachers.

3. They take much time to administer.

4. They lead to sequencing and the development of levels and hierarchies of skills. Once thirty or more skills have been identified, they must be arranged somehow on the test. The tendency has been to arrange them from easy to difficult, or low-level to high-level. Unfortunately no evidence exists in the research to support a belief in levels or hierarchies of separate skills. (See Chapter 3.) Comprehension is a holistic process in which readers use many skills simultaneously. No evidence indicates that they must learn separate low-level skills before high-level skills or that scope-and-sequence charts in comprehension skills are anything but a pedagogical (or editorial) convenience.

5. They imply that instruction may cease when a level of mastery has been reached. Teachers may not teach inferencing once a student has demonstrated that he can answer 8 out of 10 items successfully, yet inferencing instruction needs to be continued with increasingly difficult material through the upper grades (and into college). The same may be said, of course, about almost every skill included in most criterion-referenced tests.

6. Finally, criterion-referenced tests suggest a model for instruction that may be detrimental to effective comprehension teaching. Teachers who come to view reading comprehension as a composite of skills, each of which needs to be assessed separately, may be inclined to teach these skills separately, providing few opportunities for students to generalize and integrate.

Miscue Analysis

Another approach to the assessment of reading comprehension is to be found in *miscue analysis*. Using this technique, the teacher has the student read orally for 15 to 20 minutes from passages one grade level above placement level. While the student reads, the teacher follows and marks the miscues (rather than "errors") the student may make (such as substitutions, omissions, reversals, insertions, repetitions, unsuccessful attempts to correct, and intonation shifts internal to the word). Later, the teacher analyzes the miscues according to various categories:

- The *graphic proximity* category represents the student's ability to figure out an unknown word by sight;
- The *phonic proximity* category represents his or her ability to figure one out by sounding out its letters;
- The *grammatical function* category represents the student's ability to

produce errors that are at least the same part of speech as the word in the passage;

- The *syntactic acceptability* category represents his or her ability to recognize the syntactic constraints of the sentence;
- The *semantic acceptability* category represents the student's ability to use the meaning of the whole sentence when offering a word in context;
- The *meaning change* category represents the degree to which an error changes the message of the text; and
- The *self-correction* category represents the student's ability to correct errors without promptings from the teacher.

What can teachers learn from this kind of detailed analysis? They are able to discover much about an individual student's problems in understanding texts. They can determine—rather precisely—the kind of instructional assistance needed. If Robert, for example, misreads *goldfish* for *cat* in *The cat ate the goldfish*, his teacher knows that his grammatical competence is acceptable (both words fulfill the same grammatical function) but his syntactic competence is not acceptable (he fails to use the meaning of the whole sentence to guide him). If Mary, for another example, substitutes *bat* for *cat* in the same sentence, the teacher may look for her problem in the graphic or phonic proximity categories. Most important of all, as the teacher analyzes the miscues, she begins to see how a student develops his or her text-in-the-head from the printed text.

Miscue analysis provides further ways for teachers to better understand students' comprehension. Usually the teacher asks the student, who has completed the oral reading, to close the book and "retell" the story or material found in the passages read. The teacher does not interrupt but afterward asks questions she believes are important to understanding the text (such as "What can you tell me about . . . ?," "Why do you think that happened?," or "When did that happen?"). This procedure clearly allows the teacher opportunities to assess the student's text-in-the-head.

When teachers analyze the responses students make when they retell what they have read, they find that "miscomprehension" problems tend to fall into certain categories:

- Students lack appropriate prior knowledge. Sometimes they simply lack the background information needed to make sense out of the text.
- Their prior knowledge is poorly developed. They may know enough to make some connections between the new information and the old, but their "old" knowledge consists of schemata not yet fully developed. They need these schemata extended and further refined before they can comprehend a particular text.
- They confuse schemata they already have. A cue in the text reminds

them of knowledge they already have but which is inappropriate for comprehending the text.

- They already know (or think they know) what is in the text. After picking up a few cues from the beginning of the text, students form in their minds a certain interpretation. Consequently they fail to continue reading to check out their interpretation. (For more information about these sources of miscomprehension, see Chapters 2 and 4.)

Such analysis provides insight not only into the ways individual students form their interpretations of specific texts but also into the nature of the comprehension process itself. It has been said that every reading teacher should regularly complete such analyses as part of his or her continuing self-education as a professional.

Miscue analysis offers teachers more opportunities to observe the development of students' texts-in-the-head than either standardized reading tests or criterion-referenced tests. Why then is the approach less often found in classrooms?

1. Miscue analysis takes more time. Most standardized reading tests may be administered to large groups of students in less than an hour. Criterion-referenced tests may require two or more sessions to administer, but also they may be given to large numbers of students at the same time. Miscue analysis may be done with only one student at a time.

2. Miscue analysis requires more effort on the teacher's part. To catch all miscues, enter them in an appropriate inventory, and later analyze them in terms of the seven categories described above demands not only time but preparation and study by the teacher who wants to use this approach to assessment.

3. It is strictly an oral reading procedure. While it may reveal much to the sensitive teacher about how a student's mind works as he or she tries to comprehend texts, the teacher may only infer that the student goes through the same processes when reading silently.

Informal Classroom Testing

Both standardized norm-referenced and criterion-referenced tests appear to rest on less-than-firm theoretical foundations. In addition, the former may be said to provide too little information and the latter too much: reading grade levels may be discovered easily—and far more cheaply—by a variety of other classroom procedures, while discovering student ability to manage thirty or more separate skills can lead to information overload in many classrooms. Does this mean that teachers must rely on miscue analysis to measure reading comprehension? Despite its value in revealing something of how students construct their texts-in-the-head, miscue analysis has disadvantages: it requires skill and training to administer; it takes time; it may be administered to only one student at a time; it is an oral reading test; and so forth. What other measures then may teachers use to assess comprehension?

Nine suggestions are made here for testing reading comprehension. All fall under the heading "Informal Classroom Testing." Some allow only one student to be checked at a time, but most may be done in groups or classes. None requires special teacher training or necessitates additional funding. All are natural outgrowths of normal teaching activities.

Oral Retellings   The single most effective way to discover what a reader has comprehended is to ask him! If Mary's teacher wants to know how well Mary has understood a passage in the basal reader or content area textbook, she may ask: "What does that mean to you, Mary?" or "If you had to explain that to Robert, what would you tell him?" Clearly oral retellings assume some oral language skills on the part of students as well as confidence in their ability to do the task. However, if this procedure is followed regularly from primary grades through secondary school, students may have many opportunities to develop both. It provides immediate feedback, allowing teachers to observe those texts-in-the-head in the process of being created, while at the same time giving students direct encouragement to develop their own interpretations. In many classes today teachers have little idea of what responses students make to individualized reading experiences (they wait for the results of formal tests to discover if students comprehend!); and students are not really challenged to form their own interpretations (they let their eyes move over the lines, knowing that they will never be asked what they read).

Oral Paraphrases   As many have noted, the process of saying something *in one's own words* is a powerful tool for understanding. (See Chapter 6.) When a text includes a sentence or paragraph that the teacher believes may be difficult to understand, she can ask: "What does that mean to you?" or "Tell me what that means in your own words." If students are unable to paraphrase, then their teacher has grounds for thinking they are unable to understand and may return to the passage to explain it (using strategies suggested in Chapter 4). Oral paraphrasing is both a tool students may use to better comprehend and a testing device for teachers to assess comprehension.

Oral Summaries   Oral summaries have many of the advantages of simple retellings and paraphrasing but demand more intellectual activity on the part of students. They must find the main ideas of the passage, distinguish between relevant and irrelevant material provided, sequence the information they want to include, and be aware of the writer's purpose in writing the passage. All this requires practice and instruction, but summarizing experiences may begin in primary grades ("If you were a newspaper editor, what headline would you write to summarize this paragraph?") and continue through secondary school ("What is the basic idea here? What may we leave out? How shall we arrange the ideas? What's the main purpose of the paragraph or passage?"). The process of preparing summaries allows students to think through their texts-in-the head: they find out what the text means to them as they develop the summary.

Written Retellings   Written retellings, written paraphrases, and written summaries all assume an ability to write. Clearly very young children who have no command yet over the orthographic system of English cannot readily retell on paper. Their teachers, however, can write on chalkboard or wall charts the sentences children suggest. Older students should be encouraged as soon as possible to begin written responses to texts. The importance of written responses lies in the fact that short-term memory is short! When a student tries to think through his retelling of a text, he can hold his ideas in short-term memory for only a few seconds; when he thinks with a pencil and paper, he may better hold his ideas while organizing and evaluating them. Teachers may introduce written retellings into their lessons in a variety of ways: "This is such a good story it would be fun to tell it to someone else in a letter" or "Robert was absent today so let's tell him the science lesson in a short letter." (See Chapter 6 for other suggestions.)

Written Paraphrases   One way to introduce written paraphrases into intermediate grade classes is by having students write out their versions of troublesome sentences encountered in texts. For example, when one particular sentence in an assignment appears to trouble students in the group, the teacher may have them all write out their own versions. These paraphrases may then be shared and discussed, giving the teacher not only an opportunity to see how individual students interpreted the sentence but also a chance to help them all form what she believes is a better interpretation.

Written Summaries   Because summarizing includes several separate skills used simultaneously, the teacher may choose to focus on each separately first: "What is the writer's main purpose in this chapter? Let's write that down. What is the main idea? Are there other main ideas? Let's write those down. In what order does he present them? Let's note that on our papers. What can we safely leave out? Let's *not* write that down." This teaching procedure clearly guides the development of individual interpretations: an adult teacher who thinks she knows what the writer's text-in-the-head was as the text was prepared is guiding readers, step by step, through a process of reconstructing that text. Assessment may take place later when the teacher simply says "When you finish reading the chapter, write a brief summary using the steps we have discussed." The lessons in summary writing may be said to be lessons in comprehension; the final summary (without a lesson) becomes a testing procedure.

Regular Class Work   Instruction itself may be assessment! For example, a teacher who is teaching main idea recognition over a period of time need not wait until the end of a unit or block of instruction to give a test on Finding Main Ideas. Each class session provides myriad opportunities for testing. As students complete a practice exercise, they offer evidence of their ability to find main ideas; as they read assignments and point out main idea sentences to the teacher, they again present evidence of their ability (or inability) to zero in on main ideas. For another example, a teacher focusing on inferencing need not wait for a formal test to discover the effectiveness of instruction: he can note in regular class sessions student ability to make inferences in reading; he can ask students in a group to find an inference the author has made; he can stop reading and have every student write out an inference based on information provided in the text. Some may say that such assessment is entirely *too* informal and imprecise; but, because it is continuous and based on many samples of inference-making (or main idea finding), it may have its own validity and reliability. In any case, the assessment that naturally grows out of instruction is more apt to be effective for teaching purposes than that obtained from a formal test given once or twice a year.

Regular Class Tests   Teachers want to know how well they have taught something; they need to know how well students have learned so that they can provide for reteaching it—and give grades! The kind of tests they give may not be statistically sophisticated, but they can be both valid and reliable. If, after teaching ten lessons in, say, finding main ideas, a teacher gives a "home-made" test consisting of ten paragraphs in which students have to underline the main idea sentence, she has important information about her students' ability to manage this one aspect of comprehension. If she has selected those ten paragraphs from content area textbooks her class uses every day, she may have a much better assessment than she would get from either a standardized reading test or a criterion-referenced test.

Teacher-Made Tests for Specific Texts   Comprehension may not be a generalizable entity. It may be that it is seen only in terms of encounters with specific texts. It may not be something that people possess in discernible, measurable quantities (to be tested on a general measure of "comprehension") but a set of related abilities that display themselves only in certain contexts. It may not be possible to say "Robert is a good comprehender" but only that "Robert seems to comprehend this particular text or that particular text."

If this is so—or only partially so—it becomes important for teachers to test comprehension of the specific texts they teach. While finding main ideas or making inferences may be skills that, once learned, can be applied to a variety of situations, no one knows for sure. Therefore, teachers need to make their comprehension tests for the reading material students use in class.

A teacher focusing on one or two aspects of comprehension (say, finding main ideas and inferencing), as students study their fourth-grade science text-book, needs to make her comprehension test around a chapter or section of that book. She may ask

What seem to be the author's three main ideas here?

She makes an inference about X on page 99. What is it?

What inference do you make about Z as it is described on page 101?

How might you say the first sentence on page 103 in your own words?

How would you summarize this section in a few words?

The results of such teacher-made comprehension tests may reveal more about the ways students in this particular class comprehend their fourth-grade science book than the most statistically sophisticated "measuring instrument" on the market.

Suggested Readings on Comprehension Testing

The published literature on tests and measurements is vast; that on the testing of reading comprehension is only somewhat less intimidating. To assist teachers who want to know more about the testing of reading comprehension than this brief appendix can provide, several books and articles are suggested here.

Baumann, James F., and Jennifer A. Stevenson. "Understanding Standardized Reading Achievement Test Scores." *The Reading Teacher* 35 (March 1982): 648–654.

Baumann, James F., and Jennifer A. Stevenson. "Using Scores from Standardized Reading Achievement Tests." *The Reading Teacher* 35 (February 1982): 528–532.

Farr, Roger (Ed.). *Measurement and Evaluation of Reading*. New York: Harcourt Brace Jovanovich, 1970.

Farr, Roger. *Measurement of Reading Achievement: An Annotated Bibliography*. Newark, Del.: International Reading Association, 1971.

Goodman, Kenneth S. "Analysis of Reading Miscues: Applied Psycho-Linguistics." *Reading Research Quarterly* 5 (1969): 9–30.

Goodman, Yetta. "Using Children's Reading Miscues for New Teaching Strategies." *The Reading Teacher* 23 (February 1970): 455–459.

Goodman, Yetta, and Carolyn Burke. *Reading Miscue Inventory: Manual-Procedure for Diagnosis and Evaluation*. New York: Macmillan, 1972.

Johnston, Peter H. "Assessment in Reading." In P. David Pearson (Ed.), *Handbook of Reading Research*. New York: Longman, 1984.

Lapp, Diane, and James Flood. "Guide to Reading Tests and Measurements." In *Teaching Reading to Every Child*, 2nd ed. New York: Macmillan, 1983, pp. 487–545.

Moore, David. "A Case for Naturalistic Assessment of Reading Comprehension." *Language Arts* 60 (November–December 1983): 957–969.

Newkirk, Thomas. "The Limitations of Standardized Reading Tests." *The English Journal* 64 (March 1975): 50–52.

Pearson, P. David, and Dale D. Johnson. *Teaching Reading Comprehension.* New York: Holt, Rinehart and Winston, 1978.

Smith, Sharon Pugh, and Janet H. Jackson. "Assessing Reading/Learning Skills with Written Retellings." *Journal of Reading* 28 (April 1985): 622–630.

Strange, Michael. "Instructional Implications of a Conceptual Theory of Reading Comprehension." *The Reading Teacher* 33 (January 1980): 391–397.

Index

Accessibility of memories, 35
Accretion (in schema theory), 91
Acting-out literature, 95
Activating prior knowledge, 83–88
Adams, M. J., 17, 22, 190, 226
Advance organizer, 85–86, 89, 149
Affixes, 124–128, 130–131
Alexander, J. E., 118, 143
Allen, Jo Beth, 101
Analogies, 27, 107–109, 132, 133
Anaphora, 193–194, 198, 199
Anderson, J. R., 15, 21, 51, 70, 231, 245,
    246, 248, 269, 271
Anderson, R. C., 45, 47, 58, 59, 115, 143,
    157, 183
Anderson, T. H., 18, 21, 208, 225, 260, 267,
    269, 270
Andre, M. E. D. A., 267, 270
Argumentum ad hominem, 246
Armbruster, B. B., 18, 21, 58, 71, 208, 225
Array-outlining, 167–168
Artificial intelligence, 8
Assessing prior knowledge
    cloze procedure, 81–82
    direct approach, 78–79
    informal class discussion, 79
    informal concept tests, 80–81
    informal content checks, 80
    open-ended inventories, 80
    synonym and definition tests, 81
    questionnaires, 79–80
Atkinson, R. C., 35, 48
Attention, 15–16, 152
Ausubel, D. P., 85, 111, 149, 183

"Background for Reading" (in basal readers),
    94
Backward inferencing, 240
Baker, L., 258, 259, 267, 270
Barclay, C. R., 267, 270
Barnhart, C. L., 9, 21
Baron, R. A., 35, 36, 42, 47
Barron, R., 151, 183
Bartlett, F. C., 36, 42, 47
Basal readers, 6–8, 94, 146
Baumann, J. F., 284
Becker, A. L., 200, 208, 225
Bender, S. D., 115, 143
Betts, E., 157, 183
Bias, recognizing, 252–253
Biddle, W. B., 157, 183
Biggam, S. C., 261, 270
Bloom, B., 53, 70, 163, 183, 234, 270

Bloomfield, L., 9, 21
Bluth, G. J., 201, 226
Boltzmann, L., 11
Bottom-up view of comprehension process, 9
Braddock, R., 208, 225
Brainstorming as prereading activity, 101
Brandt, D. M., 201, 226
Bransford, J. D., 26, 42, 47, 86, 111, 267,
    271
Brewer, W. F., 58, 70
Brown, A. L., 258, 265, 267, 270
Brown, J. I., 123, 143
Building "new" schemata, 96–97
"Building Reading Background" (in basal
    readers), 94
Building word meanings, 120–130
Burke, C., 247, 270, 284
Burmeister, L. E., 118, 143, 209, 225, 254,
    270
Byrne, D., 35, 36, 42, 47

Calfee, R. C., 69, 70, 201, 225
Campbell, J., 26, 47
Campione, J. C., 265, 267, 270
Carr, E. M., 152, 183
Carver, R. P., 54, 55, 71
Cause and effect in inferencing, 240
Cause and effect pattern in paragraphs, 17,
    56, 66, 152, 201, 205, 256
Characterization in stories, 220, 221
Chart making as a during-reading activity,
    116
Chomsky, C., 190, 225
Chomskyan view of language, 57
Christensen, 200, 208, 209, 225
Clark, D. L., 164, 184
Classification patterns in paragraphs, 201
Cloze procedure, 81–82
Clymer, T., 84, 96, 111, 166, 183
Coding system in language, 13–15
Cognitive monitoring, 258
Cognitive skills, 51, 231
Cognitive skills in comprehension, 51
Cohen, M., 175, 183
Collins, A., 97, 111, 259, 260, 270
Comparison and contrast pattern in para-
    graphs, 17, 56, 66, 152, 201, 203, 205,
    256
Complex sentences, understanding of,
    190–191, 198
Compound words, 122, 131
Comprehension
    assumptions about, 11–19

Comprehension (*cont.*)
  definition, 67–68
  explanation of process, 60–65
  importance of, 5–6
  problems in defining, 7–8
  status of instruction today, 6–8
  strategies for teaching, 73–271
  theoretical models of process, 8–11
  writer's role and responsibilities in, 17–18,
    55–59, 61–62, 65
Comprehension levels, 53–54
Comprehension monitoring, 258–267
Comprehension process. *See* comprehension
Concept development pattern in paragraphs,
  201
Conceptually-driven processing, 44
Concluding paragraphs in extended discourse,
  216
Consequence (in story grammar), 220
Content area reading, 29, 103, 119, 145–146
Context clues activity, 132
Contextual analysis, 128–130
Contextual approaches to vocabulary build-
  ing, 140–141
Criterion-references tests, 276–278
Critical thinking-reading
  bias and slanted language, 252–253
  definition, 250–251
  emotive language, 253
  evaluating sources
  points of view, 252
  propaganda devices, 254–255
  purpose, 251
  relevancy of material, 251–252
Cultural backgrounds of readers, 59–60
Cunningham, J. W., 86, 87, 112, 149, 150,
  160, 180, 185
Cunningham, P. M., 160, 183
Cunningham, R., 165, 183
Curley, R., 69, 70, 201, 225

Dale, E., 30, 47, 115, 118, 143
Dale List of 769 Easy Words, 117
Data-driven processing, 44
Data pattern in extended discourse, 214
Davey, B., 265, 266, 270
Davis, A. R., 7, 21
Davis, B., 28, 47
Davis, F. B., 30, 47, 51, 71, 115, 143
Day, J. D., 265, 270
Decoding, 5, 9, 13–17, 62, 63, 66, 117–118,
  130–131
Deductive reasoning, 244
Deductive-inductive reasoning, improvement
  of, 245–247
Definitional paragraphs in extended dis-
  course, 216
Dehn, N., 70, 71

Deighton, L. C., 30, 47, 115, 143
Density of texts, 223
Departmentalization in language arts instruc-
  tion, 207
Descriptive paragraphs in extended discourse,
  216
Developing word meaning knowledge,
  133–141
Devine, T. G., 16, 17, 21, 29, 48, 57, 68,
  71, 95, 111, 130, 143, 165, 168, 169,
  177, 183, 202, 225, 254, 266, 270
Dewey, J., 247, 270
Dialectical model for reconstructing schema,
  97–98
Dictionary Defining Activity, 133
Directed Reading Activity (DRA), 157
Directed Reading-Thinking Activity (DR-TA),
  87, 158, 159
Disadvantaged students, 59–60, 275, 276
Discourse-centered paragraph, 200
Discussion as postreading activity, 172–173
Distinguishing relevant from irrelevant (in
  critical reading), 251–252
Dolch Basic Sight Vocabulary of 220 Words,
  117
Donlan, D., 157, 183, 209, 227
Drawing conclusions (in inference-making),
  240
During-reading activities
  immediate oral feedback, 165–166
  inserted questions, 164–165
  listing main ideas, 166–167
  outlining, 167–168
  paraphrasing, 168
  question-answering, 163–164
  self-monitoring, 169–170
  study guides, 169
  summarizing, 168–169
  time lines and charts, 166
Durkin, D., 6, 21, 27, 29, 48, 115, 117, 118,
  143, 189, 192, 225
Durrell, D. D., 231, 270

Early, M., 110, 111, 254, 270
Echoic memory, 34
Ekwall, E. E., 118, 143
Ellipsis (in sentence comprehension), 195–196
Emerson, M., 83, 111
Emotive language (in critical reading), 253
Encoding in memory, 36
Enumeration pattern in paragraphs, 17, 56,
  152, 201, 202, 205, 256
Episodic memory, 37–38, 39
Estes, T. H., 18, 21, 58, 71, 208, 226
Evaluating sources (in critical reading), 252
Explanatory paragraphs in extended discourse,
  215

Extended discourse, comprehension of, 213–222

Fact and opinion, 235–236, 256
False argumentation, 246
Farina, M. A., 241–242
Farquhar, W. W., 157, 184
Farr, R., 284
Faulty dilemma, 246
Feature analysis activity, 100
Feature-list model, 31, 37–38
Felt difficulty, 247
Five W's plus H
  as during-reading activity, 173
  as prereading activity, 154
Fix-up strategies (in comprehension monitoring), 170, 260–261
Flood, J., 9, 21, 117, 128, 144, 284
Following Directions Activity, 242
Forward inferencing, 238
Foster, D., 200, 226
Frayer, D. A., 139, 143
Frayer Model, 139–140
Frederick, W. C., 139, 143
Freebody, P., 115, 143
Frost, Robert, 28, 48, 136

General prior knowledge, 82–83
Generalization pattern in paragraphs, 17, 56, 152, 199, 201, 202, 205, 256
Generative model of the paragraph, 200
"Gifted" students, 59–60
Gipe, J. P., 140, 143
Glenn, L. G., 56, 72, 219, 227
Goals (in story plots), 221
Goetz, E. T., 58, 71
Goodman, K. S., 14, 22, 116, 143, 233, 238, 270, 284
Goodman, Y. M., 247, 270, 284
Graham, K. G., 157, 177, 184
Grammatical knowledge, 189–190
Graphic organizers, 149
Graves, M. F., 115, 116, 117, 143, 149, 164, 184
Gray Oral Reading Test, 7
Grubaugh, S., 138, 139, 140, 141, 143
Guerra, C. L., 250, 270
Guided Reading Procedure (GRP), 158–159

Hansell, T. S., 168, 184
Hansen, J., 232, 234, 271
Harste, J. C. 6, 22
Hayes, D. A., 27, 48, 107, 108, 111, 149, 184
Henry, G. H., 168, 172, 174, 184, 260, 265, 270
Herber, H. L., 29, 48, 57, 71, 201, 226
Hershberger, W., 164, 184

High interest-low vocabulary books, 16–17
Higher mental processes, 53, 231
Hittleman, D. R., 173, 184
Horowitz, R., 201, 226
Huey, E. B., 7, 22
Huggins, A. W. F., 17, 22, 190, 226
Hunt, K. W., 17, 22
Hyperbole, 196
Hypothesizing, 241–242, 250, 263

Iconic memory, 34
Illustrations
  to activate prior knowledge, 87–88
  affect on comprehension, 87, 223
  to assess prior knowledge, 89
  for building background, 94–95
  to make predictions, 155
  to make prereading summaries, 162
  as post-reading activity, 178
  as prereading activity, 149
Immediate oral feedback (as during-reading activity), 165–166
Increasing students' prior knowledge, 90–99
Individualized reading programs, 16
Indrisano, R., 84, 96, 111, 166, 183
Inductive reasoning, 244–245
Inference-making
  activity, 256
  backward inferencing, 240–241
  as cognitive process, 51
  definition, 231–234
  as explanations, 240–241
  forward inferencing, 238–240
  as predictions, 238–240
  teaching strategies, 235–241
Information processing, 8
Inhelder, B., 234, 271
Inquiry method (for reconstructing schema), 98–99
Inserted questions (as during-reading activity), 164–165
Instantiation of schema, 40, 232
Interactive model of comprehension process, 10, 61–63, 67–68
Interest and motivation, 16
Interference hypothesis (in memory), 34
Internal response (in story grammar), 220
Introductory paragraphs in extensive discourse, 215

Jackson, J. H., 285
Jaynes, J., 111, 112, 196, 226
Jenkins, C. A., 249, 270
Johnson, D. D., 8, 22, 32, 42, 48, 101, 105, 108, 112, 135, 136, 137, 144, 150, 164, 184, 240, 285
Johnson, L., 234, 271

Johnson, M. K., 26, 47
Johnston, P. H., 25, 48, 259, 271, 284

Kamil, M. L., 9, 22
Kanter, R. N., 18, 21, 208, 225
Kantowitz, B. H., 35, 36, 42, 47
Klausmeir, H. J., 139, 143
Kolesnick, W. B., 17, 22
Krumboltz, J. D., 157, 184

Lapp, D., 117, 128, 144, 284
Letter-sound correspondences. *See* sound-letter correspondences
Levels of comprehension, 53–54
Levels of reading ability, 81, 102
Levi-Strauss, C., 168, 173–174, 184
Levin, G., 201, 226
Levin, J. R., 153, 184
Lindauer, B. K., 234, 271
Linguistic competence, 13–15, 66, 189–190
Lipson, M. Y., 260, 271
Listing main ideas (as during-reading activity), 166–167
Literacy, 5–6
The Living Word Vocabulary, 118
Longer discourse, comprehension of. *See* Extended discourse, comprehension of
Long-term memory, 35–36

McGee, L. M., 224, 226
McNeil, J. D., 93, 97, 98, 112, 139, 140, 144
Maggart, Z. R., 254, 271
Main idea identification
  as during-reading activity, 166–167
  as post-reading activity, 173
Main idea sentences, 208–211, 212
Making relationships, 66–67, 101–109
Manzo, A. V., 87, 112, 158, 159, 184
Mapping (as during-reading activity), 168
Markman, E. M., 259, 267, 271
Marr, M. B., 87, 112
Marshall, N., 221–222, 226
Massaro, D. W., 9, 22
Meaning. *See* Texts-in-the-head
Meaning through feature analysis, 37–38
Meaning (in memory), 35–36
Measurement of comprehension, 7, 273–285.
  See also Testing
Mellon, J. C., 22
Memorial fragments, 43
Memory, 33–39, 43, 61–63
Menyuk, P., 20, 22
Metacognition, 258
Metaphor, 111, 196
Meyer, B. J. F., 58, 201, 226
Mikulecky, L. J., 6, 22
Miscue analysis, 278–280
Modeling by teacher, 265–266

Models of comprehension process, 9–10, 68
Modus tollens, 245
Molarsky, Osmond, 166
Monitoring (of comprehension), 258–267
Monitoring devices, 259
Moore, D., 160, 183, 285
Moore, S. A., 160, 183
Morgan, J. L., 57, 71
Morphemes, 124
Morris, C. D., 267, 271
Mosenthal, J., 219, 227
Motivation, 15–17
Multiple-meaning words, 118–119, 132

Narrative paragraphs in extended discourse, 215
Newkirk, T., 285
Nicholas, D. A., 234, 271
Niles, O. S., 17, 22, 57, 71
Non-visual information, 10
Norman, D. A., 92, 112
Norman, E. S., 157, 184
Norman, M. H., 157, 184
Norm-referenced reading tests, 274–276

Obstacles to comprehension, 262
Omanson, R. C., 234, 271
Organizational patterns
  in extended discourse, 214–222
  external, 222–223
  internal, 222–223
  in paragraphs, 201–205
  in text structure, 56–58
O'Rourke, J., 30, 47, 115, 118, 143
Outlining, 161, 167–168, 213, 217–218
Overview, Achieve, Read, Write, Evaluate, Test (OARWET), 157
Overview, Key Idea, Read, Record, Recite, Review, Reflect (OK5R), 157
Overviews, 148–150, 161
Owings, R. A., 267, 271

Page, W. D., 163, 184
Paragraph comprehension, 200–211
Paragraph functions in extended discourse, 215–217
Paragraph patterns, 200–208
Paraphrasing
  activity, 199
  as during-reading activity, 168
  as monitoring device, 260, 264–265
  as post-reading activity, 173–174
  to test, 281, 282
Paris, S. G., 234, 271
Patterns of extended discourse, 214–215
Patterns of organization. *See* Organizational patterns
Pauk, W., 157, 184

Pearson, P. D., 8, 22, 25, 32, 45, 48, 68, 70, 72, 101, 105, 108, 112, 136, 144, 149, 150, 164, 184, 240, 285
Peterson, G. A., 267, 271
Phonemes, 5, 13
Phonics, 5, 9, 117–118
Phonological knowledge, 13
Phrase grammar, 219
Physical appearance of texts, 223
Piaget, J., 234, 271
Pichert, J. W., 58, 59, 70, 71
Pictorial activators, 87
Pictures. *See* Illustrations
Pittleman, S. D., 135, 137, 144
Pitts, M. M., 170, 184, 259, 260, 271
Place (in story comprehension), 220
Plot (in story comprehension), 221
Point of view (in critical reading), 252
Polysemous words. *See* Multiple meaning words
Post hoc, ergo propter hoc, 246
Post Reading Activities and the Writing Reader, 178–179
Post-reading comprehension activities
 "creative" follow-up, 177–178
 discussion, 172–173
 follow-up of prereading activities, 172
 self-testing, 176–177
 writing, 173–176
 the writing reader, 178–179
Potter, T. C., 81, 112
Pragmatics, 8
Predicting activities for prereading, 155–156, 162, 256
Prefixes, 125–126
Prequestions, 86–87
Prereading comprehension activities
 advance organizers, 89, 149
 Directed Reading-Thinking Activity, 158
 Guided Reading Procedure, 158–159
 overviews, 148
 predictions, 155
 problems to be solved, 156
 questions, 153
 ReQuest, 159
 setting purpose, 152–156
 structural organizers, 152
 structured overviews, 149–150
 student-centered study strategies, 156–157
 teacher-directed lesson frameworks, 157–160
 vocabulary previews, 150–152
Pressey, A. S. L. A., 153, 185
Pressley, M., 153, 184
Preview, Question, Read, Record, Recite, Review, Reflect (PQ5R), 157
Preview, Question, Read, Reflect, Recite, Review (PQ4R), 157

Preview, Question, Read, State, Test (PQRST), 157
Previewing, 214, 218–219. *See also* Overviews
Prince, G., 57, 71, 219, 226
Prior knowledge
 activating, 83–88
 assessing, 77–83
 background, 25–26
 definition, 25–26
 effects on comprehension, 24–29
 examples, 26–29
 increasing, 90–99
 memory and, 38–39
 need for, 13
 relating new to known, 101–109
 role of, 18–19
 in vocabulary, 29–33, 113–144
Problem solving, 243, 247–250
Problem solving patterns in paragraphs, 201
Propaganda devices, 254–255
Propp, Vladimir, 57
Punctuation signals in sentence comprehension, 191–192, 198
Purpose for reading, 16, 152–156, 161
Pyramid outlines, 168

Question-answer pattern in paragraphs, 204
Question-answering (as during-reading activity), 163–164
Question Guide Planning Chart, 165
Question types, 164
Questions for prereading, 153–154
Questions (in story comprehension), 221–222
Quillian, M. R., 37, 48

Reaction (in story grammar), 220
Reading comprehension. *See* Comprehension
Reading comprehension skills, 52–54
Reading Guide-o-Rama, 165
Real-life experiences (in schema development), 95–96
Reasoning in comprehension, 54–55, 243–255
Reciprocal Questioning (ReQuest), 87, 159
Recognition of words, 117–118
Reconstructions (in memory), 36–37, 39
Reconstructions (in schema theory), 92–93
Refocused semantic maps, 136–138
Rehearsal (in memory), 34
Reintegrative memory, 34
Relating new to known, 101–109, 264
Reporting (as post-reading activity), 175–176
Request. *See* Reciprocal questioning
Retrieval (from memory), 35–36, 43
Rhetorical competence, 17–18, 55–56, 61–63
Rhetorical devices, 196–197
Rips, L. J., 31, 37, 48, 134, 144
Robinson, F. P., 156, 157, 177, 185, 262, 271

Robinson, H. A., 57, 71, 129, 144, 157, 184, 185, 201, 226
Rodgers, P., 200, 208, 226
Rosenblatt, L. M., 68, 71
Rosenshine, B. V., 52, 71
Rothkopf, E. Z., 164, 185
Rumelhart, D. E., 40, 43, 45, 48, 57, 72, 105, 112, 219, 226, 248, 271
Russell, D. H., 231, 250, 271

Sachs, A. W., 157, 185
Sack, A., 214, 226
Salus, M. W., 32, 48
Salus, P. H., 32, 48
Samuels, S. J., 9, 22, 87, 112
Santeusanio, R. P., 209, 210, 214, 226, 254, 271
Savage, J. F., 249, 270
Schallert, D. M., 223, 226
Schank, R. C., 70, 72, 105, 112
Schema
  accretion, 91
  activating, 40–41, 83–88
  assessing, 77–82, 96–97
  building, 90–99, 100–101, 133–141
  definition, 39–41
  functions of, 41–43
  instantiation, 40–41
  and memory, 43
  in perception, 41–42
  reconstruction, 92–93, 96–99, 133–141
  in testing, 273–284
  theory, 39–45
  in understanding discourse, 42
  use of, 43–44
Self-addressable (in memory), 35
Self-monitoring, 169–170, 258–267
Self-questioning (as monitoring device), 259–260, 262–263
Sellner, M. B., 57, 71
Semantic association (activity), 99
Semantic feature analysis, 37–38, 134–136
Semantic knowledge, 14, 29–33, 113–141
Semantic mapping, 85, 88, 105–106, 136–138, 152, 160
Semantic memory, 37–38, 39
Semantic network, 134
Sensory storage memory, 34
Sentence comprehension, 189–198
Sentence comprehension strategies, 197–198
Sequence pattern in paragraphs, 17, 56–57, 152, 201, 203–204, 205–207
Sequencing (activity), 71
Shablak, S., 165, 183
Sham enthymeme, 246
Shanker, J. L., 118, 143
Shaw, G. B., 110
Shiffrin, R. M., 35, 48
Shoben, E. J., 31, 37, 48, 134, 144

Short-term memory, 34–35
Shrauger, V. M., 210, 226
Signal words
  in paragraphs, 205–207, 211–212
  in sentences, 192–193
Simile, 196
Singer, H., 209, 227
Skills in reading comprehension, 52–54
Skills in reading comprehension tests, 275–278
Slater, W. H., 152, 185
Slot filling (in inference-making), 232
Smith, E. E., 31, 37, 48, 134, 144, 259, 260, 270
Smith, F., 10, 14, 22, 25, 38, 43, 48, 101, 112
Smith, S. P., 285
Social-cultural backgrounds of readers, 59–60
Sound, Structure, Context, Dictionary (SSCD) approach to unfamiliar words, 130–131
Sound-letter correspondences, 5, 9, 15, 117–118
Spache, G., 54, 55
Spearitt, D., 30, 48, 51, 72, 115, 144
Specific prior knowledge, 82–83
Spoken Word Activity, 138–139, 142, 143
Stadia of discourse, 200, 208
Standardized reading tests, 7, 274–276
Staton, T. F., 157, 185
Stauffer, R. G., 87, 112, 124, 144, 158, 185
Stein, B. S., 267, 271
Stein, N. L., 56, 72, 219, 227
Stetson, E. G., 157, 185
Stevenson, 284
Stieglitz, E. L., 134, 144
Stieglitz, V. S., 134, 144
Storage (in memory), 36
Story grammar, 56–57, 219–222
Story patterns, 212–213
Strange, M., 285
Structural analysis, 122–128
Structural organizers, 152
Structured overviews, 149
Student-centered study strategies, 156–157
Study guides
  during-reading, 169
  for self-monitoring, 266–267
Suffixes, 127–128
Summarizing
  activity, 171
  as during-reading activity, 168–169
  importance of, 67
  as post-reading activity, 174–175
  as self-monitoring device, 264–265
  to test comprehension, 281, 282
  writing, 211
Suprasegmental phonemes, 13
Survey, Question, Read, Recite, Review (SQ3R), 16, 153–154, 156–157, 163, 180, 250, 262–263

Survey, Read, Recite, Record, Review (S4R), 157
Surveying. *See* Previewing
Sustained Silent Reading, 96
Syllogistic reasoning, 245
Syntactic knowledge, 13–14, 189–198
Szeminsho, A., 234, 271

Tagmemic model of paragraph, 200
Taxonomies of educational objectives, 53, 163–164
Teacher-directed lesson frameworks, 157–160
Teacher-Over-My-Shoulder Guide, 165
Teaching strategies vs. learning strategies, 179–181
Telegram writing, 210
Test making by students
    activity, 162
    as post-reading activity, 176–177
Testing reading comprehension
    criterion-reference tests, 276–278
    informal classroom testing, 280–284
    miscue analysis, 278–280
    problems, 7, 273
    standardized tests, 274–276
Text
    autonomy of, 65
    density, 223
    external-internal organization, 222–223
    role in comprehension, 17–18, 55–59, 65, 66
    self-monitoring, 263–264
    teaching about, 187–222
    type and physical appearance, 223
Texts-in-the-head, 10, 61–63, 65, 67–68, 75, 113, 145, 187, 229, 231
Thinking, 67
Thinking skills, 231
Thomas, E., 157, 185
Thomas, J. L., 87, 112
Tierney, R. J., 27, 48, 68, 70, 72, 86, 87, 107, 108, 111, 112, 149, 150, 180, 184, 185
Time (in stories), 220
Time lines, 166, 221
Toms-Bronowski, S., 135, 137, 144
Top-down view of comprehension process, 9
Topic sentence, 200–201, 207, 224
Topics (as distinguished from main ideas), 209
Trabasso, T. R., 234, 271
Trace decay hypothesis, 34
Transformational grammar, 8
Transformational sentence combining, 17, 189, 190–191
Transitional paragraphs in extended discourse, 216
The Triple S Technique (Scan, Search, Summarize), 157

Tulving, E., 35, 48
Tuning (schema), 91–92
Type in texts, 223
Typographical aids, 154, 155, 162, 209

Understanding. *See* Comprehension
Understanding discourse, 42–43
Uninterrupted Sustained Silent Reading, 96

Vacca, R. T., 155, 156, 163, 165, 185
van Dijk, T. A., 16, 22
Venezky, R. L., 84, 96, 111, 166, 183
Venn diagrams, 245
Verbal Trouble Spots, 116–121
Vicarious experience, 96
Visual approaches to schema building, 94–95
Visual overviews, 149
Vocabulary. *See* Word knowledge
Vocabulary Overview Guide, 152
Vocabulary previews, 150–152

Wagoner, S. A., 258, 271
Walker, J., 168, 185
Warren, W. H., 234, 271
Webber, B. L., 194, 227
Weber, K. J., 17, 22
Whaley, J. F., 225, 227
White, R. E., 157, 185
Winograd, P., 259, 271
Word calling, 5, 15
Word knowledge
    building, 121–131, 133–141
    how acquired, 30–31
    importance of, 29–30, 61–63, 66, 115–116
    and schemata, 31–30
    semantic knowledge, 14
Word recognition, 117–118
Word roots, 123–124
Wrenn, C. G., 157, 184
Writer's responsibilities, 17–18, 55–59, 61–62, 65
Writing to comprehend
    to activate prior knowledge, 90, 101
    to assess prior knowledge, 80
    during-reading, 166–169, 171
    main ideas, 166–167, 173
    paraphrasing, 168, 173–174, 199, 260, 264–265, 281, 282
    post-reading, 173–176
    prereading, 155, 162
    problem solving, 249
    sentences, 192, 195, 197–198
    summarizing, 67, 168–169, 171, 174–175, 211, 264–265, 281–282
    in testing, 282
Writing reader, 178–179

Yourman, J., 214, 226

Zintz, M. V., 254, 271